The Fruit & Veg Finder

*Sources for 3000
commercially available
vegetable varieties
and
nearly 1500 fruits*

5th Edition
Revised Expanded Improved

Published by the Henry Doubleday Research Association
Researching, demonstrating and promoting
environmentally friendly growing techniques

With the help of Brogdale Horticultural Trust

Compiled and Edited by Jeremy Cherfas

Thanks to Morgen Cheshire, Simon Hickmott, David Mayo, Rachel Pearcey, Mike Penny, Chris Philip and Anke Wellhausen.

Cover Artwork by Pete Lawrence.

Published by the Henry Doubleday Research Association
Ryton-on-Dunsmore, Coventry, CV8 3LG

Distributed by Moorland Publishing Co. Ltd
Moor Farm Road, Airfield Estate, Ashbourne, Derbyshire, DE6 1HD

© The Henry Doubleday Research Association 1995

ISBN 0-905343-20-4

Printed in Great Britain by The Cromwell Press Ltd
Boughton Gifford, Melksham, Wiltshire, SN12 8PH

Printed on Environmentally friendly, acid-free paper from managed forests

All Rights Reserved
No part of this publication may be reproduced, stored in a retrieval system or transmitted in any form or by any means without the prior permission of the Copyright Owner.

Contents

Introduction 9
Oriental Vegetables 11
UK National Fruit Collections 13
Rootstocks for fruit trees 16
Fruit tree forms 20
Unusual or rare fruit trees 21
Fruits with good flavour 22
Awards to Fruit Cultivars 25
Top fruit varieties that can be considered for growing in the north of Britain 31
Apple varieties that have some frost resistance or avoid frost by late flowering 33
Apple varieties with decorative blossom 33
Fruit Identification 34
County origins of some UK apple, pear and plum varieties 35
Further reading 44
Suppliers 355

Amaranth (Grain) 45
Amaranth (Leaf) 45
Anredera sp 45
Apple 45
Cider Apple 95
Apricot 97
Artichoke 98
Asparagus 99
Asparagus Pea 100
Aubergine 100
Basella 101
Bean Other 101
Beetroot 102
Berry Hybrid 106
Blackberry 108
Blackcurrant 109
Blueberry 110
Broad Bean 112
Broccoli 115
Brussels Sprout 119
Bulbous Rooted Chervil 123
Burdock 123
Cabbage 124

The Fruit and Veg Finder

Cabbage Chinese	133
Cabbage Chinese Headed	133
Cabbage Other	135
Cabbage Red	135
Cabbage Savoy	137
Cape Gooseberry	140
Cardoon	140
Carrot	141
Cauliflower	151
Celeriac	163
Celery	164
Chard see Spinach Beet	167
Chenopodium capitatum	167
Chenopodium foliosum	167
Cherry	167
Chicory	171
Chicory Radicchio	172
Chinese Artichoke	174
Chinese Broccoli	174
Chinese Chives	174
Chinese Gooseberry (Kiwifruit)	174
Choy Sum (Hybrid Flowering Rape)	175
Choy Sum (Purple Flowered)	175
Chrysanthemum Greens	175
Citrus Bitter Orange	175
Citrus Citron	175
Citrus Grapefruit	176
Citrus Kumquat	176
Citrus Lemon	176
Citrus Lime	176
Citrus Limequat	176
Citrus Mandarin & Satsuma	177
Citrus Species, Hybrids & Relatives	177
Citrus Sweet Orange	177
Corn Salad	178
Cranberry	179
Cress	179
Cucumber	180
Cucumber Frame	181
Cucumber Gherkin	183
Cucumber Ridge	184

Cucumis metulliferus	185
Damson & Bullace	185
Dandelion	186
Duck Potato	186
Earth Chestnut	186
Endive	187
Madawaska Buckwheat	189
Fennel	190
Fig	191
French Bean Climbing	192
French Bean Dwarf	195
Garlic	202
Good King Henry	203
Gooseberry	203
Gooseberry Hybrid	212
Grape Greenhouse	212
Grape Outdoor	214
Groundnut	216
Horseradish	216
Horseradish Japanese	216
Huckleberry	216
Jerusalem Artichoke	216
Jicama	217
Kale	217
Kiwano	219
Kohlrabi	219
Komatsuna	220
Leaf Beet see Spinach Beet	220
Leaf Celery	220
Leek	221
Lettuce	227
Lettuce Cos	229
Lettuce Head	231
Lettuce Leaf	241
Lettuce Stem	243
Lettuce Thai	243
Loquat	243
Mangel	243
Marrow	244
Mashua	248
Medlar	248

The Fruit and Veg Finder

Melon	249
Mesclun	250
Mibuna Greens	250
Miner's Lettuce	250
Mitsuba	250
Mizuna Greens	251
Mulberry	251
Mustard	251
Mustard Greens	252
Nectarine	252
Nuts Almond	253
Nuts Cobnut & Filbert	253
Nuts Sweet Chestnut	254
Nuts Walnut	254
Nuts Walnut Hybrid	255
Oca	255
Okra	255
Onion	255
Onion Other	265
Orache	266
Pak Choi	266
Par-Cel	266
Parsley	267
Parsnip	269
Pea	271
Pea Round	271
Pea Sugar	272
Pea Wrinkled	274
Peach	278
Pear	279
Perry Pear	287
Pepper Hot	288
Pepper Sweet	289
Pepper-Tomato hybrid	292
Plantago coronopus	292
Plum & Gage	292
Potato	299
Purslane	312
Quince	312
Quinoa	313
Radish	313

Radish Storage	317
Rampion	318
Rape	318
Raspberry	318
Redcurrant	320
Rhubarb	321
Rock Samphire	322
Rocket	322
Rocket Turkish	322
Rosette Pak Choi	322
Runner Bean	323
Salad Mallow	325
Salsify	325
Scorzonera	326
Sea Kale	327
Shallot	327
Skirret	328
Solanum muricatum	328
Solanum sisfymbrifolium	328
Spinach	329
Spinach Beet	332
Squash	333
Squash Pumpkin	333
Squash Summer	336
Squash Winter	336
Strawberry	337
Strawberry Alpine	339
Swede	339
Sweetcorn	341
Texsel Greens	344
Tomatillo	344
Tomato	345
Tree Tomato	352
Turnip	352
Unusual Fruits	354
Water Chinquapin	355
Watercress	355
Watermelon	355
Whitecurrant	356
Yacon	356

Introduction

We compile *The Fruit & Veg Finder* from the published catalogues of suppliers of seeds and plants. Descriptions are generally taken from the catalogues, although other sources have also been used where appropriate. We do not include descriptions of F1 hybrids. The catalogues we use are the most up-to-date ones we can get, but in some instances may be a season behind. This should not be a problem; most seed suppliers have back stock of varieties they no longer offer and will be happy to make an additional sale. Among suppliers of plants turnover is in any case a lot less rapid.

The idea of the book is simple: to help gardeners to find the varieties they want. We hope that by compiling a catalogue of catalogues we will expand the market for some of the lesser-known varieties, thus hoping to keep those varieties, and the people who supply them, going.

With this latest edition *The Vegetable Finder* becomes *The Fruit & Veg Finder*. The help and co-operation of Brogdale Horticultural Trust has made it possible to create a volume that will be much more useful to all who want to select the best varieties of edible plants.

In so doing it could in future enable *The Plant Finder* to find a little more space in its crowded pages, by handing fruits over to us; but not, perhaps, for a year or two. Many of the nurseries whose offerings are listed in *The Plant Finder* as fruits do not recognise them as fruits themselves, and several failed to respond to our request for a catalogue. To them, variegated strawberries are not fruits but ornamental alpines, and many other varieties that produce delicious fruits are seen primarily as pretty plants. In future editions we hope to expand the scope of *The Fruit & Veg Finder* so that eventually it will indeed list all available sources of all edible plants. To that end I would ask nurseries who don't think of themselves as supplying fruit to look on this as an opportunity to extend their markets.

We have used the same nursery codes as *The Plant Finder* in most cases.

** indicates varieties that are subject to Plant Breeders' Rights; these should not be multiplied.

The variety names of vegetables are slowly continuing to sort themselves out under the influence of the powers that be in Brussels. The attempt to standardise all names continues, and the latest (17th) edition of the Common Catalogue, which regulates the marketing of seed in the European Union, has an entirely new category.

These are "old" varieties, still on the list, whose names "have been determined by the Commission". Alas, several such names were not accepted by the Commission. As a result, many of the variety names listed in the Common Catalogue were officially to cease being used on 30 June 1993. Most are still in use by seed suppliers.

Are seed suppliers scofflaws? I doubt it. I just think they are as confused as anyone by the raft of regulations that govern the marketing of plants in the European Union. It is quite a job to discover just what a variety should be called and whether it is legitimate to market it under that name, let alone whether it will be profitable to list it. The confusion sometimes apparent in these pages simply reflects the greater confusion out there in the marketplace. The problem of synonyms remains, and quite a few seed suppliers are still separately offering what is officially a single variety under two different names, often with different descriptions. No doubt this, too, is confusion rather than a cunning wheeze to increase sales. With time the names will settle down and those pesky old varieties will bother Brussels no more.

It is quite clear that the imposition of a blanket set of laws to govern the marketing of seed, no matter the quantities involved, has resulted in a loss of varieties, especially varieties suited to the needs of gardeners and small-scale growers. Now a similar pressure is being brought to bear on fruit, and it is our sincere hope that, by making it easier to find particular varieties, *The Fruit & Veg Finder* will help keep the market for those varieties alive.

Fruits by and large have an enormous advantage over vegetables, in that most are long-lived and easy to multiply. But they are still vulnerable to changes in fashion and the pressures of marketing. Brogdale Horticultural Trust does a wonderful job of collecting and preserving fruit, but it would be a tragedy if the reduced diversity so obvious in seed catalogues were to be mirrored in future in fruit lists.

Having to go through the names of the fruits in depth for the first time has given me much-needed light relief in what can at times be a tedious job. Among the gooseberries there is a particular trio of consecutive names that caused me to laugh out loud. And it was in the gooseberries too that I found the variety whose name typifies the way I have come to think of *The Fruit & Veg Finder*: Improved Mistake.

With each edition we try to expand our coverage and make the information more useful. A goodly part of that is catching and correcting errors. In this never-ending task, we welcome the help of anyone and everyone. We're not proud; if you discover anything that is wrong, please let us know.

Jeremy Cherfas
Head, Genetic Resources, HDRA

Oriental Vegetables

(with thanks to Joy Larkcom for doing the hard work)

In the 1993 edition of *The Vegetable Finder* we published a compendium of the different names under which many of the increasingly popular oriental vegetables pass. We also bemoaned the fact that there was so much confusion which, we said, makes it more difficult than it need be for people to try these unusual and rewarding additions to the kitchen garden.

We republished the list in the 1994 edition, and we make no apologies for doing so again. So far, nothing much seems to have changed in the seed catalogues. Indeed, it is still easy to find catalogues happily using the vegetable name in one language as a variety name in another language, exactly equivalent to making a big deal of a potato called Pomme de Terre. Is the muddle ever likely to be sorted out?

Bayam *is another name for*	Amaranthus
Bok choy	Chinese Cabbage Headed
Brocoletto	Choy sum
Calaloo	Amaranthus
Celery Cabbage	Chinese Cabbage Headed
Celtuce	Stem Lettuce
Ceylon spinach	Basella
Chinese lettuce	Stem Lettuce
Chinese Kale	Chinese Broccoli
Chinese White Cabbage	Pak choi
Chinese mustard greens	Mustard greens
Chinese Celery Cabbage	Pak choi
Chinese leek	Chinese chives
Chinese spinach	Amaranthus
Chinese Leaves	Chinese Cabbage Headed
Chop suey greens	Chrysanthemum greens
Crosnes	Chinese artichoke
Daikon	Radish
Edible oil seed rape	Choy sum
Flat Pak choi	Rosette Pak choi
Flat black Pak choi	Rosette Pak choi
Flowering pak choi	Choy sum
Flowering white cabbage	Choy sum
Gai lan	Chinese broccoli
Gai choy	Mustard greens

Garlic chives *is another name for*	Chinese chives
Gobo	Burdock
Hon tsai tai	Purple flowered choy sum
Hong tsoi sum	Purple flowered choy sum
Indian spinach	Basella
Indian mustard (greens)	Mustard greens
Japanese greens	Chrysanthemum greens
Japanese artichoke	Chinese artichoke
Kaai tsoi	Mustard greens
Kaai laan tsoi	Chinese broccoli
Kailan	Chinese broccoli
Kosaitai	Purple flowered choy sum
Leaf Mustard	Mustard Greens
Malabar spinach	Basella
Michihili	Chinese Cabbage Headed
Mooli	Radish
Mustard cabbage	Mustard greens
Mustard Cabbage	Pak choi
Mustard Spinach	Komatsuna
Pak tsoi sum	Choy sum
Purple flowered choy sum	Choy sum
Shungiku	Chrysanthemum greens
Spinach mustard	Komatsuna
Taisin	Pak choi
Tasai	Rosette Pak choi
Tatsoi	Rosette Pak choi
White flowering broccoli	Chinese Broccoli
Wong Bok	Chinese Cabbage Headed

UK National Fruit Collections

The National Fruit Collections were first established in Chiswick, London in the early 1800s by the Horticultural Society (now the Royal Horticultural Society) under the guidance of Thomas Andrew Knight. The first catalogue, published in 1826 and followed by a more detailed edition in 1831, listed some 1400 apples, 677 pear and 360 gooseberry cultivars, although many of these have subsequently proved to be synonyms. These were cultivated in the Society's garden at Chiswick.

It is not clear what happened to these earlier Collections but by 1936 the number of varieties at the RHS Wisley garden had dwindled to no more than 200.

The Cherry Collection originally belonged to the Kent Farm Institute, located near Sittingbourne, but passed to The Ministry of Agriculture, Fisheries and Food (MAFF) in 1965. This Collection was later relocated at Brogdale in the late 1970s.

The National Fruit Trials and the Collections were established in 1921 at Wisley, Surrey as a joint venture between the RHS and the Ministry of Agriculture, being initially managed by A. M. Rawes and subsequently by J. M. S. Potter from 1936. The Collections were relocated from Wisley to Brogdale between 1952 and 1954, when MAFF assumed complete funding. The present day Collections were largely built up from this time onwards under the direction of J. M. S. Potter until 1972, and by successive Directors of the National Fruit Trials, Brogdale Experimental Horticulture Station.

Collections were developed alongside the programme of evaluating new varieties. In the early days, the nomenclature of varieties was chaotic and caused considerable confusion to professionals and amateurs alike. This was partly due to the free exchange of propagating material between various European Countries over centuries; also immigrants to the New World took variety material with them and more often than not the variety acquired a new name in their new country. Even today, varieties can still acquire commercial synonyms, e.g. Mutsu became Crispin.

In Britain, it appeared that when a variety crossed over a parish boundary, it could often acquire a new name. Also it was not unusual for nurserymen to give a new name, so as to sell a variety as a 'new introduction' or different in some way. The apple variety Blenheim Orange has, for example, 67 published synonyms, although such a number is by no means exceptional. It was not unknown for even eminent pomologists to describe the same variety under two different names! Today varieties can be given other names for marketing or legal reasons.

In building up the Collection, Mr Potter realised the enormous confusion that still existed and initiated the colossal task of determining the correct and prior names of thousands of varieties. This work included producing lists of synonyms, wrong names, brief fruit descriptions and references. The work culminated, for apples, in the publication in 1971 of the 'National Apple Register of the United Kingdom'.

In combining the National Fruit Collections with the testing of new varieties on the same site, the National Fruit Trials were unique and this has given Brogdale a worldwide reputation as an authority on temperate fruit varieties.

In 1988, the Collections were registered with the National Council for the Conservation of Plants and Gardens (NCCPG) under the National Collections Scheme.

In March 1990, MAFF closed the National Fruit Trials as part of its implementation of the UK Governments' changes in research and development policy. Brogdale was sold to the independently created Brogdale Horticultural Trust which seeks to maintain and develop Brogdale as a centre for fruit variety research and development. However, MAFF continues to own the main National Fruit Collections per se and provides funds for their maintenance through a research commission held jointly by Wye College, University of London and the Brogdale Horticultural Trust. This represents part of the MAFF strategy to conserve diversity within crop species. The Trust is extending the scope of the Collections to encompass varieties and fruits not covered by the Ministry's portfolio.

Wye College is responsible for the scientific development of the MAFF Collections, which represent a very significant plant genetic resource of value to breeding programmes and other scientific research. Plant material and cultivar accession information are available on request to bona fide scientific and research workers who can contact the Scientific Curator at Brogdale for further information.

In addition, Wye College undertakes Plant Variety Rights testing on behalf of the Plant Variety Rights Office, for which the Collections act as a reference resource.

The Trust is responsible for maintenance of the Collections, which form part of the UK National Heritage. The Collections also serve as a valuable source of propagation material particularly of older varieties for reintroduction into commerce. Nurserymen, commercial organisations and gardeners can obtain this material (subject to Plant Breeder's Rights agreements and availability).

Members of the public can have limited access to the Collections in the company of a trained guide during the Trust's opening times or on special event days.

The catalogue of cultivars in UK National Fruit Collection

The catalogue is regularly updated and is available to bona fide research workers (on request) and to individuals and companies (£6.00 plus post and packing). Cultivar accession indices are provided for individual Collections, under four main categories: top fruit, nuts, bush fruit and vines. All cultivars are listed alphabetically.

Complementary work at Brogdale
Fruit Variety Evaluation and Development Programme

Brogdale evaluates new varieties of temperate fruits from breeding programmes throughout the world for their suitability for UK and Northern Europe. This work is funded by sponsors. Information is available to funding organisations and to corporate members of the Trust.

Post Harvest Technology

Controlled atmosphere cold storage facilities at Brogdale are used for fruit from trials and are also available for other studies. Contract storage and an increasing number of post harvest investigations are being conducted on behalf of a number of commercial organisations.

Micropropagation

Once the centre of the Ministry of Agriculture's plant tissue culture unit, Brogdale is re-commissioning its facilities. This will provide both a service to assist the variety evaluation programme in the receipt of plant material from other countries and also be able to provide a micropropagation service to the industry.

Rootstocks for fruit trees

Most tree fruit varieties are difficult to propagate from cuttings and rootstocks have therefore been used for centuries to help propagation. They also give some control over the ultimate size of the tree and, by careful choice, can extend the range of soils on which fruit trees can be successfully grown.

Apples
M27
The first fully dwarfing rootstock. It must have deep, fertile soil and be free from competition from weeds. Without annual pruning and, in some years, fruit thinning it can become stunted. Trees on M27 will always need support. M27 is excellent for vigorous varieties, e.g. triploids, in the garden. If it is grown in garden or in containers it must have regular watering, weeding and feeding to thrive. Trees will fruit in 2 to 3 years.

M9
Dwarfing rootstock selected from Paradise rootstocks at East Malling Research Station. M9 induces precocious, consistent cropping, large fruit size and is resistant to collar rot disease. It is, however, sensitive to drought, winter cold injury and fireblight as well as having a brittle root system. Varieties on M9 fruit within three years but need support. Can be used for dwarf bush, dwarf pyramid, cordon or spindle bush trees. Widely used by commercial fruit growers.

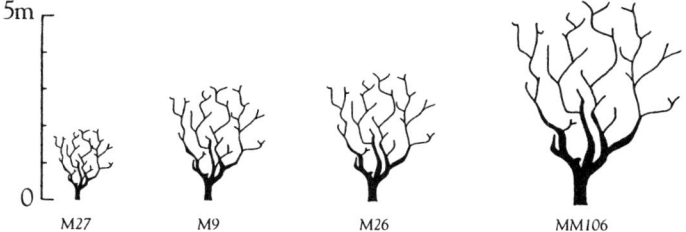

M26
Intermediate vigour. M26 is an excellent rootstock for Bramley and for growing trees in containers. It does well on soils of medium fertility. Fruits in 3 to 4 years.

MM106
Widely used stock by nurseries and produces a semi vigorous tree between M26 and MM111 in growth. It has a good cropping performance coming into fruit 3 to 4 years from planting as a maiden. Will tolerate some competition from weeds and grass but can be sensitive to collar rot on heavy, clay soils. Used for bush trees, fans and espaliers.

MM111
Vigour is slightly more than MM106 but trees on this rootstock can be grown on poorer soils, especially lighter more freely draining soils. Needs careful pruning and training to produce good crops. Useful for bush trees, half standards and small standard trees.

M25
Very vigorous rootstock but surprisingly precocious and productive. Best for growing full standard trees but does require time to train up the clear stem necessary for a standard tree.

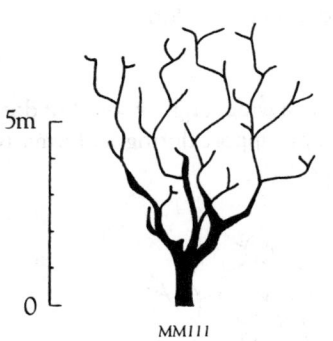
MM111

M25

The Fruit and Veg Finder

Pears

Most trees are propagated on Quince A or Quince C rootstocks. Quince C is the more dwarfing and induces slightly earlier fruiting in the tree's life than Quince A but requires a very fertile soil and permanent support.

Occasionally, pear varieties are offered for sale on the more vigorous rootstock BA29 or seedling pear. These are useful if large standard trees are required.

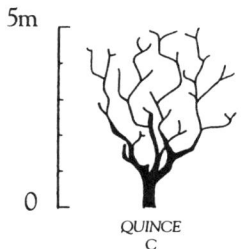
QUINCE C

QUINCE A

Plums

Pixy

The most dwarfing rootstock for plums giving trees 30 to 40% less vigorous than St Julien A. This is a precocious stock which requires support and good soil. In heavy crop years, it is essential to thin fruitlets and maintain the balance between fruity and vegetative growth. Useful for bush, dwarf pyramid or even cordon.

St Julien A

Semi-vigorous rootstock which will tolerate a wide range of soils but does tend to sucker especially if roots are disturbed. Benefits from support during its formative years. Useful for bush, fan, half standard or standard trees.

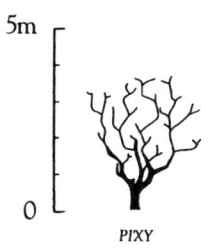
PIXY

ST JULIEN A

Cherries

Colt
A semi vigorous rootstock which can be used for fans, bush or half standard trees but has insufficient vigour to grow a standard tree. This stock induces precocious cropping and gives good fruit size.

Inmil
Very dwarf stock but trees on this are relatively unproductive and fruit size can be small. This is till a relatively new rootstock and has not been widely grown.

F12/1
Vigorous Mazzard rootstock ideal for use in traditional standard orchards but can be difficult to find in nurseries.

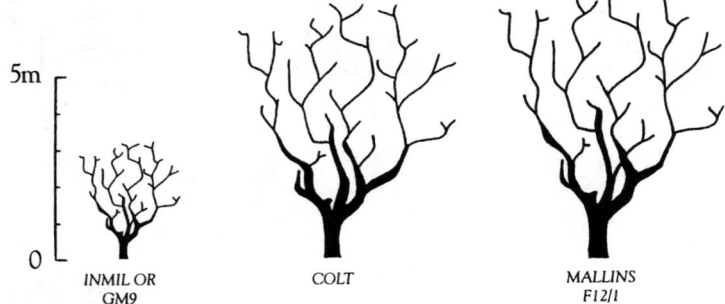

INMIL OR GM9   COLT   MALLINS F12/1

The Fruit and Veg Finder

Fruit tree forms

Fruit plants can be grown and trained in a wide range of forms depending upon space available, the number of varieties you wish to grow and the design in to which they are to fit. Correct use of winter (dormant season) and summer pruning can control tree size as will the way in which trees are trained and the rootstock upon which they are grown.

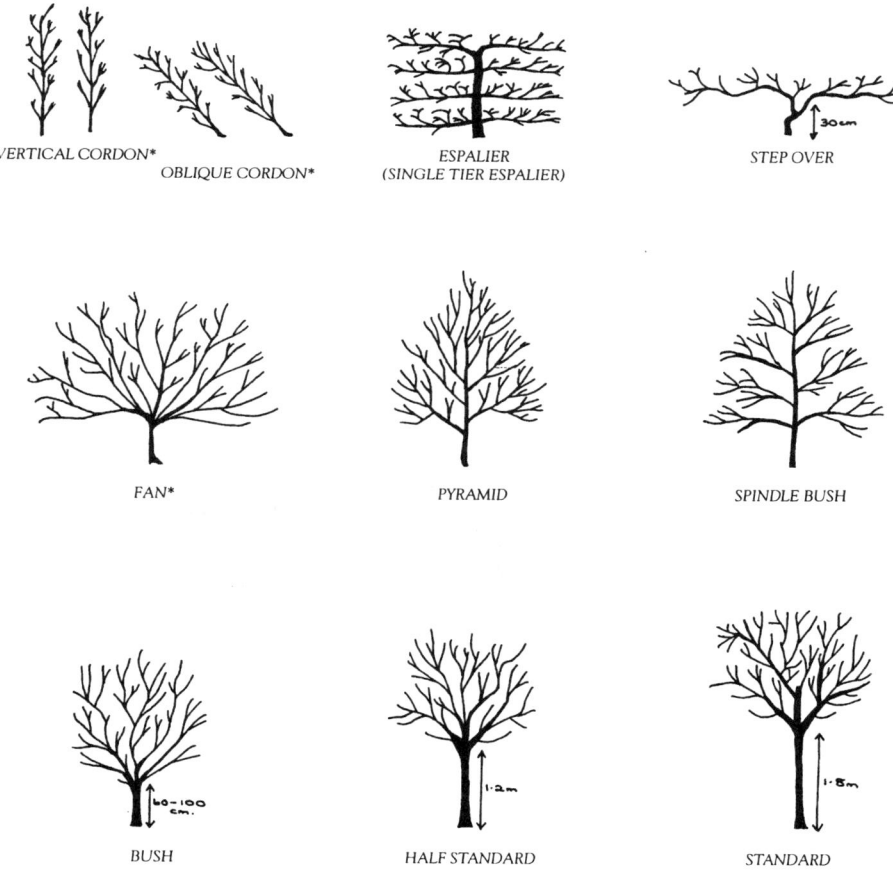

*These require wirework, fence or wall to train plants against. Soft fruit bushes can also be trained to restrict their growth and to provide features in the garden, e.g. redcurrants as cordons, gooseberries as standards (like roses).

The Fruit and Veg Finder

Unusual or rare fruit trees

Despite the huge range of varieties available from specialist nurserymen, it is still possible to have difficulty in obtaining some unusual or rare varieties. Now it is possible to acquire virtually any variety which is present in the National Fruit Collections. The Brogdale Horticultural Trust offers a "Graft or Bud While You Wait Service" each March and July. A graft or bud of the variety requested is put on to the most appropriate rootstock and supplied for growing on to produce a young tree.

Alternatively, for those who wish to propagate their own trees, both scion wood and rootstocks are available from Brogdale. Rootstocks are also available from nurseries J.C. Allgrove (Allg), Deacon's Nursery (SDea), Scott's Nurseries (CSco), Family Trees (SFam), R.V. Roger (Rog) and Edwards Fruit Trees (Edws). Complete grafting kits are available from Deacon's Nursery.

This list has been compiled from catalogues and information sent to Brogdale and does not include all nurseries who provide this service. The compilers of *The Fruit & Vegetable Finder* would be delighted to hear from any nursery that wishes to be included in this section in future editions.

This list has been prepared for guidance only and the inclusion or omission of a name should not be taken as a recommendation.

Fruits with good flavour

Flavour is often difficult to define as each individual's tastes can differ. This listing draws on the impressions of many experienced fruit experts and covers a range of eating characteristics.

Dessert apples (other than Cox)
T denotes triploid; * New or more recent introductions

Variety	Natural Season (months)	For	Against
Adam's Pearmain	12-2	Good cropper	Conical fruit
Ashmead's Kernel	12-1	Good texture	Uncertain cropper
Baker's Delicious	9	Good appearance	Small fruit; short season
D'Arcy Spice	1-3	Russet	Poor appearance
Discovery	8-9	Good shelf life	Uncertain cropper; cracked fruits; poor flavour unless ripe
Egremont Russet	10-11	A good russet	Uncertain cropper; Bitter Pit
Elstar*	12-2	Uniform, good appearance	
Epicure (Laxton's)	9	Earliest fine flavoured apple	Small fruit
Fortune (Laxton's)	9	Good shape and texture	Canker; soft flesh; biennial
Gala *	11-2	Good crop; excellent texture	Small fruit; flavour fades
Greensleeves	9-10	Heavy cropper	Flavour soon fades
Holstein T	10-12	Large fruits	Poor cropper
Jonagold T*	11-1	Heavy cropper; good texture	Very large fruit
Karmijn de Sonnaville *	10-12	Uniform size	Russet patches
Kidd's Orange Red	11-1	Good cropper	Russet patches; variable fruit size
Lord Hindlip	12-3	Large fruit; good colour	Russet patches
Lord Lambourne	9-10	Heavy cropper; even size fruits	Sticky skin
Merton Charm	9-10	Regular cropper; compact tree	Small fruit; creamy-green skin
Orleans Reinnette	11-12	Uniform, good size	Biennial; shrivels easily
Pixie*	12-3	Good keeper	Small fruit
Queen Cox	10-12	Good colour	
Red Cox (Potter)*	10-12	Good colour	
Ribston Pippin T	10-11	Regular cropper	Drops easily; poor skin finish
St Edmund's Pippin (Early Golden Russet)	9-10	Good russet	Small fruit; uncertain cropper
Spartan	12-2	Good texture	Rather small
Sunset	10-11	Regular cropper	Small fruit
Suntan T*	12-2	Compact tree	Rather acid
William Crump	12-2	Good size; late flowering	Light cropper; grey russet marking

The Fruit and Veg Finder

Culinary apples (other than Bramley)
T denotes triploid; * New or more recent introductions

Variety	Natural Season (months)	For	Against
Alderman	10-12	Large fruits	Conical fruit
Blenheim Orange T	10-11	Also good dessert	Biennial; dull skin finish
Bountiful	9-12	Precocious, compact	Moderate fruit size
Dumelow's Seedling (syn Wellington)	11-3	Good crop	Small medium fruit size
Encore	12-3	A heavy apple	Moderate cropper
George Neal	9-12	Regular crop; even size fruits	Coloured skin
Golden Noble	9-12	Round, even fruits	Moderate fruit size only
Grenadier	8-9	Good early size	Biennial tendency; dirty skin
Lord Suffield	8-9	Good early size; compact tree	Conical fruit; canker?
Rev W Wilks	9-10	Large fruits	Biennial; coloured skin
Monarch	11-3	Good appearance	Biennial; brittle wood
Norfolk Beauty	9	Large fruits	Uncertain cropper
Warner's King T	9-11	Large fruits	Canker

Dessert pears
T denotes triploid; * New or more recent introductions

Variety	Natural Season (months)	For	Against
Beurre Superfin	10	Good crop	Can rot at core in storage
Concorde*	10-12	Precocious reliable cropper	Can over crop if not thinned
Doyenne du Comice	10-11	Medium to large fruits	Irregular crops prone to scab
Fondante d' Automne	9-10	Fairly hardy	Will not pollinate some varieties
Josephine de Malines	11-1	Good crops, pinkish flesh perfumed	Tip bearer, needs warm position
Merton Pride T	9	Good crop, free spurring	Can be biennial
Onwards	9-10	Good crop, hardy	Will not pollinate Comice
William bon Chretien	9	Good reg. crops free spurring	Scab prone, will not pollinate some varieties

The Fruit and Veg Finder

Plums

Variety	Natural Season (months)	For	Against
Cambridge Gage	8-9	Consistent cropping partially self fertile	low yields
Coe's Golden Drop	9	Fruit free stone, large fruit	Self incompatible. Very difficult to crop. Grow as fan
Count Althan's Gage	8	Flower resistant to cold	Self incompatible, fruit can bruise easily
Early Transparent	8	Self-fertile, reliable crop usually	Medium sized fruit
Golden Transparent	9	Self fertile	Needs warm position
Jeffersons	8-9	Medium sized fruit	Self incompatible, will not pollinate Coe's Golden Drop
Kirkes	8-9	Blue-black; flower resistant to cold	Self incompatible. Very light cropping
Reeves Seedling	8-9	Large fruit	Self incompatible

Awards to Fruit Cultivars

Made by the Royal Horticultural Society
   AM   =   Award of Merit
   PC   =   Preliminary Commendation
   FCC   =   First Class Certificate
   AGM   =   Award of Garden Merit
* = varieties not contained within the National Fruit Collection

The AGM was re-instituted by the RHS in 1992 and besides being the highest accolade the Society can give a plant, is also useful in highlighting plants of value for gardens to consider growing.

Apples

*Albury Park Nonsuch	AM	1892	*Bella	AM	1892
Alfriston	AM	1920	Belle de Boskoop	AM	1897
Allen's Everlasting	FCC	1899		AGM	1993
Allington Pippin	AM	1894	Ben's Red	AM	1899
Annie Elizabeth	FCC	1866	Bismark	FCC	1897
Ard Cairn Russet	AM	1910	Blenheim Orange	AGM	1993
*Armorel	AM	1890	Blue Pearmain	AM	1893
	FCC	1892		FCC	1896
Arthur Turner	AGM	1945	Bow Hill Pippin	AM	1893
	AGM	1993	Brabant Bellefleur	AM	1901
Ashmead's Kernel	AM	1969	Bramley's Seedling	FCC	1883
	FCC	1981		AGM	1993
	AGM	1993	Bushey Grove	AM	1922
Atalanta	AM	1891	Byford Wonder	AM	1893
*Balchin's Pearmain	FCC	1866	Cardinal	AM	1896
*Ballinora Pippin	AM	1898	Charles Eyre	AM	1911
Ball's Pippin	AM	1923	Charles Ross	AM	1899
Barchard's Seedling	FCC	1873		FCC	1899
Barnack Beauty	AM	1899		AGM	1993
	FCC	1909	Chelmsford Wonder	AM	1891
*Bartlett's Glory	AM	1893		FCC	1891
*Bassaleg Pippin	AM	1899	*Clapham Beauty	AM	1896
*Baumann's Winter			Claygate Pearmain	AM	1901
Pearmain	FCC	1878		FCC	1921
Beauty of Bath	FCC	1887		AGM	1993
Beauty of Kent	AM	1901	*Cliveden Prolific	AM	1913
Beauty of Stoke	FCC	1890	Coronation	AM	1902

Cox's Orange Pippin	AM	1962	Greensleeves	AM 1981
	FCC	1962		AGM 1993
Crawley Beauty	AM	1912	Grenadier	FCC 1883
Crispin (Mutsu)	AM	1970		AGM 1993
Diamond Jubilee	AM	1901	Guelph	AM 1912
Discovery	AGM	1993		FCC 1913
Doctor Hogg	FCC	1878	Hambling's Seedling	AM 1893
Dumelow's Seedling	AGM	1993	Harry Pring	AM 1914
Easter Orange	AM	1897	Hector Macdonald	AM 1904
Edward VII	AM	1903	*Herbert's Prolific	AM 1918
	AGM	1993	Herring's Pippin	AM 1920
Edwin Beckett	AM	1915	*High Canons	FCC 1884
Egremont Russet	AM	1980	High View Pippin	AM 1928
	AGM	1993	*Histon Cropper	AM 1920
Ellisons Orange	AM	1911	Hormead Pearmain	AM 1900
	FCC	1917	Houblon	AM 1901
	AGM	1993	Howgate Wonder	AM 1910
Elstar	PC	1987	Hounslow Wonder	AM 1949
	AGM	1993	Idared	AGM 1993
Emneth Early	AM	1899	Improved Ashmead's Kernel	AM 1892
	AGM	1993	*Invincible	AM 1898
Encore	AM	1906	*Jacob's Strawberry	FCC 1884
	FCC	1908	Jacquin	FCC 1893
Epicure	AGM	1993	James Grieve	AM 1897
Feltham Beauty	AM	1908		FCC 1906
Fiesta	PC	1987		AGM 1993
	AM	1987	*James Kirk	AM 1905
	AGM	1993	James Lawson	AM 1918
Fortune	AM	1932	John Standish	AM 1922
	FCC	1948	Jonagold	AM 1987
	AGM	1993		AGM 1993
*Gabalva	AM	1900	Joybells	AM 1922
Galloway Pippin	FCC	1871	Jupiter	PC 1989
Gascoyne's Seedling	FCC	1887		AGM
George Neal	AM	1923	*Kane's Seedling	AM 1889
	AGM	1993	Kidd's Orange Red	AM 1973
Gladstone	FCC	1883		AGM
Golden Delicious	AGM	1993	King George V	AM 1928
Golden Noble	AGM	1993	*King Harry	AM 1892
*Goodwood Pippin	AM	1896	King of Tompkins County	AM 1900
			King's Acre	AM 1904

King's Acre Pippin	AM 1897	Mrs Phillimore	AM 1899
King of the Pippins	AGM	*Mrs Wilmot	AM 1921
King Russet	AGM	Newton Wonder	FCC 1887
Lady Henniker	FCC 1873		AGM
*Lady Falmouth	AM 1897	Norfolk Beauty	AM 1901
*Lady Pilkington	AM 1899		FCC 1902
Lady Sudeley	AM 1884	Norman's Pippin	AM 1900
Lamb Abbey Pearmain	FCC 1901	*Oakland's Seedling	AM 1894
Landsberger Reinette	FCC 1882	Ontario	AM 1898
Lane's Prince Albert	AM 1872	Opal	AM 1895
	AGM	*Orange Silvermere Seedling	AM 1892
Langley Pippin	AM 1898	Orleans Reinette	AM 1914
Laxton's Advance	AM 1932		AM 1921
Laxton's Epicure	AM 1931	*Padnall Seedling	AM 1912
Laxton's Exquisite	AM 1926	Paroquet	AM 1899
Laxton's Fortune	AM 1932	*Pay the Rent	AM 1895
	FCC 1948	Peacemaker	AM 1913
Laxton's Pearmain	AM 1922	Peasgood's Nonsuch	FCC 1872
Laxton's Peerless	AM 1920		AGM
Laxton's Superb	AM 1919	*Perkins' A1	FCC 1884
	FCC 1921	Pershore Pippin	AM 1918
*Livermere Favourite	AM 1896	Peter Lock	AM 1922
Lord Burghley	FCC 1865	Pixie	AM 1970
Lord Hindlip	AM 1896		AGM
	FCC 1898	Rambour	AM 1895
Lord Lambourne	AM 1925	*Red Leaf Russet	FCC 1875
	AGM	Red Victoria	AM 1908
Lord Stradbroke	AM 1905		FCC 1910
Madresfield Court	AM 1915	Reinette du Canada	AM 1901
Maidstone Favourite	AM 1913	*Remborough	AM 1895
May Queen	AM 1892	Renown	AM 1908
Merton Beauty	AM 1972	Rev W Wilks	AM 1904
Merton Charm	AM 1960		FCC 1910
	AGM	Ribston Pippin	AM 1962
Merton Prolific	AM 1950		AGM
Merton Worcester	AM 1950	Rival	AM 1900
*Middle Green	AM 1903	*Rivers' Codlin	AM 1892
Miller's Seedling	AM 1906	*Roi d'Angleterre	AM 1894
*Monstrous Incomparable	AM 1892	Rosemary Russet	AGM
Mother	AGM	Roundway Magnum Bonum	FCC 1864
*Mrs John Seden	AM 1898	Royal Gala (Tenroy)	AGM

The Fruit and Veg Finder   27

*Royal Late Cooking	AM	1896	White Transparent	AM	1895
Saint Cecilia	AM	1918	William Crump	AM	1908
	FCC	1919		FCC	1910
Saint Edmund's Pippin	FCC	1875	Williams Favourite	AM	1895
	AGM		Winston	AM	1951
Saint Everard	AM	1900		AGM	
	FCC	1909	(Received as Winter King)	AM	1935
Saint Martin's	AM	1896	Winter Banana	AM	1912
Saltcote Pippin	AM	1928	Woolbrook Pippin	AM	1929
Sandlin Duchess	AM	1914	Woolbrook Russet	AM	1930
Sandringham	FCC	1883	Worcester Pearmain	FCC	1875
Sanspareil	FCC	1899		AGM	
Scarlet Nonpareil	AM	1901	**Blackcurrants**		
Schoolmaster	FCC	1885	Amos Black	AM	1952
September Beauty	FCC	1885	Ben Lomond	PC	1987
Sir John Thornycroft	AM	1911		AGM	
*Stainway Seedling	AM	1899	Ben Sarek	PC	1987
*Standard Bearer	AM	1893		AGM	
Star of Devon	AM	1905	*Laleham Beauty	AM	1951
Steyne Seedling	AM	1912			
*Stone	FCC	1877	**Blackberries**		
Sunset	AGM		*Fantasia	PC	1987
Suntan	AGM			AM	1990
Tamplin	AM	1902		AGM	
*Tenro	PC	1988	*John Innes	AM	1934
Tenroy	PC	1987	*Loch Ness	PC	1989
	AM	1988		AGM	
The Queen	FCC	1880	*Merton Thornless	FCC	1941
Thomas Rivers	FCC	1892			
*Turner's Prolific	AM	1912	**Cherries**		
Tydeman's Late Orange	AM	1965	Early Rivers	FCC	1898
Tyler's Kernel	FCC	1883	Merton Bigarreau	AN	1946
*Tythby Seedling	AM	1920		FCC	1946
Venus Pippin	AM	1899	Merton Bounty	AM	1946
Wagener	AM	1910	Merton Favourite	AM	1946
Warner's King Seedling	FCC	1883	Merton Glory	AM	1971
	AGM		Merton Heart	AM	1946
Wealthy	AM	1893	Merton Premier	AM	1946
*Welford Beauty	AM	1919	Morello	AGM	
Welford Park	FCC	1872	Stella	FCC	1982
*Werder's Golden Reinette	AM	1904		AGM	

Figs
*Bourjasotte Grise	FCC	1892
Brown Turkey	AGM	
*Pingo de Mel	FCC	1892
*St Johns	FCC	1890
*Violette Sepor	FCC	1892

Gooseberry
Careless	AGM	
Invicta	AGM	
Leveller	AGM	
Whinham's Industry	AGM	

Hybrid Berries
*Loganberry	AM	1897
	FCC	1903
Loganberry LY59	AGM	
Loganberry LY654	AGM	
Tayberry	AM	1981
	AGM	

Nectarines
*Regnum	AM	1949

Peaches
*Bushwood Beauty	AM	1952
*Granny	AM	1952

Pears
Aspasie Ancourt	AM	1896
Autumn Nelis	FCC	1862
Belle Julie	AM	1894
*Bergamotte Auguste Jurie	FCC	1880
Beth	AGM	
*Beurre de Biseau	FCC	1872
Beurre de Jonghe	FCC	1875
Beurre Dubuisson	AM	1894
	FCC	1900
Beurre Fouqueray	FCC	1893
Beurre de l'Assomption	FCC	1874
Beurre Hardy	AGM	
Beurre de Naghan	AM	1907
*Beurre Perran	AM	1896
Blickling	AM	1907
	FCC	1909
Bristol Cross	AM	1951
*British Queen	FCC	1861
Brockworth Park	FCC	1870
Catillac	AGM	
Charles Ernest	AM	1900
*Collis's Hessle	AM	1906
Concorde	PC	1989
	AGM	
Conference	FCC	1885
	AGM	
Dana's Hovey	AM	1908
Directeur Hardy	AM	1897
*Dr Hogg Bergamot	FCC	1878
Double de Guerre	AM	1899
Doyenne d'Alencon	AM	1900
Doyenne du Comice	FCC	1900
	AGM	
Duchesse de Bordeaux	FCC	1885
Emile d'Heyst	FCC	1899
*Everard de Tournai	FCC	1875
*General Wauchope	AM	1901
*Glastonbury	FCC	1900
Gorham	AM	1951
*Grise de Chine	AM	1902
*Huyshe's Prince Consort	FCC	1864
Josephine de Malines	FCC	1901
	AGM	
Laxton's Foremost	AM	1934
*Laxton's Satisfaction	AM	1936
Laxton's Superb	AM	1956
Le Lectier	AM	1894
*Lucy Grieve	FCC	1874
Marguerite Marillat	AM	1899
Merton Pride	AM	1973
	FCC	1983
Michaelmas Nelis	AM	1902
*Mlle Solange	FCC	1887
Mrs Seden	AM	1912

Nouvelle Fulvie	FCC	1900
Olivier de Serres	AM	1900
Onward	AM	1967
	AGM	
Packham's Triumph	AM	1941
Passe Crassane	FCC	1874
Pitmaston Duchess	AGM	
President Barabe	AM	1897
	FCC	1898
Santa Claus	AM	1905
Sir Harry Veitch	AM	1933
*Stevenstone	FCC	1860
*S T Wright	AM	1904
Triomphe de Vienne	AM	1899
Tyson	FCC	1872
*Vineuse	FCC	1880
*Welton Beurre	FCC	1881
Williams' Bon Chretien	AM	1970
	AGM	
Winter Nelis	FCC	1902
Winter Orange	AM	1899

Plums

Czar	AGM	
Denniston's Superb	AGM	
Early Laxton	AGM	
Early Transparent Gage	AM	1898
Langley Bullace	AM	1904
	FCC	1904
Laxton's Delicious	AM	1934
Laxton's Goldfinch	AM	1952
Marjories Seedling	AGM	
Oullins Gage	AGM	
Pershore (Pershore Yellow Egg)	AGM	
Sanctus Hubertus	PC	1991
	AGM	
Severn Cross	AM	1951
Victoria	FCC	1973
	AGM	
Weirton Gage	AM	1933

Raspberries

*Autumn Bliss	PC	1986
	AM	1987
	FCC	1990
	AGM	
*Glen Moy	PC	1988
	AGM	
*Glen Prosen	PC	1988
	AGM	
*Leo	AM	1985
	AGM	
*Loganlike	PC	1990
*Malling Admiral	AM	1981
	AGM	
*Malling Delight	AM	1981
*Malling Exploit	AM	1951
*Malling Jewel	AM	1964
	AGM	
*Malling Promise	AM	1951
*November Abundance	AM	1902

Redcurrants

Laxton Perfection	AM	1923
Red Lake	AM	1949
	AGM	
Stanza	AGM	
White Grape	AGM	

Strawberries

Aromel	PC	1977
	AGM	
Auchincruive Climax	AM	1948
	FCC	1950
Cambridge Favourite	AGM	
Honeoye	PC	1991
	AGM	
Royal Sovereign	FCC	1892
Talisman	AM	1959

Miscellaneous

*Rubus nitioides	AM	1937

Top fruit varieties that can be considered for growing in the north of Britain

Apples

Alexander
Alfriston
Allington Pippin
American Mother
Beauty of Bath
Bedfordshire Foundling
Brabant Bellefleur
Carlisle Codlin
Cellini
Claygate Pearmain
Cockles Pippin
Court of Wick
Court Pendu Plat
Crawley Beauty
Devonshire Quarrenden
Duchess of Oldenburg
Dumelow's Seedling
Dutch Codlin
Early Julyan
Early Victoria
Edward VII
Egremont Russet
Ellison's Orange
Franklyn's Golden Pippin
French Crab
Gladstone
Gloria Mundi
Golden Monday
Golden Pippin
Golden Reinette
Golden Spire
Greensleeves
Greenup's Pippin
Grenadier
Hawthornden
Howgate Wonder
Irish Peach
James Grieve
Kerry Pippin
Keswick Codlin
Laxton's Royalty
Lemon Pippin
Lord Derby
Lord Suffield
Manks Codlin
Margaret
Margil
Melrose
Mere de Menage
Newton Wonder
Northern Greening
Oslin
Red Astrachan
Ribston Pippin
Royal Jubilee
Scarlet Nonpareil
Springgrove Codlin
Stamford Pippin
Summer Pearmain
Tower of Glamis
Warner's King
White Paradise
Winter Pearmain
Wormsley Pippin
Wyken Pippin
Yellow Ingestre
Yorkshire Greening

Pears
Beurre d'Amanlis
Beurre Hardy
Citron des Carmes
Clapp's Favourite
Comte de Lamy
Conference
Doyenne d'Ete
Durondeau
Emile d'Heyst
Gorham
Hessle
Improved Fertility
Jargonelle
Louise Bonne of Jersey
Marguerite Marillat
Thompson's
William's Bon Chretien

Cherries
Frogmore
Governor Wood
Kent Bigarreau
Morello

Plums, gages and damsons
Cherry Plum
Czar
Early Laxton
Farleigh Damson
Merryweather Damson
Oullin's Golden Gage
Pershore Yellow Egg
Warwickshire Drooper

Apple varieties that have some frost resistance or avoid frost by late flowering

Beauty of Bath
Charles Ross
Crawley Beauty
Discovery
Edward VII
Egremont Russet
Ellison's Orange
Epicure
Falstaff
Fortune
Greensleeves
James Grieve
Jester

Jupiter
Laxton's Superb
Laxton's Triumph
Melba
Millers Seedling
Ontario
Spartan
Sunset
Suntan
Tydeman's Late Orange
Wagener
Worcester Pearmain

Apple varieties with decorative blossom

Adam's Pearmain
Annie Elizabeth
Arthur Turner
Ashmead's Kernel
Brownlees Russet
Bushey Grove
Cornish Gillflower
Cottenham Seedling
Edward VII

George Neal
Greensleeves
Merton Russet
Morley's Seedling
Ontario
Orleans Reinette
Ribston Pippin
Rosemary Russet
Warners King

Fruit Identification

Have you got a fruit tree in your garden and want to find out its name? This is a frequent problem especially when moving into a new property or when renovating old gardens and orchards. It is possible for individuals to send fruit for naming to either the Royal Horticultural Society or the Brogdale Horticultural Trust. For apples, many Apple Day events (around 21 October each year) have an opportunity to take along fruit samples for naming. Remember that if a fruit plant is known to have been raised from seed it is unique, previously unnamed and therefore it is not possible to name – at best an expert may be able to speculate as to what one of the parents may have been.

Naming fruit is not an exact art and it is very difficult to guarantee the accuracy. At present, there are few, if any, diagnostic methods which can be routinely used on fruit to correctly identify it. The expertise, experience and knowledge of the person carrying out the identification is crucial as is a good reference collection of varieties.

When selecting fruit for naming, the following guidelines should be followed:
- Select at least 3 typical fruits from each tree to be named. Fruit should be in good condition, approaching maturity and of characteristic size, shape and colour.
- The inclusion of a shoot and foliage can sometimes be helpful.
- Number each sample and keep a record of plant from which it is taken. Sticky labels should not be used as they become detached from fruit and polythene bags.
- Pack the sample in a strong box to avoid crushing and damage in transit. Protect the sample with loose newspaper, polystyrene granules or similar materials. Avoid using containers which have had pungent products – this can mask some fruit characteristic flavours.
- Give as much detail on the history and growing of the plant as possible, e.g. age, habit of growth, source of supply. Also a note of soil type and cultural practice can be helpful.

For further details write to:

Director of Horticulture (Fruit Naming)
RHS Garden
Wisley
Woking GU23 6QB

Director (Fruit Identification)
Brogdale Horticultural Trust
Brogdale Road
Faversham ME13 8XZ

A fee is charged for these services although members of these organisations may qualify for a reduced fee.

County origins of some UK apple, pear and plum varieties

This listing of varieties by their county or region of origin is by no means complete and is intended only as a guide. It will be of particular interest to those interested in selecting local varieties for gardens or other projects and in conserving varieties of local interest. All varieties are contained within the National Fruit Collections at Brogdale.

All apples are dessert unless otherwise stated (C = culinary, CD = dual purpose)

Avon
Apple
Beauty of Blackmoor, Cheddar Cross, Exeter Cross, Gloucester Cross, Hereford Cross, Maggie Grieve, Newport Cross, Plymouth Cross, Taunton Cross, Worcester Cross
Pear
Bristol Cross, Cheltenham Cross
Plum
Avalon, Avon Cross, Excalibur, Frome Cross, Peach Plum, Severn Cross, Teme Cross, Thames Cross, Wye Cross

Bedfordshire
Apple
Advance, Ballard Beauty, Beauty of Bedford, Bedfordshire Foundling (C), Duchess of Bedford, Epicure, Exquisite, Fortune, Hambling's Seedling (C), Laxton's Early Crimson, Laxton's Favourite, Laxton's Herald, Laxton's Leader, Laxton's Pearmain, Laxton's Peerless, Laxton's Rearguard, Laxton's Reward, Laxton's Royalty, Laxton's Superb, Laxton's Triumph, Laxton's Victory, Lord Lambourne, Owen Thomas, Pioneer, September Beauty
Pear
Beurre Bedford, Harvester, Laxton's Early Market, Laxton's Foremost, Laxton's Progress, Laxton's Record, Laxton's Superb, Laxton's Victor, Satisfaction
Plum
Blackbird, Black Prince, Blue Tit, Bountiful, Delicious, Early Laxton, Goldfinch, Jubilee, Laxton's Abundance, Laxton's Cropper, Laxton's Delight, Laxton's Early Gage, Laxton's Gage, Laxton's Ideal, Laxton's Supreme, Olympia, Prosperity, Utility

Berkshire
Apple
Breedon Pippin, Charles Eyre (C), Charles Ross (CD), Encore (C), Formosa Nonpareil (C), Frogmore Prolific (C), Guelph, Hector MacDonald (C), Houblon, John Standish, Miller's Seedling, Mrs Phillimore, Paroquet, Peacemaker, Renown, Rival, Sunrise, Welford Park Nonsuch, Winston

The Fruit and Veg Finder

Pear
   William's Bon Chretien
Plum
   Damson; Prune, Marjorie's Seedling

Buckinghamshire
Apple
   Arthur Turner (C), Cox's Orange Pippin, Cox's Pomona (CD), Feltham Beauty, Langley Pippin, Small's Admirable (C), S T Wright (C)
Pear
   Sir Harry Veitch
Plum
   Allgrove's Superb, Aylesbury Prune, Langley Bullace

Cambridgeshire
Apple
   Chiver's Delight, Cottenham Seedling (C), Emneth Early (Early Victoria)(C), Green Harvey (C), Haggerstone Pippin, Histon Favourite, Hunter's Majestic (CD), Lord Peckover, Lynn's Pippin, Morley's Seedling (C), Murfitt's Seedling (C), New Rock Pippin, Red Victoria (C), Saint Everard, Wayside
Plum
   Cambridge Gage

Cheshire
Apple
   Arthur W Barnes (C), Eccleston Pippin, Elton Beauty, Lord Clyde (C), Lord Derby (C), Millicent Barnes, Minshull Crab (C), Pott's Seedling (C), Sure Crop

Cumberland
Apple
   Carlisle Codlin (C), Forty Shilling, Greenups Pippin

Derbyshire
Apple
   Beeley Pippin, Belledge Pippin, Lamb's Seedling (C), Newton Wonder (C)

Devon
Apple
   Cornish Pine, Devonshire Buckland (C), Devonshire Quarrenden, Endsleigh Beauty, Lucombe's Pine, Lucombe's Seedling, Peter Lock (CD), Ponsford (C), Star of Devon, Upton Pyne, Woolbrook Pippin, Woolbrook Russet (C)

Pear
   Huyshe's Victoria
Plum
   Dittisham Ploughman, George Calver

Dorset
Apple
   Iron Pin (C), Melcombe Russet, Mollyanne
Plum
   Bryanston Gage

Essex
Apple
   Acme, Braintree Seedling, Chelmsford Wonder (C), D'Arcy Spice, Discovery, Edith Hopwood, Eros, Essex Pippin (CD), Excelsior (C), Flame, Francis, Garnet, George Cave, Macleans Favourite, Maldon Wonder, Monarch (C), Montfort, Morris's Russet, Opal, Pearl, Queen (C), Rosy Blenheim, Ruby, Seabrook's Red, Stanway Seedling (C), Sunburn, Waltham Abbey Seedling (C)
Pear
   Gansel's Bergamot
Plum
   Prince of Wales

Gloucestershire
Apple
   Ashmead's Kernel, Bedminster Pippin, Chaxhill Red (Cider), Gloucester Royal, Hunt's Duke of Gloucester, Lodgemore Nonpareil, Northland Seedling, Tewkesbury Baron
Plum
   Blaisdon Red, Victor Christian

Greater Manchester
Apple
   Lord Suffield (C)

Hampshire
Apple
   Beauty of Hants, Beneden Early, Bramshott Rectory, Easter Orange, Hambledon Deux Ans (C), Royal Snow
Plum
   Angelina Burdett, Woolston Black

The Fruit and Veg Finder

Herefordshire
Apple
   Downton Pippin, Forester (C), Golden Harvey, Herefordshire Beefing (C), Lady's Finger of Hereford, New German, Pig's Nose Pippin, Pitmaston Pineapple, Stoke Edith Pippin, Ten Commandments, Tyler's Kernel (C), Wormsley Pippin, Yellow Ingestrie
Pear
   Broom Park, Monarch

Hertfordshire
Apple
   Brownlees Russet, Bushey Grove (C), Dawn, Fairie Queen, Hormead Pearmain (C), Lane's Prince Albert (C), New Hawthornden (C), Prince Edward, River's Early Peach, River's Nonsuch, St Martin's, Thomas Rivers (C), Voyager, Winter Hawthornden (C), Young's Pinello
Pear
   Beacon, Conference, Fertility, Magnate, Parrot, Princess, Saint Luke, Summer Beurre D'Arenberg
Plum
   Admiral, Archduke, Autumn Compote, Bittern, Blue Prolific, Blue Rock, Curlew, Czar, Damson: Early Rivers, Early Favourite, Early Transparent Gage, Golden Transparent, Grand Duke, Heron, Late Orange, Late Transparent Gage, Mallard, Monarch, President, Primate, Stint, Swan

Humberside
Pear
   Hessle

Huntingdonshire
Apple
   Huntingdon Codlin

Ireland – Northern
Apple
   Balleyfatten (C), Barnhill Pippin, Ecklinville (C), Kemp (C), Reid's Seedling, Strippy (C), Summer John

Ireland – Southern
Apple
   Ard Cairn Russet, Eight Square, Gibbon's Russet, Golden Royal, Irish Peach, Richardson

Ireland – General
Apple
Bloody Butcher (C), Brown Crofton, Clearheart, Dockney (C), Greasy Pippin, Kerry Pippin, Kilkenny Pearmain, Lady's Finger of Offaly, Munster Tulip (CD), Peche Melba, Ross Nonpareil, Sam Young, Scarlet Crofton, Thompson's Apple, Yellow Pitcher

Isle of Man
Apple
Manks Codlin (C)

Isle of Wight
Apple
Howgate Wonder (C), Isle of Wight Pippin, Jersey Beauty, King George V, Sir John Thornycroft, Steyne Seedling

Kent
Apple
Beauty of Kent (C), Bolero, Bountiful (C), Bow Hill Pippin, Brenchley Pippin, Castle Major (C), Chips (CD), Cobham (CD), Colonel Vaughan, Cooper's Seedling (C), Diamond Jubilee, Falstaff, Faversham Creek (C), Fiesta, Fred Webb, Gascoyne's Scarlet, George Neal (C), Gooseberry (C), Granny Gifford, Greensleeves, Jester, Jupiter, Kent, Kentish Fillbasket (C), Lady Sudeley, Lamb Abbey Pearmain, Lily Boxall (CD), Mabbott's Pearmain, Maidstone Favourite, Michaelmas Red, Orange Goff, Polka, Polly Prosser, Red Devil, Redsleeves, Robin Pippin, Rossie Pippin (C), St Albans Pippin, Smart's Prince Arthur (C), South Park, Sunset, Suntan, Tydeman's Early, Tydeman's Late Orange, Wanstall Pippin, Warner's King (C), Waltz
Pear
Beth, Concord, Michaelmas Nelis
Plum
Bennett's Unknown, Bush, Damson: Farleigh, Diamond, Dundale, Late Gold

Lancashire
Apple
Duke of Devonshire, Golden Spire (C), Gold Medal, Harvest Festival (C), Hutton Square, John Huggett (CD), Keswick Codlin (C), Pott's Seedling (C), Proctor's Seedling, Sowman's Seedling (C)

Leicestershire
Apple
Annie Elizabeth (C), Barnack Orange, Belvoir Seedling, Dumelow's Seedling (C), Prince Charles, Queen Caroline (C), Saint Ailred

The Fruit and Veg Finder

Plum
> Golden Monarch

Lincolnshire
Apple
> Allington Pippin, Barnack Beauty, Brown's Seedling (C), Dewdney's Seedling (C), Doctor Clifford (C), Ellison's Orange, Herring's Pippin, Holland Pippin (CD), Ingall's Pippin, Ingall's Red, Isaac Newton's Tree (C), Lord Burghley, Peasgood's Nonsuch (C), Schoolmaster (C), Sleeping Beauty (C), Uland (C)

Plum
> Ingall's Grimoldby Greengage

London
Apple
> Barchard's Seedling, Cellini (C), Chad's Favourite, Fearn's Pippin, Langley Pippin, Merton Beauty, Merton Charm, Merton Delight, Merton Joy, Merton Knave, Merton Pearmain, Merton Pippin, Merton Prolific, Merton Reinette, Merton Russet, Merton Worcester, Mitchelson's Seedling (C), Rev W Wilks (C), Storey's Seedling

Pear
> Merton Pride, Merton Star, Mrs Seden, Willie Peddie

Plum
> Langley Bullace, Merton Blue, Merton Gage, Merton Gem

Merseyside
Apple
> Florence Bennett (CD)

Middlesex
Apple
> Grange's Pearmain (C), Hounslow Wonder (C), Moris's Russet, Pinner Seedling, Royal Jubilee (C)

Pear
> Autumn Nelis, Uvedale's Saint Germain

Norfolk
Apple
> Adam's Pearmain, Admiral, Baxter's Pearmain, Beachamwell, Caroline, Foulden Pearmain, Gavin, Golden Noble (C), Green Roland, Harvey (C), Horsford Prolific, Horsham Russet, Hubbard's Pearmain, Norfolk Beauty (C), Norfolk Beefing (C), Norfolk Coleman, Norfolk Royal, Robert Blatchford (C), Sandringham (C), St Magdalen, Striped Beefing (C), Vicar of Beighton, Winter Majetin (C)

Pear
   Hacon's Incomparable

Northamptonshire
Apple
   Eady's Magnum (C), Lord Burghley, Thorpe's Peach

Northumberland
Apple
   Mrs Lakeman's Seedling (C)

Nottinghamshire
Apple
   Baron Ward (C), Beauty of Stoke (C), Bess Pool, Bramley's Seedling (C), Grantonian (C), Nottingham Pippin, Pickering's Seedling, Radford Beauty, Sisson's Workshop Newtown, Winter Quarrenden
Plum
   Damson: Bradley's King, Merryweather, Johnny Rawes

Oxfordshire
Apple
   Blenheim Orange (CD), Caudal Market (C), Corry's Wonder (C), Eynsham Challenger (C), Eynsham Dumpling (C), Foulke's Foremost, Hanwell Souring (C), Jennifer, Jennifer Wastie, Old Fred, Oxford Beauty, Oxford Conquest, Oxford Hoard, Oxford Sunrise, Oxford Yeoman (C), Peggy's Pride, Red Army, Redstart, Wardington Seedling
Plum
   White's Early Increment

Scotland
Apple
   Alderman (C), Beauty of Moray (C), Bloody Ploughman, Cambusnethan Pippin, Coul Blush, Cutler Grieve, Early Julyan (CD), East Lothian Pippin (C), Galloway Pippin (C), Hawthornden (C), Hood's Supreme, James Grieve, Lady of the Wemyss (C), Lass O'Gowrie (C), Lord Rosebery, Maggie Sinclair (CD), Oslin, Port Allen Russet, Scotch Bridget (C), Seaton House (C), Seargeant Peggy (C), Stirling Castle (C), Stobo Castle (C), Thomas Jeffrey, Thorle Pippin, Tower of Glamis (C), Warden, White Melrose (C), White Paradise (C)
Pear
   Ayrshire Lass, Craig's Favourite, Crawford, Fair Maid, Green Pear of Yair, Laird Lang, Maggie, Summer Bergamot

Plum
   Burnet, Gordon Castle, Guthrie's Late Green, Lawson's Golden

Somerset
Apple
   Beauty of Bath, Bridgewater Pippin (C), Camelot (C), Court of Wick, Fair Maid of Taunton, Golden Knob, Hoary Morning (C), Kingston Black (Cider), Loddington (C), Melmouth, Merchant Apple, Poor Man's Profit (C), Puffin, Rough Pippin, Shoreditch White, Somerset Lasting (C), Tom Putt (C)
Pear
   Beurre D'Avalon

Suffolk
Apple
   Beachamwell, Catherine (C), Clopton Red, Honey Pippin, Lady Henniker, Lord Stradbroke (C), Macleans Favourite, St Edmunds Pippin, Sturmer Pippin
Pear
   Suffolk Thorn
Plum
   Coe's Golden Drop

Surrey
Apple
   Braddick Nonpareil, Byfleet Seedling (C), Carswell's Honeydew, Carswell's Orange, Claygate Pearmain, Cleeve, Cockle Pippin, Colonel Yate (C), Comrade, Curl Tail, Dalice, Duchess's Favourite, George Carpenter, Glebe Gold, Hannan Seedling (CD), High View Pippin, John Divers (C), Joybells, Lady Isabel (CD), Margaret Taylor, Mary Green (C), Mitchelson's Seedling (C), Nanny, Palmer's Rosey, Pixie, Prince George (C), Scarlet Nonpareil, Shoesmith (C), Smiler, Victory (C), Wadey's Seedling, William Peters, Ye Old Peasgood
Pear
   Onward
Plum
   Crimson Drop, Wierton Gage

Sussex
Apple
   Aldwick Beauty, Alfriston (C), Ashdown Seedling, Coronation, Crawley Beauty (C), Crawley Reinette, Doctor Hogg (C), Eastbourne Pippin, Edmund Jupp, First and Last, Forge (CD), Golden Bounty, Golden Pippin, Hawkridge, June Crewdson, Knobby Rus-

set, Lady Sudeley, Mannington's Pearmain, Mareda, Saltcote Pippin, Sussex Mother, Wadhurst Pippin
Plum
  Victoria

Wales
Apple
  Baker's Delicious, Channel Beauty, Chaxhill Red, Cissy, Saint Cecilia

Warwickshire
Apple
  Hunt's Early, Shakespeare, Wyken Pippin
Plum
  Warwickshire Drooper

Wiltshire
Apple
  Bedwyn Beauty (C), Burn's Seedling, Celt, Chorister Boy, Dredge's Fame, Mary Barnett (CD), Roundway Magnum Bonum

Worcestershire
Apple
  Betty Geeson, Dick's Favourite (C), Edward VII (C), Gladstone, Green Purnell, Hope Cottage Seedling, King Charles Pearmain, Lord Hindlip, Madresfield Court, May Queen, Pitmaston Russet Nonpareil, Sandlin Duchess, Tupstones, Whiting Pippin (C), William Crump, Worcester Pearmain
Pear
  Black Worcester
Plum
  Apricot Gage, Evesham Wonder, Grove's Late Victoria, Hay, Pershore, Purple Pershore

Yorkshire
Apple
  Acklam Russet, Cockpit (C), Fillingham Pippin, Flower of the Town, New Bess Pool, Ribston Pippin, Sharleston Pippin, Yorkshire Greening (C)
Plum
  Winesour, Wyedale

Further reading

Fruit

Anon (1994) *Award of Garden Merit Plants*. RHS ISBN 1-874-43113-2
Baker H A (1989) *Fruit: RHS Encyclopaedia of Practical Gardening*. Mitchell Beasley ISBN 0-855-33705-2
Baker H A (1991) *The Fruit Garden Displayed*. Cassell/RHS ISBN 0-304-34016-2
Baker H & Waite R (1988) *Grapes, indoors and out: A Wisley Handbook*. Cassell/RHS ISBN 0-304-31088-3
Hessayon D G (1990) *The Fruit Expert*. PBI Publications ISBN 0-90-3505-31-2
Morgan J & Richards A (1993) *The Book of Apples*. Ebury Press ISBN 0-09-177759-3
Woodward J (1990) *Pruning Hardy Fruits*. Cassell/RHS. ISBN 0-304-311030

Vegetables

Hessayon D G (1994) *The Vegetable Expert*. PBI Publications ISBN 0-903505-20-7
Larkcom J (1991) *Oriental Vegetables*. John Murray ISBN 0-7195-4781-4
Larkcom J (1992) *The Vegetable Garden Displayed*. RHS ISBN 0-906603-87-0.
Larkcom J (1995) *Salads for Small Gardens*, and *Vegetables for Small Gardens*. Hamlyn
Pears P & Sherman B (1991) *Healthy Fruit & Vegetables: How to avoid diseases, disorders and deficiencies*. HDRA/Search Press ISBN 0-85532-689-1
Pears P & Sherman B (1990) *Pests: how to control them on fruit and vegetables*. HDRA/Search Press ISBN 0-85532-741-3
Pears P & Stickland, S (1995) *Organic Gardening: RHS Encyclopaedia of Practical Gardening*. Mitchell Beazley/RHS ISBN 1-85732-973-2

Amaranth (Grain)

Burgundy
Futu

Golden
Earliest maturing strain, yellow seed heads. (Futu)
Futu

Multicolor
Foliage is a mixture of red, green and yellow, flowerheads show similar variation. (Futu)
Futu

Quinoa
Suff

Temuco
A variety with small, white, non-bitter seeds that require little washing. Flowerheads are either bright red or bright green. (Futu)
Futu

Amaranth (Leaf)

Hijau Salad Amaranth
Amaranthus mangostanus. An excellent variety, with rounded, lime-green leaves which can be eaten raw or lightly cooked. Amaranth greens are high in minerals and contain 10-15% protein. (Futu)
Futu

Vegetable Amaranth
Red leaf 50 days. Oval heart shaped green leaves overlaid with burgundy (like a coleus) 12-18 in. bushy plant. Much more tolerant than spinach to warm soil. May be cooked like spinach and makes a flavourful addition to salads and stir fry. (Suff)
OGC Suff

Anredera sp

Madeira Vine
A frost tender ornamental vine native to the Andes which produces large quantities of succulent, slightly mucilaginous leaves which can be eaten raw or cooked. The tubers are also edible and are produced in large quantities. Grows well in pots and likes a warm sunny position, or grow it in a greenhouse. (Futu)
Futu

Apple

3022
GTwe

A W Barnes
Oct-Jan, a large brightly coloured fruit, of moderate growth.
Allg CSco

Acme
A Cox seedling, shiny, yellow flushed and striped crimson, with a good Cox flavour. Prolific and resistant to scab.
SDea SKee CSco Bowe

Adam's Pearmain
(1862) Dessert. November to March. A moderately vigorous tree. Golden yellow conical shaped fruits half flushed with dull deep red. Some russet patches. Firm, juicy and sweet with a pleasant aromatic flavour. (Brog)
Allg Cast SDea SFam WHig WJas SKee CTho CSco GTwe SFru SIgm

Advance
Late summer dessert apple. The earliest of the Laxton's, a pleasant refreshing fruit with some Cox flavour if picked early. A small, rather weak grower.
Allg SKee CSco

Akane
Jonathan X Worcester. Stores well. Raised in Japan. Medium sized fruit - red all over. Similar but better fruit than Macintosh.
SDea

Alderman
Though raised over sixty years ago this mid-season apple has only recently come to notice for its good flavour. Coloured yellow with a red flush.
SDea CSco

Alfriston
1800, Sussex (Uckfield); culinary; very late; subacid.
SKee

Alkmene
SKee GTwe Bowe

Allen's Everlasting
Very late dessert apple. Yellow flushed red, with some russet. Leave on tree as long as possible. Ripening Dec/Jan - will keep until April. Record 1864.
SDea SKee CSco GTwe

Allington Pippin
(1884) Dessert. October to December. King of the Pippins x Cox's Orange Pippin. A moderately vigorous, upright-spreading tree. Pale whitish yellow fruits with brownish red stripes. Fine-textured and juicy but rather acid. A distinct aromatic flavour. (Brog)
Allg Cast SDea WJas SKee CTho Rog CSco SFru Bowe

American Mother
(1844) Dessert. October to December. A moderately vigorous, very upright tree. A distinctly tall American apple which is very juicy and sweet with a distinctive good aromatic flavour. (Brog)
Allg SDea SFam WJas SKee CSco GTwe SFru LBuc Bowe Edws

Ananas Reinette
SKee CSco

Anna Boelens
A variety tolerant of extremely high temperatures.
SDea

Anne Marie
SKee

Annie Elizabeth
(1857) Cooker. November to April. A moderately vigorous, upright tree. Very large pale green fruits with up to half flushed with orange red stripes. Skin becomes greasy if stored. Cooks well, breaking up completely. (Brog)
> Allg Cast SDea SFam WHig WJas SKee CSco GTwe SFru Bowe Edws

Api Noir
> SKee

Api Rose
Late dessert. Recorded 1628 but thought to be of Roman origin. Highly scented, sweet dessert which stores until April.
> WJas SKee

Arbroath
see Oslin

Ard Cairn Russet
An old Irish apple, scarlet and russet netted on yellow, crisp and possessing the true russet flavour. A fair sized tree. Scab resistant.
> SDea SKee CSco GTwe

Aromatic Russet
A small red russet; a slender little tree.
> SKee CSco

Arthur Turner
(1915) Cooker. September to November. A vigorous, upright tree. Very attractive blossom. Very large pale greenish yellow fruits flushed with light purplish brown. Fruits are coarse-textured, dry and acid. (Brog)
> Allg Cast SDea WJas SKee Rog CSco GTwe Muir LBuc Bowe Edws

Ashmead's Kernel
(1700) Dessert. December to February. A moderately vigorous, upright spreading tree. A flat-round light greenish yellow apple covered with much fine grey brown russet. Fruits are juicy, a little sweet and acid with a rich aromatic flavour. (Brog)
> Allg Cast SDea SFam WHig WJas SKee CTho Rog CSco GTwe Muir

Autumn Pearmain
Early autumn dessert apple. An old lightly russetted golden apple, crisp and well flavoured, known for over 400 years. The same as Hereford Pearmain?
> SDea WJas CTho CSco

Baker's Delicious
Early autumn dessert apple. A valuable fruit, large, handsomely flushed orange-scarlet on yellow with a smooth waxy skin, juicy and refreshingly brisk. Bears well on young trees and seems free from disease.
> SDea SKee CSco SIgm

Balsam
> Cast Rog

Barnack Beauty
1840, Northamptonshire or Leicestershire. A dual purpose fruit, golden with red flush and stripes, hardy and vigorous.
Allg SKee CTho CSco

Barnack Orange
1904, Notts (Belvoir Castle); dessert; very late; aromatic.
SKee

Baron Ward
1859, Nottinghamshire; dessert; late; astringent.
SKee

Baron Wolseley
Allg

Baron de Berlepsch
Allg

Baumann's Reinette
1811. Belgium. Chiefly grown for its striking crimson skin.
Allg SKee CSco

Baxter's Pearmain
1821, Norfolk; dual; late; subacid.
Allg SKee

Beauty of Bath
(1864) - Dessert. Late July to early August. A moderately vigorous, round, spreading tree. A distinctly flat, well coloured, mottled apple. Soft, juicy and sweet with a distinctive acid flavour. Slow to come into bearing. (Brog)
Allg Cast SDea SFam WHig WJas SKee Rog CSco GTwe Bowe Edws

Beauty of Hants
1850, Hampshire; dessert; very late; aromatic.
SKee

Beauty of Kent
1820, Kent; culinary; midseason to late; acid.
Allg SDea SKee

Beauty of Moray
1883, Scotland; culinary; early to midseason; acid.
SDea SKee

Beauty of Stoke
1890, Nottinghamshire; culinary; very late; subacid.
Allg SKee

Bedwyn Beauty
Marlborough, Wilts, c 1890; sharp; culinary; late to very late.
CTho

Beeley Pippin
1880. Derbyshire. Ready late Aug - keeps until Oct. Pea green base colour, with half flushed brownish purple and russeting.
SDea SKee

Bell Apple
(syn. Sweet Sheep's Nose) Somerset; sweet; cider, culinary; mid. A distinctly shaped apple once common in Somerset and East Devon.
CTho

Belle Fille Normande
1800, France; dual; midseason to late; sweet/subacid.
　SKee

Belle de Boskoop
(1856) Dual purpose. Triploid. December to April. A medium to large upright/spreading tree. A vigorous, upright-spreading tree. Large, light greenish yellow fruits flushed with brownish orange red stripes and much light brown russet. Fruits are coarse-textured with an aromatic flavour. (Brog)
　Allg SDea SKee CSco GTwe Bowe

Bembridge Beauty
　SDea

Ben's Red
　SKee SIgm

Benoni
　Bowe

Bess Pool
Discovered in Nottingham in 1824 by Bess Pool. Very late to flower and hence frost-proof. Picked early Oct - will keep until Feb. Fruit is almost all dull crimson, with some russeting and short, broad, dark red broken stripes. Flesh is tinged green, coarse and rather dry, but with sweet pleasant flavour. Tip bearing on spreading branches. Gets slightly waxy in store.
　Allg SDea SKee CSco

Billy Down Pippin
Membury, Axminster, Devon. Supposedly a corruption of Bewley Down near Membury.
　CTho

Bismarck
1870, Tasmania; culinary; midseason to late; subacid.
　Allg SKee CSco Bowe

Blenheim Orange
(1740) Dual purpose. Triploid. November to January. A vigorous, upright-spreading tree. Has a tendency to tip-bearing. Very large greenish yellow fruits up to one half flushed with orange red stripes. Some russet. Fruits are coarse-textured and rather dry but with a rich aromatic flavour. Cooks well. (Brog)
　Allg Cast SDea SFam WHig WJas SKee CTho Rog CSco GTwe Muir

Bloody Ploughman
1883, Scotland; dessert; midseason; sweet/subacid.
　SDea

Blue Pearmain
1800, USA; dessert; very late; aromatic.
　Allg SDea SKee

Boikenapfel
　Allg

** Bolero
Shining green crisp apples to pick in Sept.
　SDea EBal

Boston Russet
A brown-green American russet, small and compact.
  Allg CSco Bowe

Bountiful
(1964) Cooker. October to January. A compact tree. Some resistance to mildew. Large, round green fruits with occasional orange-red stripes. Cooks well, requiring very little sugar. (Brog)
  Cast SDea WHig CSco GTwe Muir SFru SIgm Bowe

Bow Hill Pippin
1893, Kent (Maidstone); dessert; very late; sweet.
  SKee

Box Apple
Old, Cornwall; dessert; early to midseason; sweet.
  SKee

Braddick Nonpareil
1818, Surrey (Thames Ditton). A late greenish-yellow Nonpareil. Small.
  SKee CSco

Braeburn
A New Zealand apple - juicy and really tasty. An experiment to grow here, but with our increasing temperature through global warming it may ripen OK.
  SDea SKee

Bramley's Seedling
(1809) Cooker. Triploid. November to February. A very vigorous, spreading tree. A partial tip-bearer. A large, somewhat flattened apple extensively grown commercially. A first class cooker. (Brog)
  Allg Cast SDea SFam WHig WJas SKee Rog CSco GTwe Muir SFru

Brandy Apple
see Golden Harvey

Bridgewater Pippin
Before 1665; juicy and subacid; dessert, culinary; mid to late.
  CTho

Broad-Eyed Pippin
C1650, Old English; culinary; late; acid.
  SKee Bowe

Brownlees Russet
(1848) Dessert. December to March. A moderately vigorous, upright-spreading tree. A flat-round to short-conical deep green apple, some fruits flushed with dull red-brown. Almost entirely covered with grey brown russet. Juicy and fairly acid but with a pleasant nutty flavour. (Brog)
  Allg Cast SDea SFam WJas SKee CTho Rog CSco GTwe SFru Edws

Burn's Seedling
Marlborough, Wilts, c 1830; very sweet, scented; dessert; late.
  CTho

Burr Knot
  SKee

Bushey Grove
1897, Hertfordshire. Large fruit - flat to round. Flesh very soft. Very acid - ideal baker. Pick late Aug - keeps until Dec. Award of Merit 1922. Raised in Bushey.
SDea SKee

Buxted Favourite
SKee

Byford Wonder
Allg

Calville Blanc D'Hiver
The famous French winter apple, large and pale yellow with a pink cheek, strongly scented, but not hardy.
SKee CSco

Calville Rouge Precoce
Allg

Calville des Femmes
1850, France; culinary; very late; subacid.
SKee

Cambusnethan Pippin
C1750, Scotland (Stirling); dessert; mid to late season; subacid.
SDea SKee

Canadian Russet
SKee Bowe

Captain Kidd
Bowe

Cardross Green
SDea

Carlisle Codlin
GTwe

Carswell's Orange
1959, Surrey (Ashtead); dessert; midseason; sweet.
SKee

Catherine
1970, Kent (North Halling); dessert; late; sweet.
SKee Bowe

Catshead
(1600) Cooker. Late October to January. A moderately vigorous, spreading tree. A distinctly angular and somewhat ugly cooking apple. Similar in appearance to an outsized Lord Derby. (Brog)
Cast SDea SKee CSco GTwe Bowe

Cellini
Good regular cropping small cooker. Green becoming pale yellow, with brownish red mottling. Pick mid-Sept - keeps until end of Nov.
SDea SKee

Charles Eyre
Oct-Nov, one of the largest apples, a fine pale yellow fruit, round and evenly shaped. A small upright tree.
SKee CSco

Charles Ross
(1890) Dual purpose. Peasgood's Nonsuch x Cox's Orange Pippin. October to December. A moderately vigorous, upright-spreading tree. A large attractive apple which looks rather like a large Cox's Orange Pippin. Fruits are juicy and sweet with moderate flavour. (Brog)
> Allg Cast SDea SFam WHig WJas SKee CTho Rog CSco GTwe SIgm

** Charlotte
Cooker. Big Bramley sized apples, which bake and stew well. Green with a touch of red; melting cream coloured flesh. Pick and cook from late Sept - will store well into the New Year.
> SDea EBal

Cheddar Cross
1949, Gloucestershire; dessert; very late; aromatic.
> Allg SKee Bowe

Chelmsford Wonder
1870, Essex; culinary; midseason; acid.
> Allg SKee

Chivers Delight
(1936) Dessert. November to January. A moderately vigorous, fairly upright tree. A fairly round, pale yellow apple with up to one half flushed with orange red. Firm, juicy fruit with a pleasant flavour. (Brog)
> Cast SDea WHig WJas SKee CSco GTwe SFru SIgm Bowe Edws

Chorister Boy
Wiltshire, before 1890; juicy with a hint of strawberry; dessert; mid to late.
> CTho

Christmas Pearmain
(1893) Dessert. November to January. A moderately vigorous, upright-spreading tree. Long conical fruits becoming dull yellow and up to three quarters flushed dull orange red. Patches of dull grey russet. Firm, crisp and juicy with a pleasant aromatic flavour. (Brog)
> Allg SDea SKee CTho CSco GTwe Bowe Edws

Cinderella
> Bowe

Clarkes Royal
> GTwe

Claygate Pearmain
(1821) Dessert. December to February. A moderately vigorous tree. Fruits in appearance resemble a tall Blenheim Orange. Rather coarse-textured flesh but juicy with a rich aromatic flavour. (Brog)
> Allg SDea SKee CTho CSco GTwe SFru SIgm Edws

Clydeside
> SDea

Cockle Pippin
(1800) Dessert. December to March. A moderately vigorous, upright tree. A small conical, pale greenish yellow apple with traces of grey russet and slight brown flush. Fruits have firm, fine-textured dry sweet flesh with a pleasant flavour. (Brog)
Allg SDea SKee CTho CSco

Coeur de Boeuf
Pre 1200; France; dessert; very late; aromatic.
SKee

Colloget Pippin
(syn. Cornish Giant) Landulph, Tamar Valley, Cornwall; sharp; culinary, cider; mid. Produces a dry light cider.
CTho

Colonel Vaughan
(Syn. Kentish Pippin) Kent, 17th century; juicy, sweet, crisp; dessert; late. A heavy cropper. Popular for tarts and cider in 17th century.
Allg SKee CTho SIgm

Cornish Aromatic
(1813) Dessert. December to March. A vigorous, upright-spreading tree. A conical, greenish yellow apple with up to half flushed with dull red stripes, partly covered with fine grey russet. Fruits are firm, fine textured and rather dry with a rich aromatic flavour. (Brog)
SDea SFam WJas SKee CTho CSco GTwe SIgm Bowe Edws

Cornish Gilliflower
(1813) Dessert. November to March. A moderately vigorous, very spreading tree. A tip bearer. Golden yellow, oblong-conical
fruits flushed with orange red. Some russet. Fruits are firm, fine textured, rather dry and sweet with a rich aromatic flavour. (Brog)
SDea SFam WJas SKee CSco GTwe SIgm Edws

Cornish Honey Pin
Before 1955; sweet; dessert; second early.
CTho

Cornish Longstem
Linkinhorne, Cornwall; sharp; culinary; very late. A hard green apple that will keep until June.
CTho

Cornish Pine
(Syn. Red Ribbed Greening) Exminster, Devon, before 1920; sweet, slightly subacid, aromatic; dessert; mid to late. Cornish Gilliflower seedling.
SDea SKee CTho Bowe

Coronation
1902, Sussex. Pick mid-Sept - keeps until Dec. Yellow base with orange/red covering. R.H.S. award, 1902.
Allg SDea SKee

Cortland
1898, USA; dessert; very late; sweet.
SKee

Costard
Pre 1200, Old English; culinary; late; subacid.
SKee GTwe

Cottenham Seedling
1923, Cambridgeshire; culinary; very late; subacid.
SKee

Coul Blush
1827, Scotland; dessert; midseason; sweet.
SDea SKee

Court Pendu Plat
(1613) Dessert. December to April. A rather small to moderately vigorous, upright-spreading tree. An unusually flat apple. Flowers very late. Firm, fine-textured, juicy and sweet with a slight aromatic flavour. (Brog)
Allg Cast SDea SFam WHig WJas SKee CTho Rog CSco GTwe LBuc

Court of Wick
An old Somerset apple, recorded before 1790, once widely grown, richly flavoured, brightly coloured yellow flushed orange. Prolific.
SKee CTho CSco

Cox (Self fertile clone)
Cast SDea WHig SKee LBuc

Cox Rouge des Flandres
SKee

Cox's Orange Pippin
(1825) Dessert. November to January. A moderately vigorous, upright-spreading tree. A round conical light golden yellow apple up to three quarters flushed with orange red stripes. Fine textured, juicy, a little sweet with a rich aromatic flavour (Brog)
Allg Cast SDea SFam WHig WJas SKee Rog CSco GTwe SFru LBuc

Cox's Pomona
(1825) Cooker. October to December. A moderately vigorous, upright-spreading tree. A flat-round, highly coloured apple. Fruits do not break up completely when cooked. (Brog)
Allg SDea SKee CTho CSco

Crawley Beauty
(1870) Cooker. December to March. A moderately vigorous, spreading tree. Flowers very late. A flat-round to round pale yellow apple with one half to three quarters flushed with brownish red. Fruits can become fairly greasy. Slightly coarse-textured, dry and subacid. (Brog)
SDea SFam WJas SKee CSco GTwe SFru Edws

Crimson Bramley
Nov-Mar, the crimson skinned sport - otherwise like the type. Triploid.
SKee CSco

Crimson Cox
Another sport from Cox's Orange Pippin.
SDea

Crimson Newton Wonder
SKee

Crimson Peasgood
SKee

Crimson Queening
Dessert. 1831. A Herefordshire variety, at home in a bowl, on a show bench or in front of an artist's easel!
WJas SKee

Crispin
(1930) Dual purpose. Triploid. December to February. A very vigorous, spreading tree. A large, green, distinctly ribbed apple becoming yellow. Firm, fine textured, juicy and refreshing with a moderate flavour. (Brog)
Allg Cast SDea SKee Rog CSco GTwe SFru SIgm Bowe Edws

** Crowngold
A natural clone of Jonagold. It has a more solid bright red colour than normal Jonagold. (Brog)
Cast SKee CSco GTwe Muir Bowe Edws

Curl Tail
SKee

Cutler Grieve
SDea

D'Arcy Spice
(1785) Dessert. December to April. A somewhat weak, upright-spreading tree. A rather unattractive late keeping dessert apple. Fruits are firm, fine textured and juicy with a characteristic aromatic flavour. (Brog)
Cast SDea SFam SKee CSco GTwe SFru SIgm Bowe Edws

Dawn
1940, Hertfordshire; dual; late; subacid.
SKee

Deacon's Blushing Beauty
A very useful discovery by us here at Godshill. Fruit is bright yellow with a distinctive pink flush on the sunny side. A dual purpose apple, cooking well and later being exrtremely palatable, with a slightly subacid flavour and profusely juicy. Extremely prolific. Ready end Sept/early Oct. Irregular shape, but similar to Greensleeves, with pink face. (SDea)
SDea

Decio
Pre 480, Italy via Asia Minor; dessert; late; sweet/subacid.
SKee SFru

Delicious
Allg

Delkio
GTwe

Devonshire Buckland
Devon, before 1831; subacid, slightly sweet; dual; mid to late. Crisp, perfumed, yellow flesh.
WJas CTho

Devonshire Crimson Queen
SDea CTho

Devonshire Quarrenden
(1678) Dessert. Late August to early September. A medium sized, upright-spreading tree. A very attractive, distinctly flat apple with a pleasant, refreshing flavour. (Brog)
Allg SDea SFam WJas SKee CTho CSco GTwe Bowe Edws

Diamond Jubilee
Late dessert. One of the varieties propagated for HRH, Prince Charles.
WJas SKee

Discovery
(1949) Dessert. Mid August to mid September. A moderately vigorous, upright-spreading tree. Somewhat inclined to tip bearing. A flat to flat round apple up to three quarters flushed with bright blood red. Firm, fine textured, juicy and fairly sweet with a pleasant flavour. (Brog)
Allg Cast SDea SFam WHig SKee Rog CSco GTwe Muir SFru LBuc

Doctor Hare's
Late culinary. 1884. Originated near Leaminster. A firm and crisp culinary that will keep till May.
WJas

Domino
1883, Midlands; dual purpose; midseason; subacid.
SKee

Downton Pippin
Late dessert. 1806. A connoisseur's choice. Small, juicy best from Nov till Jan. Raised at Downton Castle.
SKee

Dredge's Fame
Salisbury, Wilts, before 1802; rich and fruity; dessert; late.
CTho

Duchess of Oldenburg
1700, Russia. Late summer dessert apple. An old striped apple, scarlet on creamy-green, sharp and juicy. A large spreading tree.
Allg SKee CSco

Duchess's Favourite
Early autumn dessert apple. An old English variety, before 1790. Much grown in the last century. Pale yellow with a crimson, shiny fruit, dark green leaves unusually healthy and resistant to disease.
Allg SKee CSco

Duke of Devonshire
(1835) Dessert. January to March. A moderately vigorous, spreading tree. A round, pale golden yellow apple rarely with a slight brownish flush. Partly covered with a netted russet. Firm, but rather dry flesh with a rich nutty flavour. (Brog)
Allg SDea SKee CTho CSco Bowe

Dumelow's Seedling
(1800) Cooker. November to April. A moderately vigorous, spreading tree. A flat-round, pale yellow apple sometimes flushed with some mottled bright orange red. Very firm and crisp, juicy and extremely acid. Cooks well, breaking up completely. (Brog)
   Allg SDea SKee CTho CSco GTwe SFru

Dunn's Seedling
An Australian apple, grown in abundance in Tasmania and imported by us. Pale yellow fruit flushed slight pink, with some russeting. A hard subacid fruit, green and flat. Pick 20th of Sept. (SDea)
   SDea

Dutch Codlin
Holland, introduced late 18th century; sharp; culinary; early to mid.
   CTho

Dutch Mignonne
Pre 1771, Holland; dessert; very late; sweet.
   Allg SKee

Early Blenheim
Somerset; dessert, culinary; second early. Similar to Blenheim Orange but earlier.
   CTho

Early Julyan
(Syn. Tam Montgomery) Pre 1800 Scotland. Early culinary. Grown for HRH Prince Charles' Highgrove gardens.
   SDea WJas SKee

East Lothian Pippin
   SDea

Easter Orange
1897 Hampshire. Hard, crisp yellow-green fruit. Scab resistant.
   SKee CSco

Ecklinville
Pre 1800, Belfast; culinary; midseason; acid.
   Allg SDea SKee

Edward VII
(1902) Cooker. Blenheim Orange x Golden Noble, December to April. A moderately vigorous, upright spreading tree. Flowers late. A flat-round pale yellow apple with a slight purplish brown flush. Rather coarse textured, juicy and acid. An excellent cooker, breaking up completely. (Brog)
   Allg SDea SFam WJas SKee CSco GTwe SFru Bowe Edws

Edwin Beckett
1915, Hertfordshire (Elstree); culinary; early to midseason; subacid.
   SKee

Egremont Russet
(1872) Dessert. October to November. A moderately vigorous, upright-spreading tree. A good quality russet variety having a rich, nutty flavour. Can be prone to bitter pit. (Brog)
   Allg Cast SDea SFam WHig WJas SKee CTho Rog CSco GTwe Muir

Elbee
   SKee

Ellison's Orange
(1904) Dessert. Cox's Orange Pippin x Calville Blanc. September and October. A fairly vigorous, upright spreading tree. Similar in appearance to Cox's Orange Pippin. Fruits have a strong aniseed flavour. Very susceptible to canker. (Brog)
   Allg Cast SDea SFam SKee Rog CSco GTwe SFru SIgm Bowe Edws

** Elstar
(1955) Dessert. Golden Delicious x Ingrid Marie. October to December. A medium sized, upright-spreading tree. A medium sized yellow apple flushed with bright red. Very juicy with good flavour. Poor colour in the centre of the tree can be a problem. Coloured sports do now exist. (Brog)
   Cast SDea WHig SKee CSco GTwe Muir SFru SIgm Bowe

Elton Beauty
Profuse early flowers are probably the reason for this cultivar's name. Fruits Oct/Nov - keeping its smooth skinned striped fruit until Jan in store.
   SDea SKee

Emneth Early (Early Victoria)
(1899) Cooker. Lord Grosvenor x Keswick Codlin. Late July to mid August. A medium sized, upright spreading tree. A useful, codlin-type early cooking apple. Tends to be biennial. (Brog)
   Allg Cast SDea SFam WJas SKee Rog CSco GTwe SFru Bowe

Emperor Alexander
   Allg

Empire
1954, New York; dessert; late; aromatic.
   SKee

Encore
1906 Berkshire. Keeping till May. Large, like a Bramley in appearance, with a red flush, particularly good flavour.
   SDea SKee CSco SFru Bowe

English Codlin
England; sharp and perfumed; culinary; early to mid. One of the oldest English apples.
   CTho

Epicure
(1909) Dessert. Wealthy x Cox's Orange Pippin. Mid August to mid September. A moderately vigorous, upright spreading tree. A round, pale greenish yellow apple up to three quarters flushed with dull brownish crimson stripes. Moderately firm and juicy with a refreshing flavour. (Brog)
   Cast SDea SFam SKee Rog CSco GTwe SFru SIgm Bowe Edws

Ernie's Russet
A large colourful Russet, located in an Isle of Wight garden. Worth a place in your collection.
   SDea

Eve's Delight
Ready in Sept. Enormous fruit, reaching 2 lb. 'The Big Apple', USA. Slater seedling to Stark's Jumbo apple.
SDea

Evening Gold
Believed locally to be an Island apple. Keeping well into Feb, this apple is like the setting sun - golden with bright orange flush. Quite palatable, even at end of storage time. A very hardy fruit - even windfalls will store. For those with a sweet tooth. Probably described as dual purpose. medium sized fruit. (SDea)
SDea

Exeter Cross
Early autumn dessert apple. Crimson, shiny fruit, dark green leaves unusually healthy and resistant to disease.
SDea SFam SKee CSco Bowe

Exquisite
Allg CSco

Fair Maid of Devon
Devon; full Sharp; cider; mid. Compact tree. Produces a high percentage of juice. Vintage quality.
CTho

Fall Russet
GTwe

** Falstaff
(1966) Dessert. James Grieve x Golden Delicious. October to December. A medium sized open tree of medium vigour and drooping habit. A round-conical yellow apple flushed with red stripes. Good skin finish. Fruits are crisp and juicy with a very good flavour. Very resistant to frost. Heavy cropper. A good pollinator. (Brog)
Cast SKee GTwe Muir SFru SIgm Bowe

Fameuse
Pre 1730, Canada via France; dessert; mid to late season; sweet.
SKee

Farmer's Glory
Bowe

Fearn's Pippin
A flattish yellow apple with a dark crimson flush; crisp and aromatic. Raised by a Mr Bagley of Fulham before 1780 and supplied to the London market over many years. Nov-Mar.
SKee

Feltham Beauty
Late summer dessert apple. A brilliant red and yellow fruit, its splendid colouration brings it into demand for summer shows.
CSco

Feuillemorte
SKee

** Fiesta
(1973) Dessert. Cox's Orange Pippin x Idared. October to January. A moderately vigorous tree with wide branch angles and a slightly drooping habit. A round, evenly shaped, attractive apple. A well coloured Cox-type apple, with a good skin finish. Fruits are crisp and juicy with a Cox-like flavour. A precocious, high yielding variety. (Brog)
   Allg Cast SDea SFam WHig SKee Rog CSco GTwe Muir LBuc SFru

Fillingham Pippin
SKee

Fireside
SIgm

Firmgold
SDea

Fisher Fortune
Bowe

Five Crowns
Pre 1580, East Anglia; dessert; late; subacid.
   SKee

** Flamenco
Late keeper. Dark red apples, with crisp tangy white flesh. With Cox in its ancestry, stores well into the New Year. Pick in early Oct and, for mellowness, keep until Christmas.
   SDea EBal

Flower of Kent
Pre 1629, Kent. Dual purpose; mid to late; subacid. The falling apple that Sir Isaac Newton watched, grown from his tree.
   Allg SKee CSco SDea SFru SIgm

Flower of the Town
Mid dessert. James Grieve type apple.
   WJas

Folkestone
SKee

Forfar
see Dutch Mignonne.

SKee

Forge
SDea SKee CSco Bowe

Formosa Nonpareil
Mid culinary. Golden Noble type culinary apple.
   WJas

Fortune
(1904) Dessert. Cox's Orange Pippin x Wealthy. September and October. A medium sized, upright-spreading tree. A round-conical pale yellow apple flushed almost completely with broken bright red stripes. Juicy and sweet with a good aromatic flavour. (Brog)
   Allg Cast SDea SFam WJas SKee Rog CSco GTwe Muir SFru SIgm

Foster's Seedling
SKee

Franklyn's Golden Pippin
An old small golden variety.
 CSco

French Crab
(Syn. Hoggs Winter Greening) France late 18th century; sharp; culinary; late to very late. Can keep until June, or eventhe following year.
 SDea CTho CSco GTwe

Freyburg
1934, New Zealand; dessert; mid to late; sweet.
 SKee

Fuji
Red sport apple from Tohoku Experimental Station, Japan. Excellently flavoured, long keeping dessert.
 SDea SKee

Gala
(1934) Dessert. Kidd's Orange Red x Golden Delicious. October to early January. A moderately vigorous, upright, fairly spreading tree. An oblong-conical yellow apple flushed and flecked with bright scarlet red. Firm, crisp and juicy and sweet with a good aromatic flavour. Prone to canker. (Brog)
 Allg SDea SFam SKee CSco GTwe Muir SFru SIgm Bowe

Galloway Pippin
Very old, Scotland (Wigtown); culinary; late to very late; subacid.
 SDea SKee GTwe Bowe

Gascoyne's Scarlet
(1871) Dual purpose. October to January. A vigorous, upright spreading tree. A flat round, pale greenish white apple up to half flushed with bright deep blood red. Firm, fine textured flesh. A little juicy and sweet with very little flavour. Fruits can become a little greasy. (Brog)
 Allg SDea SFam SKee CSco

Gavin
Raised by John Innes Institute from a Malus Floribunda X Merton Worcester. Trees consequently have arching branches, due to its parentage. Gavin's main attribute is its resistance to many nasties, i.e. apple cab and mildew. Fruit is oblong to round, with red flush on greenish base. Crisp and juicy. Ready around mid-Sept. Ideal for SW UK (where the wet produces scab problems).
 SDea SKee

Genesis II
Another release from the USA. Large fruiting cooker. Late keeping.
 SDea

Genet Moyle
 WJas CTho

George Carpenter
1902, Surrey (Byfleet); dessert; mid to late; sweet.
 Allg SKee

George Cave
(1923) Dessert. Early to mid August. A moderately vigorous, upright-spreading tree. Round-conical pale greenish yellow fruits flushed and striped with bright red. A little soft, but juicy anda little acid with a pleasant flavour. A reliable cropper. Can become a little greasy if stored. (Brog)
   Cast SDea SFam WJas SKee Rog CSco GTwe SFru SIgm Bowe Edws

George Fayers
   SKee

George Neal
(1904) Cooker. August to October. A medium to large, spreading tree. A flat-round, pale yellow apple flushed with brownish red. Fruits are rather soft, juicy and acid. Cooks well.Fruits become greasy if stored. (Brog)
   SDea SFam SKee CSco GTwe SFru SIgm Edws

Gilliflower of Gloucester
Gloucestershire; sweet, scented; dessert; early to mid.
   CTho

Gladstone
(Originally Jackson's Seedling) Worcestershire, c 1780; juicy, aromatic, sweet; dessert; early to second early. Delicious fresh from the tree.
   SDea SKee CTho SIgm Bowe

Glockenapfel
   Allg

Gloria Mundi
Raised in Germany and recorded in the USA in 1804. Very large fruit - irregular shape (oblong - flat at base). CSreamy white flesh tinged green. Pick mid-Oct - keeps until March.
   Allg SDea SKee

Glory of England
Early culinary. A Lord Derby type apple.
   WJas

Gloster 69
(1951) Dessert. Weisser Winterglockenapfel x Richard Delicious. November to March. A highly coloured, distinctly angular Delicious-type apple. Juicy and sweet with a pleasant flavour. (Brog)
   Cast SDea SKee CSco GTwe SIgm Bowe Edws

Gloucester Cross
1913, Bristol (Long Ashton); dessert; mid season; rich.
   SKee

Golden Delicious
(1890) Dessert. Grimes Golden open pollinated. November to February. A moderately vigorous, low and spreading tree. A tall, rich yellow, slightly ribbed apple of distinctive appearance. Juicy and sweet with a good aromatic flavour. (Brog)
   Allg Cast SDea SKee Rog Bowe Edws

Golden Glow
   SDea

Golden Harvey
(Syn. Brandy Apple) Possibly Hereford, early 17th century; sweet-sharp, intense; dessert, cider; late to very late. High specific gravity of juice makes very strong cider. Fruits small.
   CTho CSco

Golden Knob
Somerset, 18th century; sweet, nutty; dessert; late to very late. A little russetted apple with a fruity aromatic taste.
   SKee CTho

Golden Noble
(1803) Cooker. October to December. A moderately vigorous, upright-spreading tree. Inclined to tip bearing. A round-conical yellow apple with light patches of grey russet. Soft, very juicy and acid. Cooks extremely well. Fruits become rather greasy if stored. (Brog)
   Allg SDea SFam SKee CSco GTwe SFru SIgm Bowe Edws

Golden Nonpareil
A small golden fruit, flushed brown red.
   CSco

Golden Nugget
   SIgm

Golden Pippin
1629, England; dessert; mid to very late; rich. One of the very oldest varieties.
   SKee CSco

Golden Reinette
1650, Europe. Golden yellow with russet and a red flush.
   SKee CSco

Golden Russet
Dessert. December to March. A fairly vigorous, upright-spreading tree. A shy cropping, late russet apple similar in appearance to D'Arcy Spice. Firm, rather dry flesh with a sweet, pleasant nutty flavour. (Brog)
   Allg SDea WJas SKee CSco

Golden Russet of West New York
   SKee

Golden Spire
(1850) Cooker. September and October. A moderately vigorous, upright-spreading to spreading tree. Attractive blossom. Conical, distinctly ribbed, pale greenish yellow fruits up to half flushed with golden orange. Fruits are juicy with an acid flavour. Cooks well. (Brog)
   Allg Cast SDea SKee CTho Rog CSco

Goldilocks
(Genetic dwarf) New, France; dessert; late; sweet.
   SKee GTwe Bowe

Gooseberry
1831, Kent. Cooker. Jan-June, another late green apple yellow-green, hard and juicy in May
   SKee CSco Bowe

Grange's Pearmain
A hard greenish-yellow fruit, juicy and well flavoured. The nearest to a Newtown Pippin.
    CSco

Granny Smith
(1868) Dessert. January to April. A rather small to moderately vigorous, upright-spreading tree. A round-conical, green apple. Firm, rather coarse textured and juicy. Little flavour. Requires a long hot summer to fully mature in the UK. (Brog)
    Cast SDea SKee CSco GTwe Slgm Bowe Edws

Granny Smith Spur Type
    Bowe

Gravenstein
(1669) Dessert. Triploid. September to December. A vigorous, upright-spreading tree. A large, irregular, bright yellow apple with orange red flush on up to three-quarters of its surface. Crisp and juicy with a distinct flavour. (Brog)
    Allg SDea SFam SKee SFru Bowe

Greasy Pippin
    Bowe

Green Kilpandy Pippin
    SDea

Green Roland
1946, Norfolk; dual; late; sweet/subacid.
    SKee Bowe

** Greensleeves
(1966) Dessert. James Grieve x Golden Delicious. October to November. Produces a tree of below medium vigour, is fairly upright and rather 'twiggy'. A medium sized green apple. Fruits are crisp and juicy with a mild refreshing flavour. Prolific and precocious, but can be difficult to pick in some seasons. (Brog)
    Cast SDea WHig WJas SKee Rog CSco GTwe Muir SFru Slgm Bowe

Grenadier
(1862) Cooker. August and September. An upright-spreading tree of medium vigour. A large, somewhat flattened, pale green apple. Fairly distinctly ribbed. Firm, juicy and acid. Cooks well. (Brog)
    Allg Cast SDea SFam WHig SKee Rog CSco GTwe SFru Slgm Bowe

Hambledon Deux Ans
Originated in Hambleton, Hampshire, in 1750 or before. Dual purpose, silvery green apple, turning golden yellow. Pick late Sept - keeps until April (sometimes keeps for two years).
    SDea WJas SKee

Hambling's Seedling
1893 Bedfordshire. Jan-Mar, a good large pale yellow fruit of unusually pleasant flavour.
    Allg SKee CSco

Haralson
    Slgm

Hardispur Delicious
    Bowe

Harvey
(Syn. Dr Harvey) Pre 1629. Jan-Mar, An old East Anglian apple, long neglected but returning to favour after three centuries. Named after Dr Gabriel Harvey of Cambridge.
SDea SKee CSco Bowe

Hawthornden
Edinburgh, before 1780; subacid; culinary; mid. Scab prone but a popular old cooking apple in the eastern counties.
SDea SKee CTho

Hereford Cross
1913, Bristol. A large cromson skinned Cox seedling, crisp, sweet and juicy.
SKee CSco Bowe

Herefordshire Beefing
1780, Herefordshire; culinary; mid to late; sweet.
WJas SKee Bowe

Herring's Pippin
(1908) Dual purpose. September to November. A large, upright-spreading tree. A rather large, irregular apple with a very attractive bright red flush. Becomes greasy if stored. A little juicy with a good aromatic, almost aniseed flavour. (Brog)
Allg SDea SKee CSco GTwe

Heusgens Golden Reinette
1877, Germany. Bright shiny red and golden-yellow fruit, hard, crisp and juicy, keeping a good flavour till late. Uprightgrowth. Scab free.
SKee CSco

High View Pippin
1911, Surrey (Weybridge); dessert; very late; aromatic.
SKee

Hill's Seedling
1831, Scotland; culinary; early; acid.
SDea SKee

Histon Favourite
1883, Cambridgeshire; dessert; mid to late; subacid.
SKee

Hoary Morning
Raised in Somerset in 1819. Large fruit - flat and round. Flesh creamy white. Pale green becoming yellow, with bright red stripes. Pick mid-Sept - keeps until Dec.
Allg SDea SKee CTho Bowe

Hogg's Winter Greening
see French Crab

Holiday
Bowe

Holland Pippin
1729, Lincolnshire; culinary; very late; acid.
SKee

Holstein
(1918) Dessert. Triploid. November to January. A moderately vigorous, wide spreading tree. A distinctly heavy apple with a Cox-like appearance. Fruits are firm, coarse textured, juicy, sweet and a little acid with a rich aromatic flavour. (Brog)
 Allg SDea SKee CTho CSco GTwe SIgm Bowe Edws

Hood's Supreme
 SDea

Hormead Pearmain
1826 Herefordshire. Jan-Mar. Medium size pale green, cooking well. A small tree.
 SKee CSco

Horneburger Pfannkuchen
1851, Germany; culinary; very late; acid.
 SKee

Houblon
1901, Berkshire; dessert; mid to late; subacid.
 SKee

Howgate Wonder
(1915) Cooker. Blenheim Orange x Newton Wonder. November to March. A moderately vigorous, upright spreading tree. A very large, pale yellow apple, up to three quarters flushed with brownish red. Some orange red stripes. Fruits become very greasy if stored. Firm, juicy and with a faint aromatic flavour. Can become fairly sweet when ripe. Cooks well. (Brog)
 Allg Cast SDea SFam WHig SKee Rog CSco GTwe Muir SFru LBuc

Hubbard's Russet Pearmain
 SDea SKee

Idagold
 Bowe

Idared
(1935) Dessert. Jonathan x Wagener. November to March. A moderately vigorous spreading tree. A large, flat-round, bright red apple with a clear yellow ground colour. Very smooth and shiny. Crisp, sweet and juicy with a pleasant vinous flavour. Fruit should be allowed to remain on the tree until maximum colour is reached. (Brog)
 Allg SDea SKee CSco GTwe SFru Bowe Edws

Improved Cockpit
 Cast Rog

Ingrid Marie
(1910) Dessert. Cox's Orange Pippin seedling. October to December. A fairly large, upright-spreading tree. A medium to large, flat-round, dull dark crimson apple with very distinct large lenticels. Crisp and juicy with fair flavour. (Brog)
SDea WJas SKee CSco SIgm Bowe

Invicta
1960, Kent; dessert; late; aromatic.
SKee

Irish Peach
(1820) Dessert. Early to mid August. A medium to large, upright-spreading tree. A tip bearer. A small pale yellow apple much flushed and mottled with orange red. Rather greasy. Moderately firm and juicy with a good aromatic flavour. (Brog)
Allg Cast SDea SFam WHig WJas SKee CSco GTwe SFru SIgm Bowe

Isaac Newton's Tree
see Flower of Kent

Isle of Wight Pippin
Introduced to the island from Normandy in 1817, although in fact much older. Smallish flat fruit. Skin is yellow with orange flush, with some russeting. Flesh is tinged green, with slightly sweet flavour. Good bouquet. Early flowering, but maturing late. Very resistant to canker and mildew.
SDea Bowe

Isle of Wight Russet
A really large Russet, but not with an abundance of russeting. Sweet and juicy. Very even cropping and well worth aplace in the garden.
SDea

James Grieve
(1893) Dessert. Possibly Potts' Seedling open pollinated. September to October. A moderately vigorous and spreading tree. Around-conical, creamy yellow apple, flushed and striped with bright red. Fruits are rather soft and very juicy, with a good refreshing flavour. Fruits tend to bruise very easily. (Brog)
Allg Cast SDea SFam WHig WJas SKee Rog CSco GTwe Muir SFru

James Lawson
1918, Kent (Eynesford); dual; mid to late; sweet.
SKee

Jerseymac
SDea CSco Bowe

Jester
(1966) Dessert. Worcester Pearmain x Starkspur Golden Delicious. November to December. A compact tree with wide branch angles. Requires very little or no pruning. An extremely attractive bright red apple with a yellow green ground colour. Anexcellent skin finish. Very greasy. Fruits are crisp and juicy with good texture and flavour. Blossom resistant to frost. A precocious, high yielding variety. (Brog)
Cast SDea SKee CSco GTwe Bowe

John Apple
Very old, France; dessert; mid season; sweet.
SKee Bowe

John Standish
A shiny scarlet Somerset apple of splendid appearance, clean, free from disease, crisp and juicy but lacking in distinctflavour. Upright growth.
SDea GTwe

Jonagold
(1943) Dessert. Triploid. Golden Delicious x Jonathan. November to March. A moderately vigorous, fairly wide spreading tree. A large, bright yellow apple up to one half flushed and mottled bright red. Juicy and sweet with a good rich flavour. Several coloured sports now exist. (Brog)
Allg Cast SDea SFam WHig SKee CSco GTwe SFru SIgm Bowe

** Jonagored
The most brightly coloured sport of Jonagold. Triploid.
CSco GTwe Bowe

Jonathan
An American apple, crisply juicy and tender, pleasantly flavoured when ripe, generally greenish-yellow, but flushed crimson in the sun.
Allg SDea SKee CSco Bowe

Jordan's Weeping
Mid dessert. Unusual variety with arching branches from Norfolk. Its weeping habit make it a suitable specimen tree for a lawn or border.
SDea WJas

Josephine
A real russet - late flowering and hence frost resistant. Prolific fruit. Nutty, dry flavour.
SDea

Joybells
A real russet - late flowering and hence frost resistant. Prolific fruit. Nutty, dry flavour.
Allg SKee GTwe Edws

Jubilee
1980, France; dessert; late; sweet.
SKee

** Jupiter
(1966) Dessert. Triploid, Cox's Orange Pippin x Starking. November to December. A vigorous tree with wide branch angles. A round-conical, slightly angular apple with an attractive orange red flush with stripes on a greenish yellow ground colour. Fruitsare juicy with a Cox-like flavour. (Brog)
Allg Cast SDea WHig WJas SKee Rog CSco GTwe SFru LBuc SIgm

Kapai
(Syn. Red Jonathan) American apple. Juicy and tender. Selffertile.
Bowe SDea

Karmijn de Sonnaville
1970, Holland; dessert; very late; aromatic.
SDea SKee GTwe SFru Bowe

Katy
(1947) Dessert. James Grieve x Worcester Pearmain. September to October. Produces a tree of medium vigour. A small to medium, bright scarlet apple with a pale yellow ground colour. Fruits are juicy with a pleasant flavour. An excellent pollinator. Cropping is heavy and regular. (Brog)
Allg Cast SDea SFam WHig SKee CSco GTwe Muir SFru LBuc SIgm

Kent
(1949) Dessert. Cox's Orange Pippin x Jonathan. November to February. A moderately vigorous, upright-spreading tree. A conical greenish yellow apple up to three quarters flushed and striped with orange red. Some grey russet present. Fruits are slightly coarse textured, juicy and with a pleasant aromatic flavour. (Brog)
SDea SFam SKee CSco GTwe Muir Bowe Edws

Kentish Fillbasket
Pre 1820, Kent; dual; mid season; sweet.
SKee

Kentish Pippin
see Colonel Vaughan.

SKee

Kentish Quarrenden
Old, Kent; dessert; late; perfumed.
SKee

Kerry Pippin
1807, Ireland. Early autumn dessert apple. A very old Irish variety, crisp and juicy.
SKee CSco GTwe

Keswick Codlin
(1793) Cooker. September to October. A moderately vigorous, upright-spreading tree. A typical codlin type and is distinctly angular and rather ugly. Fruits are rather soft, dry and acid. (Brog)
Allg Cast SDea SKee Rog CSco GTwe

Kidd's Orange Red
(1924) Dessert. Cox's Orange Pippin x Delicious. November to January. A moderately vigorous, spreading tree. A conical, greenish yellow apple almost completely flushed with bright deep orange red. Some stripes. Patches of scaly grey russet. Firm, crisp, juicy and sweet with a rich aromatic flavour. (Brog)
Cast SDea SFam WHig SKee CSco GTwe SFru SIgm Bowe Edws

Kilkenny Pippin
GTwe

King Charles Pearmain
(Syn. Rushock Pearmain) Before 1876, Worcester; sweet, juicy and rich; dessert; mid to very late.
SKee CTho

King George V
1898, Isle of Wight; dessert; very late; subacid.
Allg SKee

King Harry
Allg

King Luscious
From the USA. Large fruit of bright red. Keeps well into Jan.
SDea

King Russet
This is a sport from King of the Pippins. Matures to follow on from St. Edmund's Russet. Nutty flavour. Crops around similar production to Cox. Fruit is completely russeted. Recentreport from Ministry of Agriculture suggested it to be a promising cultivar.
SDea SFru

King of Tompkins County
1804, USA; dessert; late; aromatic.
Allg SKee CSco

King of the Pippins
(1800) Dessert. October to December. A moderately vigorous, upright tree. A medium sized oblong conical golden yellow apple up to three quarters flushed with brownish orange. A few bright red stripes. Fruits are firm, fine textured, juicy and subacid with a slight aromatic flavour. (Brog)
Allg Cast SDea WHig SKee CTho CSco GTwe SFru LBuc Bowe

King's Acre Bountiful
1904, Hewreford, the old Kings Acre Nurseries; culinary; midseason; acid.
WJas SKee CSco

King's Acre Pippin
(1897) Dessert. Sturmer Pippin x Ribston Pippin. December to March. A moderately vigorous, very spreading tree. A large, dull green apple partly covered with a dirty, fine grey brown russet. A few fruits with a dull brownish red flush. Firm, juicy with a rich aromatic flavour. (Brog)
SDea SFam WJas SKee CTho CSco SFru

King's Favourite
SKee

Knobby Russet
SKee GTwe

Lady Bacon
Cornwall.
SKee

Lady Henniker
Original tree raised by John Perkins, Head Gardener to Lord Henniker of Thornham Hall, Eye, Suffolk, in 1840. It was, in fact, developed from a cider pip found in the must of a cider brew. Awarded a first class certificate by the R.H.S. in 1873. Well known dual purpose apple - similar to Ribston. Picked late Sept - will keep until Jan. Coloured green, becoming clear gold and yellow. Creamy white flesh. Coarse textured and good subacid flavour. Ideal for Christmas.
SDea WJas SKee GTwe

Lady Lambourne
1945, Berkshire; dessert; mid season; aromatic.
SKee Bowe

Lady Sudeley
(1849) Dessert. August to September. A moderately vigorous, upright-spreading tree. A round-conical apple almost completely flushed with orange red on a golden yellow ground colour. Several bright red stripes. Juicy and a little acid, with a good flavour. Becomes greasy if stored. (Brog)
Allg SDea SKee CSco GTwe SFru

Lady Williams
SKee

Lady of the Lake
SDea

Lady of the Wemyss
1831, Scotland; culinary; late; acid.
SDea SKee

Lady's Finger of Lancaster
1824, Lancashire; dual; late; subacid.
SKee

Lady's Finger of Offaly
Mid to late season dessert.
SDea SKee

Lamb Abbey Pearmain
1804, Kent (Dartford); dessert; late; aromatic.
WJas SKee

Landsberger Reinette
1840, Germany; dessert; mid to very late; perfumed.
SKee

Lane's Prince Albert
(1840) Cooker. December to March. Produces a spreading tree of medium vigour. A large pale green round apple. Some fruits up to half flushed with orange. Fine textured, very juicy and acid. Cooks well. A regular cropper. (Brog)
Allg Cast SDea WJas SKee Rog CSco GTwe Muir SFru SIgm Bowe

Langley Pippin
1898, London (Chelsea); dessert; early; aromatic.
Allg SDea SKee

Lass O'Gowrie
1883, Scotland; culinary; early; sweet/subacid.
SDea SKee

Laxton's Early Crimson
Late summer dessert apple. Worcester X Gladstone. Crimson fruit, soft but crisp if picked in time, juicy and refreshing.
CSco

Laxton's Pearmain
Like a duller red Cox in appearance; crisp and pleasantly flavoured, a small upright tree.
CSco

Laxton's Rearguard
The latest Laxton, a small upright tree.
Allg WJas SKee CSco

Laxton's Reward
A flattened crimson skinned fruit, of good quality, cropping freely and keeping well.
Allg CSco

Laxton's Royalty
(1908) Dessert. Cox's Orange Pippin x Court Pendu Plat. January to March. An upright tree of medium vigour. Fairly late flowering. A small apple similar in appearance to Cox's Orange Pippin but more flattened. Fruits are crisp and a little juicy with quite good flavour. (Brog)
Allg SDea SFam CSco GTwe Bowe

Laxton's Superb
(1897) Dessert. Wyken Pippin x Cox's Orange Pippin. November to January. A vigorous tree with abundant rather slender new growth. Subject to biennial bearing. A round-conical, medium to large greenish yellow apple almost completely covered with a deepreddish purple flush. A few broken stripes. Very juicy and sweet with a pleasant refreshing flavour. (Brog)
Allg Cast SDea WJas SKee Rog CSco GTwe SFru LBuc Slgm Bowe

Laxton's Triumph
Bowe

Leathercoat Russet
(Syn. Royal Russet) England, 16th century; sweet and sharp; dessert; late to very late. Mentioned by William Shakespeare.
SKee CTho Bowe

Leeder's Perfection
1912, Norfolk.
SKee

Lemon Pippin
Dual purpose. November to March. A vigorous, upright-spreading tree. A medium sized, greenish yellow apple with some light patches of grey russet. Can become greasy if stored. Firm, coarse textured and dry with a faint aromatic flavour. (Brog)
Allg SDea WJas SKee CTho Bowe

Lemon Queen
SDea

Lewis' Incomparable
(Syn. Nancy Jackson) Pre 1790; England; culinary; late; subacid.
   SKee

Liberty
USA. All over red. Disease resistant. Pick mid-Sept - keeps until Feb. Highly productive. Crisp and juicy. Tasty, good looking and show potential.
   SDea

Liddel's Seedling
   SDea

Linda
   SKee

Listener
North Devon; sweet; dessert, cider; early.
   CTho

Lobo
   Bowe

Loddington
(Syn. Stones?) 1820; Kent; dual; early - mid; subacid.
   SKee

Lodgemore Nonpareil
An old Gloucestershire apple, very late ripening.
   CSco

Lodi
1911, Newark, New Jersey, USA. Culinary; early; acid. Jul-Aug. Earliest cooker. Pale green. Tree makes a graceful arching form. Montgomery X Whitetransparent.
   SDea SKee Bowe

London Pippin
East Anglia, before 1530; subacid; dessert; mid to very late. A very old market variety, probably shipped to London by barge. Grown in Somerset since before 1580.
   CTho

Lord Burghley
1834; Lincoln; dessert; very late; sweet. Large dessert apple. Pick mid-Oct and will keep until April. Average size, appearing greenish brown with large russet dots.
   Allg SDea SKee GTwe

Lord Derby
(1862) Cooker. October to December. A moderately vigorous, upright-spreading tree. A very large greenish yellow apple, occasionally with a little purplish brown flush. Rather coarse textured and somewhat dry. Cooks well. A well-known cooking apple. (Brog)
   Allg Cast SDea WHig SKee Rog
   CSco GTwe Muir Bowe Edws

Lord Grosvenor
1872; England; dual; early - mid season; subacid.
   SKee GTwe Bowe

Lord Hindlip
1896; Worcestershire; dessert; very late; sweet. A sharp, pleasantly flavoured crimson fruit. Award of Merit in 1896 and a First Class Certificate in 1898 by R.H.S. Fruit is medium to large. Greenish yellow, covered with brownish crimson flush and a few dark red stripes. Flesh is cream tinged green, firm but juicy and of good aromatic flavour. Picked in mid-Oct - will keep until March.
Allg SDea SKee GTwe

Lord Lambourne
(1907) Dessert. James Grieve x Worcester Pearmain. September to November. A spreading, almost weeping tree of medium vigour. A flat round, medium sized greenish yellow apple up to three quarters flushed with deep red. Some broken red stripes. Becomes very greasy if stored. Juicy and sweet with a good aromatic flavour. (Brog)
Allg Cast SDea SFam WHig WJas SKee Rog CSco GTwe Muir SFru

Lord Rosebery
1934; Scotland; dessert; early - mid; sweet.
SDea SKee

Lord Stradbroke
1934; Scotland; dessert; early - mid; sweet.
Allg SKee

Lord Suffield
1836; Lancashire; culinary; early; acid.
Allg SKee SIgm Bowe

Lovacka Renata
SDea

Love Beauty
SDea

Lucombe's Pine
1800, Exeter, Devon. Rich, aromatic, pineapple-like; dessert; mid to late. Raised at the nursery of Lucombe and Pince, St Thomas, Exeter.
CTho

Lucombe's Seedling
Exeter, Devon, before 1830; subacid, spicy; dessert; mid to very late. Raised by Lucombe and Pince. Grown in West Cornwall in 1920s as Newquay Prizetaker for market.
SKee CTho

Mabbot's Pearmain
A nice flavoured old variety, yellowish with a brownish flush, small and prolific.
SDea CSco SIgm

Madresfield Court
1915; Worcestershire; dessert; mid season; rich. Raised by William Crump. Unusually tall apple; high quality fruit; tip bearing. Fruit is medium sized, dull green flushed crimson, striped with red, some russeting. Flesh is tinged green, firm,
sweet and juicy. Picked late Sept - will keep until Dec.
Allg SDea WJas SKee

Maggie Sinclair
SDea

Maidstone Favourite
1913; Kent; dessert; early; very sweet.
SKee

Maltster
Pre 1830; Cambridgeshire; dessert; mid season; sweet.
WJas SKee GTwe

Manks Codlin
Pre 1815, Isle of Man; sweet; culinary; early. Excellent early baked apple.
SKee CTho

Mannington's Pearmain
1770; Sussex; dessert; late; rich.
SKee

Margaret
(Syn. Red Joanetting) Pre 1665; England; dual; early; subacid.
SKee

Margil
(1750) Dessert. October to January. A rather weak, upright-spreading tree. In appearance rather like a small Ribston Pippin. Rather greasy if stored. Firm fleshed, rather dry and sweet with a rich aromatic flavour. (Brog)
SDea SFam SKee CTho CSco GTwe SIgm Bowe

Marriage-Maker
Pre 1883; England; dessert; mid - late; sweet.
SKee

Mary's Apple
Developed and grown by a lady who lives close to Queen Victoria's favourite house - Osborne House, Cowes, I.W. This great apple is late keeping and every year produces prolific crops of large green dual purpose fruit. Strong grower and worth a space this season.
SDea

May Queen
(1888) Dessert. November to May. A very weak, upright-spreading tree. A golden yellow, flat-round apple, almost completely flushed with bright dark red. Blood red stripes. Rather greasy if stored. A little juicy and rather acid with only a moderate flavour. (Brog)
SDea SFam WJas SKee CSco

McCutcheon
SIgm

McIntosh
Allg WJas SKee Bowe

Meads Broadling
SKee

Measdale Favourite
SKee

Melba
1898; Canada; dessert; mid - late; sweet/ subacid.
SKee

Melon
An old variety, about 1830. Yellow, red and green. Sweet. Keeping until Jan. German origin.
SDea

Melrose
1937, USA. Jonathan X Delicious. A modern shiny crimson fruit, crisp and cropping well. Not to be confused with the old Scottish variety White Melrose.
SDea SKee CSco GTwe Bowe

Merchant Apple of Ilminster
Pre 1872, Somerset; subacid/sweet; dessert; mid.
CTho

Mere de Menage
Till Mar., a large crimson fruit, a good cooker, cropping well and forming a large spreading tree.
Allg CSco SIgm

Merton Beauty
Early autumn dessert apple. A large handsomely striped fruit, of the Ellison's Orange type, crisp and pleasantly flavoured.
CSco SFru Bowe

Merton Charm
1933, John Innes Institute, Cambridge. Early autumn dessert apple. A newish Cox cross, rather small dull greenish-yellow, brown flushed, juicy, aromatic and of good flavour, cropping heavily from an early age.
SFam SKee CSco Bowe

Merton Joy
A Cox-Sturmer cross, crisp, juicy, nicely flavoured, rather dull greenish-yellow with an orange-red fush, cropping well.
Bowe

Merton Knave
(1948) Dessert. September. A moderately vigorous, fairly spreading tree; a little weeping. A round, bright scarlet red apple. Very greasy if stored. Soft, juicy and sweet with a pleasant flavour. Flesh tinged pink beneath the skin and near core. (Brog)
SDea SFam CSco GTwe SFru Bowe

Merton Pippin
Bowe

Merton Prolific
A dull greenish-yellow fruit with brown-red flush, of no special flavour, but prolific and hardy.
CSco Bowe

Merton Russet
1921; Cambridgeshire; dessert; very late; sweet. A large russet, notably colourful in flower. Strong aromatic apple. Delicious flavour - juicy and crisp. Disease-free. Makes a large and vigorous tree. Fruit is large and darkly russeted. Self fertile. Sturmer Pippin X Cox.
Allg SDea SKee CSco Bowe

Merton Worcester
1914; Cambridgeshire; dessert; mid; sweet. Early autumn dessert apple. A Cox-Worcester cross, the Cox infuence improvingthe Worcester flavour.
SDea SKee CSco Bowe

Michaelmas Red
1929; Kent; dessert; mid; sweet. Early autumn dessert apple. A nicely coloured later Worcester, superior in flavour, not tip bearing.
WJas SKee CSco GTwe Bowe

Miel D'Or
Cornwall.
SKee

Miller's Seedling
1848; Berkshire; dessert; early - mid; sweet.
WJas SKee Bowe

Millicent Barnes
Raised by Barnes of Chester in 1903. A cross of Gascoigne'sScarlet and Cox. An exhibition variety. Greenish yellow flushedwith bright red. Pick mid-Sept - keeps until Dec.
SDea

Mollies Delicious
SKee

Monarch
(1888) Cooker. Peasgood's Nonsuch x Dumelow's Seedling. November to January. A vigorous, upright spreading tree. A flat-round, pale yellow apple up to one half flushed with pinkish red. Becomes extremely greasy if stored. Bruises easily. Fairly juicy and subacid. Coarse textured and rather soft. (Brog)
Allg Cast SDea SFam WJas SKee Rog CSco GTwe Bowe

Monarch Advanced
Dual purpose; very late; subacid.
SKee

Mondial Gala
SKee

Monmouth Green
SIgm

Moss's Seedling
Raised in Wiltshire, a Cox seedling. Or was it discovered by N. Talbot of Newport, Shropshire, in 1953? Outyielded Cox. Fruit is round and sweet, keeping even until Feb in store. Greenturning yellow. Ideal to store, retaining flavour.
SDea CSco Bowe

Mrs Crittenden
1891; Kent; dessert; late; sweet.
SKee

Mrs Phillimore
1896; Berkshire; dessert; late; sweet.
Allg SKee

Nancy Jackson
see Lewis' Incomparable

Nettlestone Pippin
A seedling from a cross between James Grieve and Cox's Orange Pippin. This is a most attractive apple. Ready mid-Sept.Cox size, brightly striped red and gold, with the James Grieve shape. Quite juicy. Slight russeting. Skin is shiny and slightly waxy, like James Grieve. Sunny side is all red with yellow and russet stripes a really attractive apple. Ideally eaten from the tree and last season stored until the end of Oct.
SDea

New Hawthornden
Allg

Newton Wonder
(1887) Cooker. Dumelow's Seedling x Blenheim Orange. November to March. A very vigorous, upright-spreading tree. A very large, flat-round yellow apple with up to three quarters flushed with brownish red. Some short, broken red stripes. Becomes greasy if stored. Moderately juicy and subacid. Cooks very well. (Brog)
Allg Cast SDea SFam WHig SKee Rog CSco GTwe SFru SIgm Bowe

Newtosh
Allg

Newtown Pippin
Late season dessert. Bright green with brown tinges. Fruitsometimes oblong.
SDea

Nittany Red
Yellow with red flush. Keeps until Oct.
SDea

Nonpareil
1500, France; rich, vinous, aromatic; dessert; very late. A rather weak grower but will store until May. Needs a sunny site to ripen fully. Small, dull in colour, but richly flavoured.
SKee CTho CSco

Norfolk Beauty
1901; Norfolk; dual; early - mid; slightly acid. Keeping till Christmas. A large pale yellow apple, flushed red.
Allg SKee CSco Bowe

Norfolk Beefing
(1807) Cooker. December to April. A vigorous, upright spreading tree. A flat-round, medium to large dark purplish red apple. Very firm, coarse textured, juicy and very acid. (Brog)
Allg SDea WJas SKee CTho CSco Bowe

Norfolk Coleman
SKee Bowe

Norfolk Royal
(1908) Dessert. September to December. A moderately vigorous, upright tree. A conical bright scarlet apple with pale yellow ground colour. Some stripes. Very greasy if stored. Moderately firm, crisp, very juicy and sweet with a pleasant flavour. (Brog)
Cast SDea SKee CSco GTwe SIgm Edws

Norfolk Royal Russet
A sport of the Norfolk Royal, with a russet skin.
WHig CSco GTwe Bowe

Norfolk Summer Broadend
Old; Norfolk; dessert; mid; subacid.
SKee

Northern Greening
SKee

Northern Spy
Allg

Nutmeg Pippin
(Syn. Cockle Pippin) Early 19th centry; sweet, aromatic; dessert; very late. Much prized in the 19th century for a late keeper. A pleasant little golden fruit, crisp and juicy. Small dessert variety. Green becoming yellow, orange overlap, with netted russeting. Pick Oct - keeps until March.
SDea SKee CSco Bowe

Oaken Pin
Pre 1876, Devon, the Exe valley; juicy, sweet and aromatic; culinary; mid to late. Once very common on Exmoor. A good bearer.
CTho

Old Pearmain
Pre 1200, England or France; rich; dessert; late. Highly esteemed in the past for cider.
SDea SKee CTho

Ontario
Allg

Opalescent
1899; USA; dessert; very late; sweet. A large dual purpose fruit, cropping well, of quite spectacular colour, shiny crimson and yellow.
SKee CSco

Orange Goff
1842; Kent; dessert; very late; acid.
SKee

Orkney
Local traditional apple.
SKee

Orleans Reinette
(1776) Dessert. November to January. A vigorous, upright-spreading tree. A flat round, golden yellow apple up to three quarters flushed dull orange red with some short red stripes. Firm, juicy and sweet with a Blenheim-like flavour. (Brog)
Allg Cast SDea SFam WHig WJas SKee CTho CSco GTwe SFru SIgm

Oslin
(Syn. Arbroath) Very old; Scotland from France; dessert; early - mid; aromatic.
SDea SKee

Owen Thomas
1897; Bedfordshire; dessert; early; aromatic. Early autumn dessert apple. A pleasant dessert, but not keeping long.
SKee CSco

Paroquet
1897; Berkshire; dessert; late; subacid.
SKee

Patricia
1920; Canada; dessert; mid; perfumed.
SKee

Paulared
New superior variety from the USA. Early Aug/Sept. Dessert;mid; sweet.
SDea SKee

Peacemaker
1913; Berkshire; dessert; mid; sweet.
SKee

Pearl
Essex, 1933; subacid, sweet, rich; dessert; mid. A Cox type that never became popular, introduced by Seabrooks, cropping well, crisp and juicy with a good Cox flavour and said to be frost resistant.
Allg SDea CTho CSco

Peasgood's Nonsuch
(1858) Cooker. A Catshead cross. September to December. A moderately vigorous, spreading tree. Rather subject to canker. A very large, round apple up to three quarters flushed pale orange red on a yellow ground colour. Some short red stripes. Moderately juicy and a little sweet. Cooks well. (Brog)
Allg SDea SFam SKee CSco GTwe SFru Bowe Edws

Peck's Pleasant
1832; USA; dessert; very late; aromatic.
SKee

Pendragon
(Cornish clone of Sops in Wine) Devon/Cornwall; sweet; second early to mid. Known by various names. Old trees scattered throughout Devon and Cornwall. A striking purple red stemmed and fruited form. Flesh of fruit red to core.
CTho

Peter Lock
Buckfastleigh, Devon, early 19th century; sweet, scented; dessert; very late. Cooks to a sweet, smooth puree.
CTho

Peter's Pippin
seedling of ours from open pollinated Granny Smith. Cox-like flavour. Gold and red colouring, with some russeting. Larger than Cox. (SDea)

SDea

Peter's Seedling
Sister seedling of Peter's Pippin. Ideal sized apple for children. No waste. Profuse cropping. Pick late Aug. Smaller fruits, which are completely red all over.
SDea

Pickering's Seedling
Pre 1869; Nottinghamshire; dessert; mid; sweet.
SKee

Pig's Nose Pippin
SKee

Pine Golden Pippin
Old; England; dessert; late; subacid.
SDea SKee

Pitmaston Pineapple
(1785) Dessert. Golden Pippin seedling. September to December. A moderately vigorous, upright tree. A distinctly small conical, golden yellow apple, partly covered with fairly fine grey brown russet. Firm, juicy and slightly sweet with a rich, distinctive flavour. (Brog)
SDea Cast SFam WJas SKee CTho CSco GTwe SFru LBuc Edws

Pitmaston Russet Nonpareil
Pre 1814; Worcestershire; dessert; late; rich.
SKee CSco

Pixie
(1947) Dessert. Thought to be a seedling from Cox's Orange Pippin or Sunset. December to March. A moderately vigorous, wide spreading tree. A flat round yellow green apple, flushed and striped with orange red. Crisp and juicy with a good aromatic flavour. A high quality, heavy cropping apple. (Brog)
Cast SDea WJas SKee CSco GTwe SFru LBuc SIgm Bowe Edws

Plum Vite
Devon, before 1880; sweet, subacid; dessert; early. Gives juicy apples in late July.
CTho

Plympton Pippin
Tamar Valley; subacid; culinary; late. Very large green apples.
CTho

** Polka
Dessert. Bright green and red fruit, crisp and juicy. Pick and eat late Sept. Self fertile.
SDea LBuc

Polly Prosser
SKee

Polly Whitehair
Truro, Cornwall; sweet; culinary; late. Tall, vigorous. Masses of white blossom.
SDea SKee CTho

Pomeroy
(Syn. The Old Pomeroy) Pre 1851 Somerset; crisp, sweet, juicy, highly flavoured; dessert; mid to late. A very old variety once extensively grown.
CTho

Pomme Royale
Bowe

Ponsford
Devon, 19th century; acid; culinary, cider; very late. An excellent old variety. Vigorous, healthy.
SKee CTho CSco

Port Allen Russet
SDea

Potts' Seedling
1849; Nottinghamshire; culinary; mid; acid.
SKee

Princess Pippin
Mid dessert; early 1800's; A distinctive and lovely apple. (Syn. King of the Pippins, Golden Winter Pearmain, Stanardine (Shropshire).)
WJas

Proctor's Seedling
Allg

Queen
(1858) Cooker. September to December. A moderately vigorous, upright-spreading tree. A distinctly flattened and highly coloured cooking apple. Rather soft flesh, juicy and distinctly acid. (Brog)
Allg SDea SKee CTho CSco

Queen Caroline
1820; Nottinghamshire; culinary; late; acid.
SKee

Queen Cox
A coloured selection of Cox's Orange Pippin. (Brog)
Cast SDea WHig SKee CSco Muir SIgm Bowe Edws

Racky Down
Cornwall.
SKee

Ray's Seedling
Allg

Red Astrachan
Old; Russia (England 1816); dual; early; subacid.
SKee

Red Beauty of Bath
Bowe

Red Blenheim
SKee

Red Charles Ross
This red cultivar complements its popular parent. Compact growth and colourful fruit makes this a winner. Apart from colour, identical to parent. Self fertile.
SDea SFru

Red Cox's Orange Pippin
SKee

Red Delicious
CSco Bowe

Red Devil
(1975) Dessert. Discovery x Kent. September to December. Compact tree habit. A medium to large, bright red apple. When ripe, the flesh turns pink under the skin. Crisp and juicy with a good flavour. A heavy cropper. Some resistance to mildew. (Brog)
Cast WHig SKee GTwe SIgm Bowe

Red Ellison
(1948) A coloured selection of Ellison's Orange (Brog)
Cast SDea CTho Rog CSco Bowe

Red Fuji
Red sport of the original.
SDea

Red Gravenstein
CSco GTwe

Red James Grieve
This red cultivar is now available and makes James Grieve even more popular!
SDea SKee Bowe

Red Jonathan
see Kapai

Red Laxton's Superb
SKee

Red Melba
Late summer dessert apple. A brightly coloured Canadian apple, crimson in the sun, pinkish or pale green in shade, smooth, juicy, tender and pleasantly refreshing. A prolific cropper and most useful as a garden fruit. Resistant to scab.
CSco Bowe

Red Miller's Seedling
SDea CSco SIgm Bowe

Red Newton
SKee

Red Ruby
Old variety discovered in old orchard in the Teign Valley.
CTho

Red Starking
SKee

Red Sudeley
SDea

Red Victoria
Early dessert. Grown for the National Trust's Hanbury Hall from their tree. A red sport of Early Victoria/Emneth Early.
GTwe

Redfree
GTwe

Redsleeves
Aug/Sept; mid. Raised at East Malling Research station (now H.R.I. East Malling) in Kent from Exeter Cross X a seedling selection and introduced in 1985 - a good heavy cropping garden variety with resistance to scab and mildew, the flesh is crisp and very juicy. A sister seedling to Greensleeves.
Cast SDea GTwe SIgm Bowe

Reinette Dorge de Bordiker
GTwe

Reinette Rouge Etoilèe
SDea SKee

Reinette du Canada
An old variety of the Blenheim type, richly flavoured in a warm season, inclined to canker. A large spreading tree. Triploid.
Allg CSco SFru SIgm

Reinette du Canada Grise
Possibly Normandy, before 1770; acid at first, becoming sweet; dessert, culinary; late to very late. Popular in France for tarts and late eating.
CTho

Rev Greeves
Green cooker that keeps until March. Scottish origin.
SDea

Rev W Wilks
(1904) Cooker. Peasgood's Nonsuch x Ribston Pippin. August to November. A rather small, spreading tree. Tends to be biennial. A very large, conical greenish white apple faintly flushed and mottled with pale orange. Becomes greasy if stored. Crisp, juicy and subacid. Cooks well; breaks up completely. (Brog)
Allg Cast SDea SFam WJas SKee Rog CSco GTwe Muir SFru SIgm

Ribston Pippin
(1707) Dessert. Triploid. October to January. A moderately vigorous, spreading tree. A medium sized round conical yellow apple, up to three quarters flushed with brownish orange. Some red stripes. Rather greasy if stored. Firm and juicy with a rich aromatic flavour. (Brog)
Allg Cast SDea SFam WJas SKee CTho CSco GTwe SFru LBuc SIgm

Rival
1900; Berkshire; dessert; mid - late; subacid. A good dual purpose apple. A Peasgood X Cox apple, raised by Charles Ross in 1900. A flat, slightly conical, large yellowish green fruit with red stripes. A solid juicy subacid flesh. Very vigorous spreading tree. Does well in the north.
Allg SDea SKee CSco

Rivers' Early Peach
Bowe

Robin Pippin
GTwe Bowe

Rock
SDea

Rome Beauty
Originated in USA in 1800s. Attractive dessert apple. Usually available in markets in UK from Feb to May. Medium sized pale yellow apple flushed orange to scarlet. Definite red stripes. Soft, juicy flavour. Pendulous growth when matured.
SDea

Rosamund
see Red James Grieve

Rosemary Russet
(1831) Dessert. November to March. A moderately vigorous, upright-spreading tree. A conical pale yellow apple up to half flushed with bright reddish brown. Firm, rather acid and juicy with a good flavour. (Brog)
Allg Cast SDea SFam WJas SKee CTho CSco GTwe SFru SIgm Bowe

Ross Nonpareil
(1802) Dessert. November to January. A moderately vigorous, upright-spreading tree. A medium sized round-conical greenish yellow apple up to one half flushed and striped orange red. Partly covered with fine, grey brown russet. Firm, dry flesh with a rich aromatic flavour. (Brog)
Allg SDea SKee CSco GTwe

Rough Pippin
Somerset, before 1880; sweet to subacid; dessert; mid/late. Firm flesh, crisp yellow-green. Will hang on tree till end of October. Variable in shape.
CTho

Roundway Magnum Bonum
Devizes, Wilts, c 1860; sweet, aromatic, pear-like; dessert; very late. Raised by W. Joy at Roundway Park, Devizes. Remarkable for its delicious pear-like flavour. Received Award of Merit (first class) in 1864. Dual purpose. Silver green to pale yellow. Flesh brownish orange. Pick Oct - keeps until Feb.
SDea SKee CTho CSco

Roxbury Russet
1620; USA; dessert; very late; subacid.
SKee

Royal Jubilee
1888; London (Hounslow); dual; late; subacid. Till Dec. A good late flowering variety cropping regularly. Introduced by Bunyards.
Allg SKee CSco

Royal Russet
(1597) Dessert. December to March. A large, flat apple almost entirely covered with rough brown russet. Flesh is tender with a sweet subacid flavour. (Brog)
Allg Cast SDea CSco GTwe

Royal Snow
Pre 1833; Hampshire; dessert; very late; sweet.
SKee

Royal Somerset
Somerset, before 1818; juicy, sweet; culinary, cider; mid to very late.
CTho

Rubens
SKee

** Rubinette
(1966) Dessert. Golden Delicious x Cox's Orange Pippin cross. October to December. A moderately vigorous tree. Some resistance to mildew. A conical, yellow apple with brilliant red stripes. Tends to produce small fruits on very young trees. Crisp and juicy with an excellent flavour. (Brog)
   Cast WHig WJas CSco GTwe SIgm Bowe

Russet Seedling
   SKee

S T Wright
1913; England; culinary; mid; acid.
   Allg SKee

Saint Alban's Pippin
1883; Kent; dessert; mid; sweet.
   SKee

Saint Augustine's Orange
Old; Kent; dessert; late; aromatic.
   Allg SKee

Saint Cecilia
1900; Wales; dessert; very late; sweet. Never widely grown, but in regular demand from those who know it. Of the Cox's Orange parentage, raised by Barham's of Bassaleg, Monmouth, from open pollinated Cox. Award of Merit in 1918. High quality dessert fruit. Green to pale yellow, with broken red stripes. Pick early Oct - keeps until March.
   SDea WJas SKee CSco Bowe

Saint Edmund's Pippin
(1875) Dessert. September to October. A moderately vigorous, upright-spreading tree. A golden apple almost entirely covered with fine light brown russet. Juicy and slightly acid with a good flavour. One of the earliest russet apples to ripen. (Brog)
   Cast SDea SFam SKee CTho CSco GTwe SFru LBuc SIgm Bowe Edws

Saint Everard
1900; Cambridgeshire; dessert; early; aromatic. Early autumn dessert apple. A nice fruit, said to be from Cox's Orange and Margil.
   Allg SKee CSco SFru

Saint Magdalen
1890; Norfolk; dessert; very late; sweet.
   SKee

Saltcote Pippin
1918; Sussex (Rye); dessert; very late; aromatic.
   SKee

Sam Young
Pre 1818; Ireland; dessert; mid - late; subacid. A very old Irish russet, green brown.
   SKee CSco GTwe

Sandlands
   SDea

Sandringham
1883; Norfolk; culinary; mid - late; subacid.
   Allg SKee

Sanspareil
1880; dessert; very late; aromatic. Sweet, fruity, juicy; culinary, dessert; late to very late. A fairly large crisp well-flavoured fruit, greenish at first ripening to a handsome orange-yellow with a crimson cheek. Remarkably fertile and disease free.
SKee CTho CSco

Saw Pits
SKee

Scarlet Bramley
Allg

Scarlet Crofton
Pre 1600; England; dessert; mid; sweet.
SKee

Scarlet Newton
Allg

Scarlet Nonpareil
1773; Surrey (Esher); dessert; very late; rich.
SKee

Scarlet Pimpernel
(Syn. Stark's Earliest) 1938; USA; dual; early; acid. Late summer dessert apple. A very early American variety, pale green or white with a crimson-scarlet cheek, crisp and juicy, cropping well if pollinated by another early flowering sort. Scab resistant.
WJas SKee CSco Bowe

Schoner van Nordhausen
Allg

Schoolmaster
Allg

Scotch Bridget
Allg SDea SKee

Scotch Dumpling
SDea GTwe

Seabrook's Pearl
see Pearl

Allg

Seaton House
SDea SKee

Shakespeare
Late dessert; A yellow skinned, interesting old variety.
WJas

Sheep's Nose
Old; Somerset; culinary; mid; acid. Unusual shape!
SDea SKee

Shenandoah
Culinary; late; acid.
SKee

Shoesmith
Late Sep/mid Dec; mid; Raised in Surrey from Lane's Prince Albert X Golden Noble and first exhibited in 1930 - handsome cooking variety producing very large fruits; exhibition variety. Rather soft, a little coarse textured, very juicy and sub-acid. Cooks well.
SIgm

Shorty Mac
1970; Canada; dessert; mid - late; sweet.
SKee

Sir John Thorneycroft
Very late season dessert.
Allg SDea

Small's Admirable
Allg

Smart's Prince Arthur
Raised by Smart of Sittingbourne in 1883. Medium to large apple. Green to yellow, flushed with purple stripes. Flesh is pale yellow tinged green. Very firm, sweet and juicy. Pick early Oct - will keep until April.
SDea

Smoothee
Bowe

Sops in Wine
West Country, probably medieval; sweet; culinary, cider; mid to late. Vigorous heavy bearer, resistant to canker. Flesh is flushed red as if sopped in wine.
SKee CTho

Spartan
(1926) Dessert. McIntosh x Yellow Newtown Pippin. November to February. A moderately vigorous, upright-spreading tree. A round conical dull deep purple apple. Crisp and juicy with a refreshing vinous flavour. (Brog)
Allg Cast SDea SFam WHig WJas SKee Rog CSco GTwe Muir SFru

Spencer
1926; Canada; dessert; very late; sweet.
SKee

Splendour
Bowe

Spur Mac
Another popular red apple in the States. Ripens late Aug.
SDea GTwe

Stamford Pippin
SDea

Star of Devon
Late season small dessert from Devon.
SDea

Stark
Discovered in Orofino, Idaho, USA in 1938. Early, bright coloured dessert. Massive crops. Pick early Aug. Eat from tree.
SDea

Stark's Earliest
see Scarlet Pimpernel

Stark's Late Delicious
SDea

Starking
1921; USA; dessert; very late; sweet.
SKee Bowe

Starkrimson
1953; USA; dessert; very late; sweet.
SKee

Starkspur Golden Delicious
The "real" Golden Delicious. 1959; USA; dessert; very late; sweet. In this case the phrase "too well known to need description" is indeed true. Prolific and free from disease, it is a good garden fruit, often of better quality than shop fruit.
   Cast SKee CSco Bowe

Steyne Seedling
Mid to late season dessert.
   SDea

Stirling Castle
(1831) Cooker. September to December. A weak, spreading tree. A flat-round pale yellow apple, some fruits flushed with orange brown. Rather greasy if stored. Soft, juicy and acid. (Brog)
   Allg SDea SKee CSco GTwe Bowe

Stobo Castle
Pre 1900; Scotland; culinary; early - mid; subacid.
   SDea SKee

Stoke Edith Pippin
Late dessert; 1872; Herefordshire variety rescued from near extinction. Nov-Mar. Sweet apple with nicely perfumed flavour.
   WJas SKee

Stoup Leadington
   SDea SKee

Striped Beefing
1794; Norfolk; culinary; very late; acid. Very late, pale green with red stripes, vigorous and fertile.
   SKee CSco

Stubnose
   SKee

Sturmer Pippin
(1831) Dessert. Ribston Pippin x Nonpareil. January to April. A moderately vigorous, upright-spreading tree. An oblong-conical greenish yellow apple up to one half flushed with dull purplish brown. Very firm and juicy with a rich aromatic flavour. Requires a warm season to mature properly. (Brog)
   Allg Cast SDea SFam WJas SKee CSco GTwe SFru SIgm Bowe Edws

Summer Golden Pippin
Pre 1800; England; dessert; early; rich. Late summer dessert apple. Pale yellow skin, with a brown-red flush, crisp and juicy.
   SKee CSco

Summer Granny
   SDea

Summerred
1961; Canada; dessert; early; sweet. Dessert. Excellent variety with bright solid red firm crisp fruit with a good flavour. Pick early Sept. for eating Sept-Oct.
   SKee GTwe Bowe

Sunburn
1920; Essex; dessert; late; aromatic.
   SKee Slgm Bowe

Sunnydale
   SDea

Sunset
(1918) Dessert. Cox's Orange Pippin seedling. October to December. A moderately vigorous, upright-spreading tree. A small, flat-round golden yellow apple, striped and flushed with orange red. Firm and crisp with a good aromatic Cox-like flavour. (Brog)
   Allg Cast SDea SFam WHig SKee Rog CSco GTwe Muir SFru LBuc

Suntan
(1955) Dessert. Triploid. Cox's Orange Pippin x Court Pendu Plat. October to February. A vigorous, wide spreading tree. A fairly large, flat-round golden yellow apple, flushed and striped with orange red. Juicy and rather acid with a mild aromatic flavour. Can be prone to bitter pit in some seasons. (Brog)
   Allg SDea WHig SKee CTho CSco GTwe SFru Bowe Edws

Surprise
   GTwe

Taunton Cross
Early autumn dessert apple. One of the Long Ashton seedlings, brightly coloured and disease resistant.
   CSco

Ten Commandments
Mid dessert; 1883; A Herefordshire variety. Small fruit. Dark red.
   SDea WJas GTwe Bowe

** Tenroy (Royal Gala)
   Cast SKee GTwe Muir Edws

Thomas Rivers
Herts, c 1890; acid; culinary; second early to mid. Named in honour of the famous fruit breeder who raised it.
   SDea SKee CTho Bowe

Thorle Pippin
1831; Scotland; dessert; early; sweet.
   SDea SKee

Tibbetts Pearmain
   Allg

Tillington Court
   WJas

Tom Putt
(1700s) Cooker. September to November. A vigorous, very spreading tree. A medium sized flat-round greenish yellow apple, up to three quarters striped and blotched with dull red. Becomes very greasy if stored. Crisp, juicy and acid. Cooks well. Formerly often used as a cider apple. (Brog)
   Allg Cast SDea WHig WJas SKee CTho CSco GTwe Slgm Bowe

Tower of Glamis
Old; Scotland; culinary; very late; perfumed.
   Allg SDea SKee CSco Bowe

Transparent Bois Guillaume
SKee

Transparent de Croncels
1869; France; dessert; early - mid; sweetish.
SKee

Twenty Ounce
Pre 1844; USA; culinary; late; subacid. As suggested by its name, very large fruit. Good colour.
Cast WJas SKee GTwe Bowe

Twinings Pippin
Pre 1872; Cornwall?; dessert; mid; rich.
SKee

Tydeman's Early
(1929) Dessert. McIntosh x Worcester Pearmain. August to September. A moderately vigorous, very spreading tree. Inclined to tip-bearing. A round-conical dull yellow apple almost entirelycovered with an attractive bright crimson flush. Becomes greasy if stored. Crisp and juicy with a good vinous flavour. (Brog)
Allg Cast SDea WJas SKee Rog CSco GTwe Bowe Edws

Tydeman's Late Orange
(1930) Dessert. Laxton's Superb x Cox's Orange Pippin. December to April. A vigorous, upright spreading tree. A round-conical yellow apple, flushed and striped with dull dark purplish red. Firm, crisp and juicy with a rich aromatic flavour. (Brog)
Cast SDea SFam SKee Rog CSco GTwe SFru Bowe Edws

Tyler's Kernel
1883; Herefordshire; dual; late; subacid.
Allg SKee

Upton Pyne
1910; Devonshire; dessert; very late; aromatic.
SDea SKee CTho Bowe

Veitches Perfection
Devon, 19th century; dessert, culinary; mid to late. Bred by the Veitch nursery of Exeter.
CTho

Vickey's Delight
SDea

Vista Bella
(1956) Dessert. Complex parentage involving Julyred. Late July to early August. A medium sized, upright-spreading tree. A round, yellow green apple almost entirely covered with a maroon flush and a heavy bloom. Crisp and juicy with a characteristic McIntosh flavour. (Brog)
Cast SDea SKee CSco GTwe Bowe Edws

Wagener
1791; USA; dessert; very late; sweet. An old American variety keeping crisp and juicy until March, of good flavour, golden-yellow when ripe with a carmine cheek. Remarkably prolific and hardy and free from scab. Raised by Abraham Wagener of Dover, New York State. Jan-Apr.
Allg SDea SKee CSco Bowe

Waltz
Dessert. Dark red and green apple, sweet and juicy. Good keeper. Self fertile.
SDea LBuc

Wanstall Pippin
1800; Kent; dessert; mid - late; sweet.
SKee Bowe

Warden
Pre 1575; Worcester; very large fruit; Feb; culinary.
SDea

Warner's King
(1700s) Cooker. Triploid. September to February. A vigorous, upright-spreading tree. A large, pale greenish yellow flat round apple, sometimes with a slight purplish brown flush. Becomes greasy if stored. Soft, juicy and very acid. Cooks well. Somewhat subject to bitter pit. (Brog)
Allg SDea WJas SKee CSco SFru Bowe

Washington
Allg

Wayside
Allg

Wealthy
1860; Minnesota USA; dual; mid - late; subacid. A dual purpose American apple. A Cherry Crab cross, best eaten from the tree in Oct. Good for baking and apple juice. Fruit flat to round, pale yellow flushed carmine. Crisp and abundant fruit
sub-acid and with good bouquet. Tree is moderate growth, but cropping heavy.
Allg SDea SKee

Weight
SDea

Welcome
Bowe

Wellspur Red Delicious
GTwe

Welsh Russet
An enormous Russet. Completely russeted all over. The size of Peasgood's Nonsuch. Its origin is unknown. Slightly sharp, but not to cooking sharpness. Not easy to bite, due to its larger size! Keeps well into March.
SDea

Wheeler's Russet
Edws

White Joaneting
(Syn. White Jenneting) England, before 1600; subacid; dessert; early. The first of all earlies. Ripe in July. Late summer dessert apple. Very early, small yellow fruit, crisp and fresh. An ancient variety, known before 1600, but there is some doubt as to its identity.
CTho CSco

White Melrose
Very old; Scotland; culinary; mid - late; subacid. Early Oct/Nov. An unusual cooker, being seedless. Yellow, smooth skinned and keeping until Feb, when it will be palatable for dessert. Skins become waxy with age - at dessert quality time. Cooking potential is great, cooking to a froth. Makes a dome shaped tree.
SDea SKee GTwe

White Paradise
Old; Scotland; culinary; mid; subacid.
SDea SKee

White Transparent
Pre 1800; Russia. Late summer dessert apple. The first to ripen in late July, a smooth, waxy, milky-yellow fruit, crisp andvery juicy, pleasantly sharp and cooking well. Scab free and prolific. Rather slow growing.
Allg SDea SKee CSco

William Crump
Dessert. Cox's Orange Pippin x Worcester Pearmain. December to February. A fairly vigorous, upright tree. A round conical rich yellow apple almost completely covered with bright deep red flush. Some short, broken red stripes with light patches of grey russet. Rather greasy. Firm, juicy and sweet with a rich aromaticflavour. (Brog)
Cast SDea WJas SKee CSco GTwe SFru Bowe Edws

Winston
(1920) Dessert. Cox's Orange Pippin x Worcester Pearmain. December to April. A moderately vigorous, upright spreading tree.A round-conical, greenish yellow apple up to three quarters flushed with dull purplish red. Some distinct red stripes. Firm, juicy and sweet with a good aromatic flavour. (Brog)
Allg Cast SDea SFam SKee Rog CSco GTwe SIgm Bowe Edws

Winter Banana
1876, but was it raised in Worcestershire or Indiana, USA? Dessert; mid - late; aromatic. A smooth shiny red/yellow apple. Pick early Oct - keeping until March. Award of Merit (R.H.S.) in1912. Flesh yellow. OK in hot climates.
Allg SDea SKee Edws

Winter Greening
Allg

Winter Peach
Possibly USA, before 1850; acid, spicy; dessert, culinary; late to very late. Will keep until April. Tender, juicy flesh.
CTho

Winter Pearmain
Very old; England; dessert; very late; sweet.
SKee

Winter Quarrenden
1896; Nottinghamshire; dessert; late; perfumed. A late Quarrenden, having similar character of Devonshire Quarrenden. A small hard red apple that will store reasonably well.
SDea SKee

Winter Queening
Norfolk, before 1818; sweet, rich, perfumed; dessert, culinary; mid to very late. A very old variety, possibly medieval. A hardy, good bearer. Often confused with Winter Pearmain.
SDea CTho

Withington Basket
Allg

Woolbrook Pippin
Sidmouth, Devon, 1903; sweet, aromatic; dessert; mid to late. Bred by Stevens and Son of Sidmouth from a Cox's Orange pip.
CTho CSco

Woolbrook Russet
Sidmouth, Devon, 1903; juicy, acid; culinary; late to very late. Bred by Stevens and Son. A useful, rich late cooker.
SKee CTho CSco SFru Bowe

Worcester Pearmain
(1874) Dessert. Thought to be Devonshire Quarrenden seedling. September to October. A moderately vigorous tree. Inclined to tip-bearing. A round-conical, pale yellow apple almost completely flushed with bright blood red. Firm, a little juicy and sweet with a pleasant flavour. (Brog)
Allg Cast SDea SFam WHig WJas SKee CTho Rog CSco GTwe Muir

Wormsley Pippin
1811; Herefordshire; dessert; mid; aromatic. Raised by Thomas. A. Knight. Very nearly extinct.
WJas SKee

Wyken Pippin
(1700s) Dessert. November to February. A rather weak, upright tree. A flat-round, greenish yellow apple with prominent, sometimes russetted, lenticels. Firm, juicy and sweet with a good aromatic flavour. (Brog)
SDea SFam SKee CSco GTwe

Yellow Ingestre
Allg SKee WJas CSco

Yellow Newton
Allg

Yellowspur
SKee Bowe

Yorkshire Aromatic
SDea

Young America
SIgm

Zabergau Renette
1885; Germany; dessert; late; subacid.
SKee

Cider Apple

Alford
SKee

Ashton Bitter
CTho GTwe

Ashton Brown Jersey
CTho

Black Dabinette
CTho

Breakwell's Seedling
CTho CSco

Brown Snout
CTho CSco

Brown's Cider
GTwe

Broxwood Foxwhelp
CTho CSco

Bulmers Norman
SKee CSco Bowe

Camelot
CTho

Captain Broad
CTho

Chaxhill Red
CTho

Chisel Jersey
CTho CSco

Cider Lady's Finger
CTho

Court Royal
CTho

Crimson King
CTho CSco

Crimson Victoria
CTho

Dabinette
Late October to November. A small compact tree. Medium bittersweet. A good cropper of high quality. (Brog)
Allg SDea SKee CTho CSco GTwe LBuc Bowe

Dove
CTho

Dufflin
CTho

Ellis Bitter
CTho GTwe LBuc

Fillbarrel
CTho CSco

Frederick
CSco

Golden Bittersweet
CTho

Goring
CTho

Halstow Natural
CTho

Hangy Down
CTho

Harry Masters Jersey
SDea CTho CSco

Hollow Core
CTho

Improved Dove
CSco

Improved Lambrook
CTho CSco

Improved Redstreak
CTho CSco

Johnny Andrews
CTho

Kingston Black
November. Medium bittersharp. A medium sized tree. The best variety for vintage cider. (Brog)
 SDea SKee CTho CSco Bowe

Lady's Finger of Hereford
WJas

Langworthy
CTho

Major
CTho

Michelin
SDea CTho CSco GTwe

Morgan Sweet
SDea SKee CTho CSco

Nehou
CSco

Northwood
CTho

Paignton Marigold
CTho

Payhembury
CTho

Pig Snout
CTho

Porter's Perfection
CTho CSco

Redstreak
CTho

Sercombes Natural
CTho

Slack Ma Girdle
CTho

Somerset Redstreak
CTho CSco

Stembridge Cluster
CSco

Stembridge Jersey
CSco

Stoke Red
CTho CSco

Sweet Alford
CTho CSco Bowe

Sweet Bay
CTho

Sweet Cleave
CTho

Sweet Coppin
CTho CSco

Tale Sweet
CTho

Taunton Fair Maid
CTho

Taylors
SDea CSco

Town Farm No 59
CTho

Tremletts Bitter
SDea CTho CSco

Vilberie
CSco

White Close Pippin
CTho

Yarlington Mill
SDea SKee CTho CSco

Apricot

Alfred
Late July. A vigorous, spreading and hardy tree. Very productive. Large fruits. Firm, juicy with a sweet rich flavour. Freestone. (Brog)
  Cast SDea SKee CSco GTwe Muir ERea SFru Bowe

Aprigold
WHig ERea

Bredase
SDea

Chojura
WHig GTwe Bowe

Early Moorpark
Mid July. Large round to oval fruits. Yellow mottled and dotted with crimson on exposed side. Very rich flavour. (Brog)
  Allg Cast SDea SFam GTwe ERea SFru SIgm

Farmingdale
Allg SDea SKee SFru

Goldcot
SDea

Golden Glow
ERea

Hermskerk
Allg SKee

Hongaarse
SDea

Hosui
GTwe CSim

Kosui
GTwe

Kumoi
SDea WHig LBuc Bowe

Moorpark
(1760) August. Large roundish fruits, deep orange with brownish red flush and darker dots. Firm fleshed and very juicy. Excellent flavour. (Brog)
SDea WHig SKee Rog CSco GTwe Muir ERea SFru Bowe Edws

New Large Early
(1873) Mid July. Large round-oval fruits. Pale apricot skin. Melting, juicy flesh with a good flavour. (Brog)
Cast SDea SKee CSco GTwe ERea SFru Bowe

Nijisseiki (20th Century)
SKee Bowe

Royal Orange
Bowe

Shinko
GTwe

Shinseiki
SDea WHig GTwe Bowe

Shinsui
SDea WHig SKee Bowe

Shipleys
Allg

Tross Orange
SDea

Artichoke

Green Globe
A gourmet variety. Harvest the large flower heads while the fleshy scales are still packed tight. Boil until tender and serve with melted butter. (Unwi)
Brwn Chil EWK Foth John JWB Mars Milt Mole OGC SbS

Green Globe Improved
With sharp spines greatly reduced and larger, heavier bearing, consistent quality globe-shaped heads, this is a much improved variety. (T&M)
T&M

Purple Globe
For those who like "haute cuisine". The thick, fleshy artichoke bottoms can be prepared in several ways. The globe artichoke is a very decorative garden plant that flowers beautifully with large, purple flowers. It should be planted in asunny sheltered position and be protected in winter. (Bakk)
Bloo EWK Futu OGC SbS Wall

Vert de Laon
One of the most suitable for cultivation in the UK. Its flavour is judged to be superior to imported artichokes. It gained an award of merit in the RHS trials. (Benn)
Benn

Violetta di Chioggia
A luxury vegetable that is easily raised from seed. This variety produces a delicious and attractive purple headed artichoke. Decorative enough for the flower border. Select the best plants and propagate by division. (Some heads will be green from this seed). (Suff)
SbS Suff

Asparagus

F1 Accell
Bloo SbS

F1 Andreas
Dob Foth

Argenteuil Purple Imported
SbS

F1 Backlim
RSlu

F1 Boonlim
Benn RSlu SMM Sore

F1 Carlim
RSlu

Cito
This French variety has consistently given outstanding results with yields of over 0.5 lb per crown. Longer spears than traditional varieties that are just as tasty and tender. A light crop may be harvested during the first year. Quite delicious. (Foth)
Sutt

Connover's Colossal
This is an excellent standard variety which is an early and heavy cropper. Being open pollinated you get more seed for your money but have to wait an extra season for the first crop. (Suff)
Benn Chil Dob EWK John JWB Mars Milt Mole OGC Rog

F1 Dariana
Mars

F1 Franklim
Benn EWK John Mars OGC RSlu Sore Suff T&M

F1 Gijnlim
Brwn RSlu Sore

F1 Jersey Knight Improved
T&M

F1 Limbras
Bloo Unwi

Limburgia
Excellent asparagus with a mild flavour. Limburgia is as soft as butter and not stringy. High yield. (Bakk)
Bakk

Lucullus
The first all-male variety, it produces a much heavier crop than older varieties where the female plants are weakened by seed-bearing. The spears are longer, slimmer and straighter. (Mars)
Mars

Mary Washington
A very strong growing and productive strain producing long, thick spears in May and early June. There is some confusion between the two varieties Mary Washington and Martha Washington, which is not clarified by any books we have been able to consult.
SbS

Merrygreen
Green asparagus, very tender. Thick spears. Grows without earthing up. Very agreeable flavour. (Bakk)
Bakk

F1 Thielim
RSlu

F1 Venlim
Brwn RSlu Sore

Asparagus Pea

Asparagus Pea
A member of the legume family with delightful brick-red flowers. The pods should be picked very small, before they toughen.
Bloo Brwn Chil Dob EWK Foth Futu JWB OGC SbS SMM

Aubergine

F1 Adona
RZ

F1 Antar
EWK

F1 Atar
SbS

Bambino
A true genetic baby vegetable with super early maturity, growing only 12ins tall. Before you know it you will have lots of large, attractive lavender flowers and then clusters of shiny 1inch fruits. These thumb-sized fruits are delicious popped under the grill for a couple of minutes and served hot or can be used in many ways. Excellent plant for container culture or the small garden, wherever space is limited. (T&M)
Bloo T&M

Black Beauty
Excellent, open-pollinated variety. Dark purple-black, pear-shaped fruits of good flavour. (Foth)
Bloo Foth John Mole SbS

F1 Black Enorma
Bloo T&M

F1 Black bell
John Yate

F1 Bonica
Dob Foth SbS

F1 Dobrix
Toze

F1 Easter Egg
John

F1 Large Fruited Slice-Rite
Mars

Long Purple
Very easy to cultivate, preferably in a warm, sunny position. It will give a high yield of beautiful, purple fruit. (Bakk)
Bakk Chil EWK JWB OGC SbS Tuck Wall

F1 Long Tom
OGC SbS

F1 Moneymaker
Brwn EWK Foth Milt Mole SbS Sutt Toze Wall

New York Purple
John

New York Round Purple
SbS

F1 Onita
SbS Suff

F1 Ovana
Sutt

F1 Palomo
SbS

F1 Rima
S&G

F1 Short Tom
SbS Suff

F1 Slice Rite
SbS Tuck

Slice Rite 23
The large, black, oblong fruits can weigh as much as 500g/1lb. Very heavy cropper. (Unwi)
Unwi

F1 Vista
Bakk

Basella

Indian Spinach
Not a variety name, but an alternative for Basella.
OGC Suff

Bean Other

Extra Early Ben Yard Long Bean
Vigna uniquiculata. Eaten as far afield as India and the West Indies, this giant, novel bean can be grown successfully in a greenhouse in the British Isles. (Foth)
Foth

Fiskeby V Soy Bean
Suff

Gion Green Soy Bean
EWK OGC SMM Suff

5th Edition

Liana Asparagus Bean
A novelty item recommended for growing in a greenhouse or maybe in a warm sheltered position outside in the Southern counties. The long (15-24in.) pods are slim and best cooked cut into 1 inch pieces. The name Asparagus Bean refers to its delicious flavour. (John)
John SMM

Ruby Moon
Mars

Yard Long Bean
An interesting variety that can reach 8ft in height with pods that grow to 18in long. Harvest pods when they are the thickness of a pencil. (OGC) Could be a synonym of Liana Asparagus Bean.
OGC Suff

Beetroot

Action
Mars

Albina Vereduna
(Formerly Snowhite) The ice-white flesh has a sweet flavour surpassing red beetroot, and the curled and wavy leaf is a vegetable delicacy high in vitamins. (T&M)
T&M

Avon Early
SbS

Barbietola di Chioggia
(Beetroot of Chioggia) An old traditional Italian beet. An excellent variety with unusual white rings when the beet is sliced. Cooks to pale pink. Lovely mild flavour. (Suff)
Chil OGC SbS Suff T&M

Bikores
The most bolt resistant variety. Bred for fresh market quality, internal colour is excellent. Bikores can be used for both early and late crops. (Brwn)
Brwn EWK John Mole SbS VanH Wall

Boldet
Bred to combine uniform shape, smooth skin and resistance to bolting with the good internal colour. A bold early variety. (Toze)
SbS Toze

Boltardy
Globe - good colour and flavour. Resistant to bolting. Can be sown earlier than most beetroots, but make sure that the soil has warmed up by using cloches. Otherwise sow late April to July. Crops August to November. (D&D)
Brwn Cart Chil Dob EWK Foth Howe John JWB Mars

Boltardy Beatnick
SbS

The Fruit and Veg Finder

Bonel
Definitely one both for devoted beetroot lovers and first time growers, you won't be disappointed. It is a lovely globe variety with marvellous internal colour and superb succulence. High yields, excellent bolt resistance and long cropping make this exceptional. (Foth)
 Foth SbS

Boston
Smooth skinned round beets with excellent internal colour. Slow bolting. (Toze)
 SbS Toze

Bull's Blood
A real old variety which is grown especially for its spectacular red/purple leaves. Best picked young. (Suff)
 SbS Suff

Burpees Golden
Yellow flesh, delicious to eat. (JWB)
 Brwn Chil Dob EWK John JWB Milt OGC SbS SMM Suff

Cheltenham Green Top
A broad-shouldered, long-rooted, medium-sized variety. (Dob)
 EWK John JWB MAS Mole SbS Suff Toze Wall

Cheltenham Mono
Broad shouldered long beet, perfect for storing. Each seed cluster produces only one seedling. (Mars)
 Mars SbS Toze

Crimson Globe
see Detroit

Crimson Intermediate
see Cylindra

Crimson King
see Detroit

Crimson King
Smooth skin and deep red flesh, circular in shape and of fine flavour and appearance. Keeps well. (OGC)
 EWK OGC SbS

Cylindra
Grows above ground in a cylindrical shape. Good flavour. Harvest young. (D&D)
 Brwn EWK John JWB Mars Milt SbS Suff T&M Tuck Unwi

D'Egypte
see Egyptian Turnip Rooted

Detroit
A fine globe beet for general use. Excellent colour and taste. (Tuck)
 MAS Mole OGC SbS SMM Suff Tuck VanH

Detroit 2
A small, ball-shaped dark red beet. A wonderful flavour and ideal for bottling, pickling, freezing. (Foth)
 Brwn Mars Sutt T&M

Detroit 2 Crimson Globe
 Foth Cart

Detroit 2 Dark Red
Extremely good beet for storing with beautiful, deep red flesh. This variety, too, has an excellent flavour, and a very heavy crop to last you through the winter. (Bakk)
Bakk

Detroit 2 Little Ball
A small, ball-shaped dark red beet. A wonderful flavour and ideal for bottling, pickling, freezing. (Foth)
Dob EWK Foth JWB SbS Sutt Tuck Wall

Detroit 2 Nero
Foth RSlu

Detroit 2 New Globe
Very productive with roots of exceptional quality and uniformity suitable for all uses. (Bree)
Dob John S&G SbS Yate

Detroit 2 Spinel
Very uniform baby beets ideal at 1.5ins. diameter but remaining tender, true and tasty when bigger even late in the season. Ideal for pickling or canning and preferred by top restaurants. (T&M)
T&M VanH

Detroit 6 Rubidus
RSlu T&M

Detroit Crimson Globe
Recommended for all purposes, nice quality. (JWB)
Howe John JWB

Detroit Globe
Large sized roots for maincrop use. Very suitable for exhibition. (EWK)
Chil EWK SbS Wall

Detroit Loki
Special, bolt resistant selection of the well-known "Detroit" beetroot with smooth-skinned, deep red, globe-shaped roots and tender flesh which cooks quickly. Delicious harvested small, yet also stores well. (Bakk)
Bakk

Dragon
A medium early Detroit type with round roots, a smooth skin and small tops. The roots are uniform in shape and size with a dark red internal colour and no white rings. Good bolt resistance for a Detroit type and particularly suitable for freezing. (Foth)
Foth

Dwergina
A short topped Detroit type with intense colour, smooth texture and superb sweet flavour. Remains quite small even at maturity. (Suff)
Chil OGC SbS

Egyptian Flat
see Egyptian Turnip Rooted

Egyptian Turnip Rooted
Smooth flattish-round roots have beautifully coloured deep red flesh and an exceptionally fine flavour. (Bakk)
SbS

Extra Early Globe
see Detroit

Forono
Improved intermediate type. Half long stump ended roots of extra good flavour. (EWK)
   Bakk Dob EWK Foth OGC SbS Sutt Yate

Globe
see Detroit

Golden
see Burpees Golden

Golden Ball
   SbS Wall

Kyros
Excellent winter food for animals in the winter. (JWB)
   JWB

Libero
Very quick growing main crop variety. Tender, tasty roots that can be sown through to mid-summer. (EWK)
   EWK RZ SbS Wall

Mammoth Long
   Rob

Modella
Replacing Monopoly, monogerm, globe type one seed per cluster, no bolting. (JWB)
   JWB S&G

Monaco
Smooth-skinned globe Beetroot with uniform internal coloration. Fine flavoured variety. (Dob)
   Dob

Moneta
   Sutt Tuck

Monodet
Produces only one seedling from each seed cluster, reducing the amount of thinning required. Globe roots, crimson-fleshed, free from rings. Good bolt resistance. (Mars)
   Mars SbS Toze

Monogram
An excellent dark red, well flavoured globe beet with good vigour, smooth skin and superb rich red colour when sliced. Each seed produces only one seedling. (T&M)
   John SbS T&M Toze Unwi

Monopoly
Outstanding variety derived from and having the qualities of Boltardy. Each seed produces only one seedling. (T&M)
   Brwn Cart Dob Foth OGC SbS T&M

Motown
   S&G

Nobol
   SbS SbS

F1 Pablo
   Bakk Brwn Milt SbS Sutt Toze Tuck VanH

Pronto
Mole SbS Sutt Wall

Ran Uniball
Suitable for early, main and second crop-production. Quick growing, bolting-resistant and giving very good yields of uniformbeets. (Bree)
S&G

F1 Red Ace
Foth John Rob Sutt T&M

Regala
The best round Detroit type for early sowing. The deep red beet, with rings, have comparatively little foliage and store particularly well. (Unwi)
John SbS Suff Unwi

Replata
Very early. Quality outstanding. Very resistant to bolting. (Mars)
Mole SbS

Rotunda
Howe

Rubigala
SbS

Slowbolt
SbS

Snowhite
see Albina Vereduna

F1 Wodan
Mars

Berry Hybrid

Black Chokeberries
LBuc

Black Loganberry
SDea Bowe

Boysenberry
July-August. Large, purple, roundish oblong fruits with a wild blackberry type flavour. A heavy cropper. Moderately vigorous, thin and thorny canes. (Brog)
SDea WHig Rog CSco GTwe Muir LBuc

Brandy Wine
SDea

Dewberry
Bowe

Hildaberry
WHig

Japanese Strawberry
Bowe

Japanese Wineberry
August. Small, red, sweet and juicy berries which all ripen together. Produces quite low yields. Very decorative canes which are covered with soft red bristles. (Brog)
SDea WHig Rog CSco Muir CSim Bowe

Jostaberry
July. Blackcurrant x gooseberry. Very large, blackcurrant type fruits. Heavy yielding. A large, vigorous, upright bush. Resistant to American gooseberry mildew. (Brog)
   SDea WHig GTwe Muir LBuc Bowe

King's Acre Berry
Muir

Loganberry - LY59
Mid July-August. Large dark red fruits with a sharp taste. Excellent for culinary purposes. A moderately vigorous, thorny plant. (Brog)
   Allg SDea Rog GTwe Bowe

Loganberry LY654 (Thornless)
Mid July-August. Large dark red fruits with a sharp taste. Excellent for culinary purposes. A thornfree variety slightly less vigorous than LY59. (Brog)
   Allg Cast SDea WHig SKee Rog CSco GTwe Muir LBuc Bowe Edws

Marionberry
Bowe

Silvanberry
Muir

Sunberry
Mid July-late August. Medium sized, dark purple fruits with good flavour. Very vigorous, thorny canes. (Brog)
   WHig SKee CSco GTwe Muir

Tayberry
Early July-mid August. Larger fruits, sweeter and more flavour than the loganberry. Moderately vigorous, prickly canes. (Brog)
   Cast SDea WHig Rog CSco GTwe Muir LBuc Edws

Thornless Boysenberry
Cast CSco Bowe

** Tummelberry
Cast GTwe

Veitchberry
August-September. Large, sweet, juicy dark red berrries withexcellent flavour. Stout, wiry, thorny canes. (Brog)
   WHig Rog GTwe Muir Bowe

Wineberry
GTwe

Worcesterberry
Late June. A small, purple-black gooseberry type fruit. Flavour similar to a gooseberry. Excellent for jam and freezing. A vigorous, upright, thorny bush. Resistant to American gooseberry mildew. (Brog)
   SDea WHig Rog CSco GTwe Muir Bowe

Youngberry
SDea Bowe

5th Edition

Blackberry

Ashton Cross
Early to mid August. A medium sized, round firm berry. A good but rather acid flavour. Very high yielding. Very vigorous and prolific, thorny canes. (Brog)
SDea WHig GTwe Muir LBuc Bowe Edws

Bedford Giant
Late July. A large blackberry with large drupelets. Juicy and very sweet. Medium to strong thorny canes. (Brog)
Cast SKee GTwe Muir Bowe Edws

Black Satin
SDea Bowe

** Fantasia
GTwe Muir Edws

Godshill Goliath
SDea

Himalayan Giant
Mid August. A large, round berry with medium sized drupelets, produced on large trusses each carrying a large number of fruits. Juicy with a moderate flavour when ripe. A heavy cropper. Very strong, prickly canes. (Brog)
Allg SDea SKee Rog CSco GTwe Bowe Edws

John Innes
Rog CSco Bowe

Kotata
Cast

** Loch Ness
Late August to mid October. A large, firm blackberry with a pleasant flavour. Moderate to heavy cropper. Vigorous, thorn freecanes. Suitable both for dessert and freezing. (Brog)
Cast SDea WHig GTwe Muir LBuc Bowe

Merton Thornless
SKee Rog GTwe Bowe

No Thorn
SDea

Oregon Thornless
Late August. A medium sized berry with a sharp flavour. Moderately vigorous thornfree canes. (Brog)
Allg Cast SDea WHig CSco GTwe Muir Bowe Edws

Parsley Leaved
SDea

Silvan
Cast GTwe Edws

Smoothstem
Bowe

Thornfree
September. Very large fruits with good flavour. Thorn free canes. (Brog)
Allg SDea GTwe Bowe Edws

Waldo
Early July. Large, firm fruit with excellent flavour. Especially noted for the small size of seeds. A heavy cropper. Moderately vigorous, thornfree canes. (Brog)
Cast WHig Muir LBuc Bowe

Blackcurrant

Amos Black
Bowe

Baldwin
Late July. A medium sized berry with good flavour. Fruit hangs well. Heavy cropper. A moderately vigorous, fairly compact bush. Fruits rich in vitamin C. (Brog)
Allg Cast SDea SKee CSco GTwe Bowe Edws

** Ben Alder
SDea GTwe

** Ben Connan
GTwe Muir

** Ben Lomond
Late July. Large, plump berries with a rather acid but good flavour. Short strigs. A medium sized, upright bush of fairly compact habit. Late flowering. A heavy and regular cropper. Can be used for fresh fruit or processing. (Brog)
Allg Cast SDea WHig SKee Rog CSco GTwe Muir LBuc Bowe Edws

Ben Loyal
GTwe

Ben More
Late July. Large berries. Late flowering. Fairly heavy cropper. Produces a good quality juice. A medium sized, upright bush. (Brog)
Cast SDea SKee CSco GTwe Bowe

Ben Nevis
Late July. Medium to large berries borne on short strigs. Late flowering. Moderately vigorous, upright bushes. Fairly heavy yields. (Brog)
Cast SDea SKee Rog GTwe Bowe

** Ben Sarek
Mid July. Large berries with good flavour. Early flowering but some frost tolerance. A heavy and regular cropper. A small compact bush with rather spreading branches which need support. Resistant to mildew. An ideal garden variety. (Brog)
Allg Cast SDea WHig SKee CSco GTwe Muir LBuc Bowe Edws

** Ben Tirran
Cast WHig GTwe LBuc

Black Reward
Bowe

Blackdown
Bowe

Blacksmith
GTwe Bowe

Boskoop Giant
Early July. Large, juicy, fairly sweet berries, with a thin, rather tender skin. A large, vigorous, spreading bush producing only a moderate crop. Flowers prone to frost damage. Not recommended for planting in small gardens or in the North. (Brog)
> Allg Rog CSco GTwe Bowe

Cotswold Cross
Bowe

Daniel's September
GTwe Bowe

Goliath
Bowe

Green's Black
Bowe

Jet
Mid-late August. Small berries borne on very long strigs. Late flowering. A heavy cropper. A large, vigorous bush. Some resistance to mildew. (Brog)
> Cast WHig Rog CSco GTwe Bowe Edws

Laxton Giant
CSco GTwe Bowe

Malvern Cross
Bowe

Mendip Cross
Rog GTwe Bowe

Seabrook's Black
WHig Bowe

Silvergieter's Zwarte
Bowe

The Raven
Bowe

Tor Cross
GTwe Bowe

Wallace Seedling
Bowe

Wellington XXX
Mid July. A medium to large berry with a fairly tough skin. Sweet and juicy with a good flavour. Early flowering. A heavy cropper. A vigorous, spreading bush. (Brog)
> Allg Cast SKee Rog CSco GTwe LBuc Bowe Edws

Westwick Choice
Bowe

Blueberry

Amm Blue
Bowe

Berkley
Mid-season. Large, firm, slightly aromatic berries which are resistant to cracking. A tall, spreading, rather open and very productive bush. (Brog)
> SDea GTwe Treh LBuc Bowe

Blue Crop
Early. Large, light blue, firm berries with a slight aromatic flavour. Resistant to cracking. Excellent dessert quality. A vigorous, upright bush. A good cropper. (Brog)
SDea WHig GTwe Muir Treh LBuc Bowe

Blue Ray
Bowe

Bluetta
GTwe Treh Bowe

Collins
Bowe

Coville
Muir Treh Bowe

Dixi
Bowe

Duke
GTwe

Erliblue
SDea GTwe Muir

Goldtraube
SDea WHig GTwe Bowe

Grover
Bowe

Heerma 1
Bowe

Herbert
GTwe Muir Bowe

Ivanhoe
Bowe

Jersey
SDea Bowe

Mader
Bowe

Northland
GTwe Bowe

Parrot
GTwe

Patriot
Treh Bowe

Rostina
Bowe

Rubens
Bowe

Spartan
GTwe Bowe

Sunrise
GTwe

Toro
GTwe

Un-named selection
CSco

Weymouth
SDea Bowe

Broad Bean

Acme
see Masterpiece Green Longpod

Aguadulce
John

Aquadulce Claudia
Very hardy variety for early spring or autumn sowing. Mediumlong pods with white beans. Ideal for freezing. (EWK)
   Cart Dob EWK Foth Howe John JWB Mars MAS Milt Mole

Aquadulce Loreta
A vigorous, early autumn or early spring sowing type. Ready 1 week before Aguadulce, producing well-filled pods with 7 delicious beans per pod. Excellent vigour and frost resistance. (T&M)
   T&M

Bailey
S&G

Bonny Lad
This is excellent for small gardens. The plants are from 15-18 in. high and produce 3 or 4 stems each bearing a cluster of smooth, 5 in. long pods. (Dob)
   Cart Dob

Bunyards Exhibition
Difficult to beat for all-round performance. Crops heavily with "long-pod" beans full of flavour. Good for autumn or spring sowing. (Foth)
   Brwn Cart EWK Foth Howe John MAS Milt Mole OGC SbS

Colossal
see Conqueror

Conqueror
Long pods widely used for exhibition. Plump beans of excellent flavour. (Sutt)
   Mole Wall

Dreadnought
Outstanding quality for late spring sowing. Sturdy quick growing plants with good size pods. (EWK)
   Chil Dob EWK John S&G SbS SMM Sutt Wall Yate

Express
A very prolific variety producing many well-filled pods about 8 inches long containing 5 or 6 plump, greenish-white seeds. Flavour and quality very good. (Dob)
   Dob EWK John Mars OGC RSlu SbS Shar SMM Suff T&M

Futura
A bicolour flowering bean with a large, slightly curved pods which ripen evenly and contain four to five beans. A little shorter and more robust than other white seeded varieties. It is one of the earliest spring sown varieties; early to mature from an early spring sowing. Reaches a full grown height of 2 ft. 6 in. (Foth)
   Foth Mole RZ SbS

Giant Exhibition Longpod
see Dreadnought

Giant Four Seeded Green Windsor
John

Giant Four Seeded White Windsor
John

Green Longpod
see Masterpiece Green Longpod

Green Windsor
EWK OGC SbS Suff Wall

Hylon
An outstanding variety producing pods of great length. Freezes well and highly recommended for exhibition. (Sutt)
JWB Sutt Tuck

Imperial Green Longpod
Produces pods some 15in. long, each containing up to 9 large, green beans. (Dob)
Dob Foth John T&M Toze

Imperial Green Windsor
Deep green colour, excellent cropper. (CGar)
John Shar Toze

Imperial White Longpod
Extremely long, broad pods containing 9 to 10 beans. Excellent for exhibition. (Mars)
John Mars Unwi

Imperial White Windsor
Long podded with well-filled pods. Seeds are good size. (Sutt)
Cart John Sutt

Ite Beryl
A well-known white seeded processing variety where it is used because of its small seeds. Beryl has few rivals for size, plant type and lateness. (Bree)
S&G

Jade
Developed from Feligreen, it gives a heavy crop of light green beans which retain their colour after cooking. The smaller size of the beans makes them ideal for freezing. Sturdy plants, shorter than most, with upright pods. (Mars)
Mars

Johnson's Wonderful
An early longpod type giving a heavy yield of good quality beans. (OGC)
OGC SbS

Jubilee Hysor
Up to 9 large succulent white beans much more closely packed into the pods than usual, thereby making shelling faster and easier. (Dob)
Brwn Dob Foth Mars Shar

Masterpiece Green Longpod
Excellent length of pod and table quality. A fine green-seeded broad bean and also excellent for deep freezing. (Sutt)
Brwn; OGC Cart Chil EWK Howe John JWB MAS Milt Mole

Medes
Shar

Metissa

Fine-seeded broad bean. This white-flowering variety is insensitive to unfavourable weather conditions. Metissa is a strong broad bean which, in addition, offers a surprisingly high yield. (Bakk)
Shar Toze

Red Epicure

A fine long pod of exhibition standard, with deep chestnut-crimson seeds. Some of the colour is lost in cooking, but it still retains the superb flavour. (Unwi)
Unwi

Relon

Produces an abundance of long, plump pods containing an average of 8-9 green seeds of excellent quality and flavour. Of tallish habit, a vigorous and most reliable variety. (Dob)
Dob Sutt

Statissa

Bronze seeded variety with true broad bean flavour. Consistently outyielded Express and other heavy yielding varieties. It averages 4 mid-size beans per 5in. pod. Early. (T&M)
OGC Shar T&M

Stereo

An unusual variety with white beans half the normal size, which can be eaten in the style of petit pois. It has a high yield and a habit which makes picking easy. Ht: 4ft. (Brwn)
Brwn Yate

Superaguadulce

Largely used for autumn sowing, earlier and more compact than the English strain, and we consider this the largest podded variety in its class. (Brwn)
Brwn Shar

Talia

If, like the writer, you get real enjoyment and flavour out of the frozen baby-sized broad beans now available, you will lovethis modern variety. A reversal of the trend where big is beautiful, it has been bred to produce beans of a very small, delicious size - only about half an inch long - at about five to the pod and a pale lime green in colour. The plants are of mediumheight, of good standing ability and with straight, erect pods. (Chil)
Chil

The Sutton

A compact and bushy variety, little over 1ft high, ideal forsmall gardens. Excellent flavour. (Mars)
Brwn EWK Foth John JWB Mars Milt Mole OGC SMM Suff

Threefold White

An excellent variety widely used by the canning and freezingindustry. The pods are about 6-7 in. long and the beans are smaller than most other varieties, with a white eye. It is a spring sowing variety. Height 3-3.5 ft. (John)
Bakk John JWB

Topic

Sutt

White Windsor
Will not stand frost, so must not be planted out or sown in the open until all danger of frost is past. (OGC)
EWK JWB OGC SbS

Witkiem
see Meteor

Witkiem Major
A very fast and early variety giving large yields of long, thick pods. A little after Vroma. (Foth)
Mole T&M Toze Unwi VanH Wall

Witkiem Manita
An early maturing variety suitable for early spring sowings. (Bree)
Brwn EWK John OGC S&G Shar Tuck Yate

Witkiem Maxim
Howe

Witkiem Vroma
An excellent spring sowing variety, it is early enough to crop at the same time as autumn sown varieties without lost yield. Good harvests of medium-size pods containing 5 or 6 white seeds. (Foth)
Dob Foth Mars

Broccoli

F1 Arcadia
EWK Howe John Yate

Autumn Calabrese
Large green "heads" followed by side shoots. (Unwi)
Unwi

Autumn Spear
An abundance of delicious green spears from September to November. (Sutt)
Sutt

Broccoletto
A speciality from Italy. A quick sweet flavoured broccoli producing a single head at about 9 in. tall. (OGC)
Bloo OGC SbS Suff

F1 Cape Queen
SbS

F1 Captain
Howe

F1 Caravel
RSlu T&M

F1 Christmas Marvel
Mars

F1 Citation
Dob

F1 Colonel
Howe Yate

F1 Corvet
Brwn Cart Dob EWK Foth John JWB Mole OGC RSlu SbS

F1 Cruiser
John Mole RSlu SbS

5th Edition

F1 Dandy
  SbS

De Cicco
  see Ramoso calabrese

F1 Dundee
  Yate

El Centro
  Produces a good crop of side-shoots over a lengthy harvesting period. (Mars)
  Mars

F1 Emerald City
  Howe Toze Yate

F1 Emperor
  Foth OGC RZ SbS Toze Unwi

F1 Eusebio
  John

F1 Express Corona
  Sutt

F1 Fife
  S&G

F1 Flash
  RSlu

F1 Floccoli
  T&M

F1 Gallant
  Yate

F1 Ginga
  S&G Toze Yate

F1 Green Belt
  Howe John Milt S&G SbS Toze Yate

F1 Green Comet
  EWK Foth JWB Mole SbS SMM T&M Wall

F1 Green Duke
  John JWB SbS Suff

Green Sprouting
  Medium-sized central heads produced in summer followed by a profusion of sprouts. Do not sow later than mid-May. (Dob)
  Cart Chil Dob EWK Foth John JWB Mole OGC SbS SMM

F1 Green Valiant
  John

F1 Jewel
  Foth

F1 Laser
  RSlu

F1 Legend
  S&G

F1 Marathon
  Brwn Howe John Milt S&G SbS Toze Tuck Yate

F1 Mercedes
  JWB Mars OGC SbS

Morse's 4638
  SbS

Nine Star Perennial
Multi-heading variety; will produce up to ten small white heads from each plant. (EWK)
Brwn Chil Dob EWK JWB Mars Mole SbS Sutt

F1 Northern Dancer
Foth

Pacifica
A general purpose non-hybrid mid-season variety. Not as uniform as the F1 hybrids and gives a spread of cropping over several weeks. (Toze)
SbS Toze

F1 Packman
Howe SbS Toze Yate

F1 Pinnacle
Bakk SbS

F1 Pirate
SbS

F1 Premium Crop
SbS Toze

F1 Prima
SbS

Purple Cape
S&G Toze

Purple Sprouting
Produces delicious purple flowered shoots in great profusionas early as February. High in vitamin B. (Suff)
Chil EWK Mole SMM Suff Sutt Unwi VanH

Purple Sprouting Early
Extremely hardy and will provide a succession of delicious tender shoots. Easy to grow. (Foth)
Bloo Brwn Cart Dob Foth Howe John JWB Mars Milt

Purple Sprouting Late
April heading. (OGC)
Bloo Brwn EWK Howe John JWB Mars Milt OGC RSlu S&G

Purple Sprouting Red Spear
A newly introduced early variety, producing fine quality spears. (Brwn)
Milt SbS Toze

Purple Sprouting Redhead
SbS Toze

Ramoso
(De Cicco). This is an old Italian variety for spring or autumn cropping. Non-uniform in maturity and producing over a long season. After the main head is cut a large yield of spears (side shoots) is produced. Delicious and tender. (Suff)
SbS Suff

Red Arrow
A vast improvement on existing strains, cropping 1 week earlier and yielding up to 20% more. Vigorous plants producing lots of vitamin rich, tender flower buds. (T&M)
Dob OGC SbS T&M Toze Tuck Wall

Red Lion
Purple headed variety to mature in the autumn. Produces deep, well coloured heads that are well protected. (Toze)
Toze

F1 Regilio
Bloo Howe Mole Wall

Romanesco
A very distinctive type of broccoli, maturing in late autumn. Lime-green heads up to 6 in. across, consisting of many "pinnacles" of curd. Extremely soft. texture and magnificent flavour. For May sowing only. (Mars)
Brwn Cart Chil Dob EWK JWB Mars OGC SbS Suff Sutt

Rosalind
Mars Toze

F1 Roxette
Yate

F1 Royal Banquet
Unwi

Rudolph
A very early variety producing large purple spears. Gives an extra long harvesting period if planted with a standard type. Harvest January - On. (Brwn)
Brwn SbS Toze

F1 SG1
SbS

F1 Samurai
Howe John Milt SbS Toze Yate

F1 Shogun
Brwn EWK Foth Howe John Milt Mole OGC S&G SbS SMM

F1 Skiff
RSlu

F1 Southern Comet
Bakk Mole SbS Toze Wall

F1 Sprinter
John

F1 Stolto
SbS

F1 Sumosun
VanH

F1 Topstar
Unwi

F1 Trixie
Mars OGC T&M Unwi Yate

F1 Vantage
EWK SbS

F1 Viking
Howe

White Sprouting
Delicious shoots like tiny cauliflowers are produced when vegetables of this type are usually scarce. (Bree)
Bloo Cart Chil EWK Mole OGC S&G SMM

White Sprouting Early
Ready March when there are few other vegetables. Very hardy. (Mars)
Foth Howe John JWB Mars MAS RSlu SbS Suff Toze

White Sprouting Improved
Delicious creamy-white shoots for use in March-April. (Sutt)
Sutt

White Sprouting Late
Pure white "mini cauliflowers" holding into May. (Mars)
Brwn Dob EWK Howe John JWB Mars MAS Milt RSlu SbS

White Star
Stock has been rigorously re-selected to give higher yields than existing strains plus a much higher quality spear. (T&M)
SbS T&M Toze Tuck

Brussels Sprout

F1 7159
Toze

F1 Acropolis
Mole SbS

F1 Adeline
Howe John

F1 Adonis
S&G T&M

F1 Adri
SbS Yate

F1 Ajax
S&G SbS

F1 Amoroso
RSlu

F1 Aries
Mole SbS

F1 Ariston
S&G

Ashwell Strain
Produces good, firm sprouts. (JWB)
John JWB

Bedford
For picking between December and February. Plants of medium height closely packed with firm, dark green sprouts of fine flavour. (Dob)
Dob

Bedford Blue Vein
A late sprout which stands well and produces a large crop of dark green sprouts on tall stems. (Suff)
EWK JWB SbS Suff Wall

Bedford Darkmar 21
Lots of firm sprouts with a fine flavour. (Foth)
Brwn Foth John JWB Mole OGC SbS Tuck VanH Wall

Bedford Fillbasket
A open pollinated sprout producing large solid buttons from October to December. (Suff)
Chil EWK MAS SbS Suff Sutt VanH Wall

Bedford Winter Harvest
Dark green medium-sized sprouts from October to February. Strong, very hardy plants. (Sutt)
Sutt

F1 Boxer
Mole SbS VanH

F1 Buttons
Foth

Cambridge No 5
Large sprouts - ready December/January. (D&D)
Bloo EWK John JWB MAS OGC SbS Suff Wall

F1 Cascade
Dob John SbS

F1 Cavalier
John Mole SbS T&M Toze VanH Wall

F1 Citadel
Bloo Cart Dob EWK JWB SbS SMM Sutt T&M VanH Wall

F1 Claudette
EWK OGC SbS Toze Yate

F1 Collette
EWK Howe SbS SMM Yate

F1 Content
Mars SbS

F1 Cor Valiant
Mole S&G SbS Wall

F1 Corinth
S&G

F1 Cyrus
S&G

F1 Diablo
Milt Toze VanH

F1 Dolmic
John Mole T&M Wall

F1 Domica
SbS

Early Half Tall
A very early variety which gives a heavy crop of buttons from top to bottom of the stalk. Should be ready from September and should stand throughout November. (OGC)
Bloo John Mole OGC SbS Wall

F1 Edmund
S&G Toze

Evesham Special
A good, well-established variety with firm, early crops. Large, tasty sprouts on medium plants. Ideal for growing in exposed positions. (Foth)
Brwn Foth John Milt Mole SbS Wall

F1 Evident
SbS

F1 Extent
SbS

F1 Fortress
EWK Foth John Mars OGC SbS Suff Tuck Unwi Wall

F1 Gabion
John RSlu

F1 Gavin
John

F1 Golfer
Mole SbS

F1 HZH021
John

F1 Hunter
SbS

F1 Icarus
S&G T&M Wall

F1 Igor
SbS

F1 Ilias
S&G

F1 Jackeline
Howe

F1 Kundry
S&G

F1 Lunet
John Mars Mole RSlu SbS Wall

F1 Mallard
Unwi

F1 Masterline
Brwn Howe

F1 Montgomery
Mars Milt Toze

F1 Nicoline
Bakk

Noisette
An old French variety; gourmet vegetable. Small tight sprouts with very distinctive nutty flavour. (Suff)
OGC SbS Suff

F1 Odette
EWK Howe SbS SMM Toze Tuck Yate

F1 Oliver
Brwn John JWB Milt OGC S&G Toze

F1 Ottoline
Howe John

F1 Patent
SbS

F1 Pauline
Howe John

F1 Peer Gynt
Brwn Cart Dob EWK Foth John JWB Mars Milt Mole OGC

F1 Perfect Line
SbS

F1 Philemon
S&G

F1 Predora
Mars Mole SbS VanH

F1 Prelent
Mole SbS

F1 Prince Marvel
EWK SbS Wall

F1 Rampart
Brwn Dob EWK John Milt Mole OGC RSlu SbS Suff Toze

Red
see Rubine

F1 Richard
S&G Toze

F1 Roger
John JWB S&G SbS Toze Unwi

Roodnerf
An excellent maincrop, ready from November onward giving a good yield of firm, medium-sized sprouts. Remains sound and can be picked over a long period. (Dob)
Dob

Roodnerf Early Button
High yield of medium-sized sprouts of excellent quality for picking at Christmas. Sprouts keep well on the stem over a long period. (Sutt)
Sutt

Roodnerf Seven Hills
see Seven Hills

Roodnerf Stiekema
An excellent variety from which you can harvest all winter long. Beautiful, tight sprouts, excellent quality. (Bakk)
Bakk

Rous Lench
Dwarf habit, excellent cropper. (JWB)
SbS

Rubine
A red sprout to give a little variation to winter vegetables. Excellent flavour and becoming popular in the fresh market. (OGC)
Chil Foth JWB OGC SbS SMM Suff Wall

F1 Saxon
Sutt

Seven Hills
A late Brussels sprout, which will give a bountiful crop ready just after Christmas and will stand through January. (OGC)
Cart EWK OGC SbS Wall

F1 Sheriff
John Mars Mole SbS T&M Tuck VanH Wall

F1 Smasher
VanH

F1 Stan
Rob Wall

F1 Stephen
JWB S&G Wall

F1 Stockade
SbS

F1 Suzette
Yate

F1 Talent
SbS

F1 Tavernos
S&G T&M

The Wroxton
SbS

F1 Topline
Brwn Howe John JWB Toze

F1 Trendline
Howe

F1 Troika
Dob Foth John SbS

F1 Uniline
Howe

United
Bred by combining the best of Bedfordshire type inbred linesto give a more uniform open pollinated Ashwell's stock. (Toze)
SbS Toze

F1 Victor
SbS

F1 Wellington
Foth John Toze Unwi

F1 Widgeon
Sutt

Bulbous Rooted Chervil

Turnip rooted chervil (Chaerophyllum bulbosum)
Once grown widely for its roots. Germination is difficult, needing a cold winter. Selection might improve this vegetable with ease.
Futu

Burdock

Burdock
A bushy plant with large leaves and purple thistle like flowers. Blooms July-Sept. An important blood purifier. Has anti-bacterial properties and is used for many skin problems. Useful also for rheumatism and arthritis. The root may be boiled as a vegetable and the stalk, prior to flowering, may also be cooked. Habitat: waste ground. (Suff)
Futu Suff

Mitoya Shirohada
New for 1995 is this replacement for Watanabe Early no longer available. Earlier, whiter and finer surfaced, the roots have a tender texture and good flavour. It can be sown in both spring and autumn and produces splendid, uniformly thick roots upto 3ft. in length. Try serving them whole! (Chil)
Chil

Watanabe Early
A very rapid grower, producing long, slender roots about 30ins. long with flesh of a fine texture and of a good flavour. (Chil)
  Foth John

Cabbage

F1 Admiral
  Toze

F1 Advantage
  Sutt Toze Tuck

F1 Alabama
  Howe

Alpha
  see Golden Acre

Amager
  SbS

F1 Anton
  S&G

F1 Apex
  SbS

April
Early spring cutting variety forming dwarf compact hearts. (EWK)
  Bloo EWK Howe John JWB Mole SbS Suff Sutt Tuck

F1 Aquila
  SbS

F1 Arena
  Yate

F1 Aristocrat
  SbS Toze

F1 Augustor
  S&G

Avon Crest
Best of the spring cabbages for standing. (JWB)
  SbS

F1 Balbro
  SbS

F1 Bartolo
  John Mole SbS Toze

F1 Big Ben
  SbS

F1 Bison
  Howe John SbS

Biwama
  SbS

Brunswick
Very large heads for autumn and early winter use. Will stand for a long time without splitting. (EWK)
  EWK John MAS SbS SMM VanH Wall

Brunswijker
  see Brunswick

Budereich
The standard variety for autumn cutting. Solid deep green ballheads weighing up to 3 lbs. Very uniformly shaped therefore most suitable for exhibition work. (VanH)
SbS VanH

F1 Cape Horn
EWK Foth JWB SbS Yate

F1 Carnival
Toze

F1 Castello
Foth John Mars SbS T&M Wall

F1 Celtic
Howe Mole Sutt Yate

F1 Charmant
Howe John Toze Yate

F1 Chessma
Howe

Christmas Drumhead
Solid flat-topped hearts. Ready December. (D&D)
Bloo Dob EWK John JWB Mars Milt Mole OGC SbS SMM

Christmas Drumhead Early
A blue-green drumhead maturing Oct-Nov from sowings made outdoors April-early May. (Sutt)
Sutt

Christmas New Late
SbS Toze

F1 Clarinet
S&G

Coleslaw
Superb quality autumn and early winter cabbage. Fine white heads for shredding, will keep for a long time. (EWK)
EWK

F1 Colt
S&G

Copenhagen Market
John SbS

Cotswold Queen
Somewhat later in maturity than Offenham, this makes better heads. (OGC)
Bloo John OGC SbS Toze Yate

F1 Custodian
Mole SbS Wall

Delicatesse
Sbs

F1 Delphi
John Mole RSlu SbS Wall

F1 Delus
RSlu

Derby Day
A tip-top ballhead. Should be ready in early June. (Foth)
Bloo Brwn Foth John JWB Mars Milt Mole SbS Toze

Ditmarscher Forcing
see Golden Acre

Dorado
Howe John SbS Toze

F1 Duchy
Brwn SbS T&M

F1 Dumas
RSlu

F1 Duncan
Brwn Howe John Mars Mole SbS Toze Unwi VanH Wall

Durham Early
Autumn sowing variety for spring cutting. Small firm hearts of excellent quality and flavour. (EWK)
Bloo EWK Howe John JWB Mars MAS Milt Mole SbS Sutt

Durham Elf
A small high class selection of Durham Early. (Bree)
Brwn Howe John S&G SbS Yate

Earliest of All
Our own introduction into the commercial market. Excellent ball head type of compact habit and very early to mature. Can be grown at close spacing. (EWK)
EWK

Early Drumhead
see Brunswick

Early Flat Dutch
see Brunswick

Early Jersey Wakefield
A very old variety that deserves to be grown more today. Heads are shaped like an upside down ice cream cone, dark waxy green and very compact. Weighing 2-3 lbs. superb eating quality and stands without splitting. May also be sown March/April for cutting during August/Sept. (Suff)
Suff

Early Queen
One of the best Spring Cabbages. Sow in late summer for early Spring Greens or later for tight heads. (Suff)
EWK SbS Suff

F1 Elisa
Howe S&G Toze Yate

Ellam's Early Dwarf
Good flavoured oval heads for eating March-May. (D&D)
EWK John JWB SbS Wall

F1 Emerald Cross Summer Monarch
JWB

F1 Enfield (2811)
S&G

Enkhuizen Glory
John SbS

F1 Erdeno
S&G

F1 Erma
Howe

F1 Espoir
Howe John Toze

F1 Estron
SbS

F1 Eureka
Yate

Express
A very high-quality selection with little core. Pointed solid heads. (Mars)
Brwn Chil Dob EWK Foth JWB MAS Mole OGC SbS Suff

F1 Felix
Foth

F1 Fidelio
John

First Early Market 218
A fine large leafy dark green cabbage well suited to the "greens" trade and also for heading. (Bree)
Bloo Brwn Howe John Mole RSlu S&G SbS SbS Toze

First of June
A dark Primo type. Small head, uniformity and compactness. Can be used for general purpose drilling for succession in the summer. (Toze)
SbS Toze

F1 Flagship
OGC SbS Tuck

F1 Fortune
EWK SbS

F1 Freshma
EWK Howe John SbS Toze Yate

Gloria
see Green Boy

Golden Acre
Early cabbage, weighing 1.5 kg. Can be harvested in early summer. (Bakk)
Brwn Cart Chil Dob EWK Foth John JWB Mars MAS Milt

Golden Acre Baseball
SbS

Golden Acre Earliest of All
A fast cabbage for late spring and summer use. Matures within 12 weeks. Very firm and delicious for coleslaw or cooked. (Suff)
SbS Suff

Golden Acre Extra Early
John Mole SbS

Golden Acre May Express
Fine ballhead maturing 7-8 weeks from planting. Excellent cooked, and also raw shredded in salads and coleslaw. (Sutt)
SbS Sutt

Golden Acre Primo
Round head. Good for salads, coleslaw. Harvest June - July. (Bloo)
Bloo Howe John OGC Wall

Golden Acre Progress
Very early variety with small round solid heads. (BREE)
SbS

Golden Acre Rapidity
SbS

F1 Golden Cross
EWK Howe John JWB Mole S&G SbS Toze

F1 Goldma
Howe

F1 Goodma
John

Gouden Akker
see Golden Acre

F1 Green Boy
SbS

F1 Green Coronet
SbS

F1 Green Express
John SbS Yate

Green Wonder
SbS

Greensleeves
For early greens to cut before Early Market. This variety bred to reduce the "stalkiness" so common in greens harvested at this period. (Toze)
SbS Toze

Greyhound
Very early compact pointed hearts, can be grown close together. (EWK)
Bloo Cart John Mars Milt SMM Tuck Unwi VanH Wall

Greyhound
see Express

Harbinger
John SbS

F1 Hawke
Dob JWB Sutt

F1 Hermes
RSlu

F1 Hidena
John JWB SbS Toze

F1 Hispi
Bakk Brwn Cart Dob EWK Foth Howe John JWB Milt

F1 Histona
VanH

Holland Late Winter
A Dutch white winter cabbage which produces large, firm round heads. Good both cooked or eaten raw in salads and coleslaw. (Foth)
Bloo EWK Foth John OGC SbS Sutt Tuck Wall

Holland Late Winter E50
John

Holland Winter
The average weight of these cabbages, which store well for a long time, can be as much as 4-5 kg. Beautiful colour and good flavour. (Bakk)
Bakk JWB

Holland Winter E50
see Langedijk 4

Holland Winter White Extra Late
see Langedijk 4

F1 Horizon
RSlu

F1 Hornspi
John

F1 Hyjula
Mole SbS

Improved Hispi
see Kingspi

Jersey Wakefield
Early pointed variety, forming small firm hearts. (Bree)
John SbS Toze

June Giant
see Golden Acre

June Star
see Princess

F1 Kalorama
Brwn Howe John

F1 Karma
Howe

F1 Kilor
S&G

F1 King Greens
RSlu

F1 Kingspi
Mars

F1 Krautman
Bakk VanH

Langedijk 3 Starkwinter
Toze

Langedijk 4
The traditional white dutch cabbage for cutting October/November. Will keep for weeks if stored in a ool, airy place. (Unwi)
John Mars SbS Toze Unwi VanH

Langedijk 4 Decema
Attractive drumhead for maturing late autumn. Very resistant to weather damage. Can be cut as required over the early winter period. (Brwn)
Brwn Mole SbS Wall

Langedijk Superstar
SbS

Late Green Winter
SbS

Late Winter Giant
see Langedijk 4

F1 Lennox
VanH

Lincoln Imp
SbS

F1 Marathon
S&G

Marner Allfruh
Open pollinated variety with small, solid round heads covering a good cutting period. Sow February-March, plant 18 in. apart, harvest July-August. (OGC)
EWK Howe John SbS

Marner Rocco
SbS

F1 Marquis Greens
RSlu

F1 Marvellon
SbS T&M Wall

F1 Mayfield
Toze

F1 Metino
RSlu

F1 Mighty Globe
SbS

F1 Milord
Toze

F1 Minicole
Brwn Dob EWK Foth John JWB Milt Mole OGC SbS SMM

F1 Multiton
John

F1 Musketeer
S&G

Myatts Early Offenham
For quality dark green hearts. (JWB)
JWB

F1 Nobilis
Yate

Noblesse
SbS

F1 Nordri
RSlu

Offenham
Strong growing with large pointed heads for late April maturity. (EWK)
Bloo EWK OGC SbS Wall

Offenham 1 Little Kempsey
SbS

Offenham 1 Myatts Offenham Compacta
A very uniform stock which is very early and dark green. (Bree)
Brwn Howe John Mars Milt Mole RSlu S&G SbS Toze

Offenham 2 First and Best
SbS

Offenham 2 Flower of Spring
For late eating (March onwards). Sow in September. Nice flavour. (D&D)
Chil Dob EWK Foth John JWB Mole OGC SbS Sutt Tuck

Offenham 3 Kempsey
SbS

Offenham 3 Wintergreen
Howe RSlu S&G Bloo EWK John JWB Mars OGC SbS Suff

5th Edition

Offenham BG 283
SbS

Offenham Compacta
see Offenham 1 Myatts Offenham Compacta

Offenham Hardy Offenham
Bred to give a pointed dark green late variety for the second half of May. (Toze)
Toze

F1 Patron
SbS

F1 Pedrillo
John SbS Toze

F1 Perfect Ball
T&M

Pewa
SbS Yate

F1 Piton
S&G

Pixie
Very early. The compact plants produce very tight hearts and have few other leaves. Suitable for close spacing and ideal for small gardens. (Mars)
Brwn Dob JWB Mars Milt SbS Sutt T&M Toze Unwi

F1 Pointer
Yate

F1 Polestar
SbS

F1 Polinius
John Mars SbS Toze

Primax
SbS

F1 Primero
Dob

Primo
see Golden Acre

F1 Prince Greens
RSlu

F1 Princess
SbS

F1 Prisma
Howe

Prospera
EWK Mole SbS Wall

F1 Puma
Toze Yate

F1 Quickstep
Mars T&M

F1 Quisto
S&G

F1 Ramco
S&G

F1 Rapid
SbS

F1 Rinda
RSlu

The Fruit and Veg Finder 131

Robinson's Champion
Large ox and cow cabbage for stock feed. (JWB)
John JWB MAS Rob SbS

F1 Rodon
SbS

Roem van Enkhuizen
see Enkhuizen Glory

F1 Scanbo
Yate

F1 Scanner
Yate

F1 Scanvi
Yate

Scarisbrick
SbS

F1 Scout
SbS

F1 Selma
Howe

F1 Slawdena
John Toze

F1 Sparkel
Dob Foth

F1 Speedon
SbS

F1 Spirant
SbS

F1 Spirit
SbS

F1 Spitfire
Dob Mole OGC SbS Toze Wall

F1 Spring Hero
Bloo Dob EWK Foth Howe John JWB Mars Mole OGC SbS

Spring Time
SbS

Standby
Autumn ballhead. Stands well until wanted in September/October period without bursting. (Toze)
SbS Toze

Steenkop
see Stonehead

F1 Steppe
SbS

F1 Stonehead
Brwn Dob EWK Foth Howe John JWB Milt Mole OGC S&G

F1 Storan
SbS

Summer Monarch
see Emerald Cross

F1 Super Action
SbS

F1 Supergreen
Toze

F1 Trevor
S&G

Utility
John

F1 Vanguard
Mars Toze

F1 Vantage Point
EWK SbS

Vienna
see Green Wonder

Volga
Mole

Wheelers Imperial
An old variety but still a fine early. Small pointed heads. (Dob)
Cart Chil Dob EWK John JWB Mole SbS SMM Sutt Tuck

Wiam
Very solid round heads. Matures in September and holds well. Especially sweet sort for use raw, in salads. (Mars)
Mole SbS

F1 Winchester
S&G

Winnigstadt
An older, still very popular cabbage. Tightly wrapped leaveswith hard, pointed hearts. (Dob)
Bloo Chil Dob EWK Foth John JWB Mars MAS Mole OGC

Winnigstadter
see Winnigstadt

Wintergreen
see Offenham 3 Wintergreen

Cabbage Chinese

Shaho Tsai
SbS

Cabbage Chinese Headed

F1 Asten
RZ

F1 Blues
Toze

F1 Chiko
John

China Express
see Tip Top

F1 China King 14
Chil

Early Jade Pagoda
see Michihili

F1 Eskimo
Suff

F1 Festival
John

F1 Green Rocket
EWK John SbS

F1 Harmony
Sutt

F1 Hobbit
Brwn Yate

F1 Hypro
RSlu

F1 Jade Pagoda
EWK Suff Toze Yate

F1 Kasumi
Brwn Howe John Mars Milt SbS Toze

F1 Kingdom
John

F1 Mariko
SbS

Michihili
SbS

F1 Monument
Bakk John

F1 Nagaoka
SbS Toze

F1 Nagaoka 50 Days
Mole Wall

F1 Nagaoka 60 day
Foth

F1 Nemesis
Howe

F1 Okido
SbS

F1 Orange Queen
Bloo EWK SbS Suff T&M

Parkin
S&G

Pe-tsai
Not a variety name.
Chil EWK OGC SbS Suff

F1 Ruffles
Dob Sutt

Santo
SbS

Santo Serrated Leaved
Very hardy, this is an open leaved cabbage with decorative serrated leaves. Autumn/winter or spring vegetable. Excellent as a quick growing seedling crop to be cut when a few inches high. (Suff)
Suff

F1 Shanghai
Suff

Shantung
Nice to look at, nice to eat, this is an early, semi-headingvariety of spreading habit with light green leaves that are smooth and tender. Dense interior leaves that blanch well. Heads weigh about four or five pounds. (Chil)
Chil

F1 Tango
SbS Toze

F1 Tip Top
John JWB OGC SbS Tuck EWK SbS Suff

F1 Tip Top 12
Chil

F1 Tip Top China Express
Bakk Toze

F1 Tonkin
SbS

Tsoisam
Milt Suff

F1 WR 60 Days
SbS

Wong Bok
see Pe-tsai

Cabbage Other

Couve Tronchuda
A splendid cabbage-like plant growing to 2 ft. or more across, with closely set leaves with thick, white, fleshy ribs forming a loose kind of head. The leaves and head are very tender to eat, and the midribs, said to have a distinct and agreeable flavour, cooked like Sea Kale. It withstands frost well - indeed it helps to develop the flavour - but it is probably best grown like a half-hardy annual. (Chil)
Chil

Jersey Walking Stick
The long straight stems can be dried, producing attractive lightweight wood that makes into walking sticks. Mature height 5-7 ft. and if left for another season will reach 16 ft. The edible tops resemble kale. (Foth)
Chil Foth T&M

Cabbage Red

F1 Autoro
John Toze VanH

F1 Hardoro
EWK John OGC SbS

F1 Kempero
John

Langedijk Red Autumn
see Langedijk Red Medium

Langedijk Red Late
Excellent variety for storing that can be harvested from September. Sturdy plants with a weight of approx. 3.5kg. (Bakk)
Bakk Sbs

Langedijk Red Medium
An early deep red variety. (Dob)
Dob John

Langedijker Bewaar
see Langedijk Red Late

Langedijker Herfst
see Langedijk Red Medium

5th Edition

F1 Marima
Howe

Niggerhead
SbS

F1 Normiro
John

F1 Rebus
S&G

Red Drumhead 2
A large globe cabbage for pickling, cooking and winter salads. Sow in July for winter. (D&D)
Chil EWK John JWB Mars Mole OGC SMM Sutt Tuck Wall

Red Dutch
see Red Drumhead

Red King
see Langedijk Red

Red Kissendrup
Later maturing than Meteor. Deep red colour. Sown in spring it keeps well in the autumn and early winter. (Toze)
SbS Toze

Red Meteor
Sow early spring in frames or outdoors for late summer crops. (Toze)
Toze

F1 Red Winner
Brwn Yate

F1 Redar
S&G

F1 Reddy
S&G

F1 Revue
S&G

F1 Rodeo
SbS Tuck

F1 Rodima
Howe Yate

F1 Rona
RSlu

F1 Rondy
SbS

Roodkop
see Red Drumhead

F1 Rookie
Foth SbS

F1 Ropex
SbS

F1 Roxy
RSlu

F1 Ruby Ball
EWK Foth John JWB Mars Milt SbS Suff

Volga
SbS

F1 Vorox
RSlu

5th Edition

Cabbage Savoy

F1 Alaska
S&G

Alexanders No 1
Uniform, solid heads mature in the New Year and hold longer than any other variety well into spring. (Mars)
John Mars

Alexanders No 1 Lincoln Late
SbS

F1 Aquarius
John JWB

F1 Arisma
Howe

F1 Atlanta
S&G

Avon Coronet
SbS

Best Of All
Excellent garden variety producing firm flattish heads. (Tuck)
Cart Dob EWK John JWB Mole OGC SbS SMM Suff Tuck

F1 Bingo
John T&M

F1 Cantasa
John

F1 Celsa
Bakk John

F1 Celtic
Brwn Dob EWK Foth John JWB Mars OGC SbS SMM Sutt

F1 Chirimen
Milt Toze Yate

F1 Concerto
Toze Yate

F1 Corsair
Dob

F1 Daphne
Toze

De Pontoise 3
see January King

Decema Extra
SbS

F1 Denver
S&G

F1 Hamasa
Bakk EWK SbS

Hammer Herba
Mole

Herfstgroene
see Novum

F1 Ice Queen
SbS Unwi Wall

F1 Icecap
S&G

The Fruit and Veg Finder 137

January King
Excellent strain for Winter use. Solid heads with distinct colouring. Very hardy. (EWK)
 Chil EWK Foth JWB Mars OGC SbS SbS SMM Suff Unwi

January King Hardy Late Stock 3
Very uniform stock selected over many years by an English breeder. It is extremely hardy and will stand well into March andApril. (Mars)
 Brwn Cart Dob Howe John Mars Milt Mole RSlu SbS

January King Improved Extra Late
SbS

January King Improved Late
SbS

F1 Julius
John S&G T&M Toze

Langedijk 4 Decema
SbS

Late Drumhead
A very popular old variety that is ready for cutting February/March from a May/June sowing. (Suff)
 Bloo JWB SbS

F1 Lucetta
John

F1 Marabel
John SbS T&M Toze VanH

F1 Menuet
Toze Yate

F1 Midvoy
Brwn SbS

F1 Mila
S&G

F1 Morgan
John

Novum
SbS

F1 Novusa
John Mars Toze

Ormskirk
Large variety, good frost resistance. (D&D)
 EWK OGC Suff VanH

Ormskirk 1
A very hardy grey-green crinkled leaved savoy maturing December to January and standing for a long time. (Unwi)
 Unwi

Ormskirk 1 Ormskirk Late
Hearts in January/March, very hardy and solid with lovely flavour. (Mars)
 Brwn Chil Dob John Mars Milt SbS Wall

Ormskirk 1 Rearguard
Sutt

Ormskirk Early
SbS

Ormskirk Extra Late
True Savoy type with dark green crimpled foliage. Will cut even into April. (Tuck)
Mole SbS Tuck

Ormskirk Medium
SbS

F1 Ovasa
John VanH

F1 Paravoy
SbS

F1 Paresa
John Toze Yate

Perfection Drumhead
SbS Wall

F1 Primavoy
SbS

F1 Protovoy
Dob SbS Sutt VanH

F1 Rhapsody
Yate

F1 Rigoletto
Toze Yate

F1 Saga
RSlu

Savoy King
Unsurpassed for yield, uniformity and vigour, it has solid heads of superb flavour. (Foth)
Brwn EWK Foth SbS SMM T&M Unwi

F1 Silva
Sutt

Snovoy
SbS

Starski
A vigorous variety producing good solid heads which store well. Some frost resistance and it retains its colour through the Winter. (OGC)
EWK OGC SbS Yate

F1 Stilon
RSlu

F1 Taler
Mars RSlu

F1 Tarvoy
EWK Howe John SbS T&M Tuck

F1 Tasmania
S&G SbS

F1 Tombola
SbS

F1 Tundra
Bloo Brwn Dob Howe John JWB Mars Milt Mole OGC SbS

Winter King
Excellent cabbage with a good flavour, suitable to remain in the field for a long time, as well as for prolonged refrigerated storing. (Bakk)
Bakk Mars SbS

Winter King Harda
An outstanding variety with good frost resistance for cutting December to March. (Suff)
Mole SbS

Winter King Shortie
SbS

F1 Winter Star
SbS

F1 Winterton
John Toze

F1 Wintessa
EWK John SbS Suff Toze

F1 Wirosa
Brwn Howe John JWB Mole SbS Toze Tuck VanH Yate

F1 Wivoy
Dob Howe John Mars SbS Toze

F1 Yslanda
John

Cape Gooseberry

Cape Gooseberry
Half hardy annual with spreading shoots, the pale green "lantern" flowers contain edible round yellow fruits. Grows in greenhouse or sheltered border. (OGC)
Bakk Bloo Dob OGC Suff Sutt

Cossack Pineapple
Futu

Golden Berry
Producing orange berries up to 1 in. across which are a tangy sweet mixture of pineapple and strawberry. Each fruit is enclosed in a papery Chinese lantern-like casing. Grow like bush tomatoes. Will crop outdoors in South in a sunny sheltered site, otherwise best in a cool greenhouse. (T&M)
Foth T&M Unwi

Cardoon

Cardoon
Related to the Globe Artichoke but grown for its blanched stems. Use as an alternative to fennel or celery. (OGC)
Chil JWB OGC SbS SMM

Gigante di Romagna
A marvellous decorative architectural plant for the vegetable or flower garden. Tie up the long stalks to blanche the inner heart like celery. Harvest December. Needs lots of space. (Suff)
Suff

Carrot

F1 Allegro
SbS

Amini
Sutt Yate

Amsterdam Bak
see Amsterdam Forcing 3

Amsterdam Forcing
see Amsterdam Forcing 3

Amsterdam Forcing 3
Early carrot, extremely suitable for sowing early in a cold frame. Good for cultivation in the open. (Bakk)
Bakk Dob EWK Foth John JWB Mars Milt Mole OGC SbS

Amsterdam Forcing 3 Sweetheart
Excellent colour and shape, blunt ended with little core. For forcing or early crops, outside or under glass. Sow: Feb - Apr. Harvest: May - Jul. Shape: cylinder. (Brwn)
Brwn SbS Unwi

Amsterdam Outdoor
see Amsterdam Forcing 3

F1 Anglia
S&G Wall

Astra
Nantaise type medium early variety. Length 15-17cms. Good resistance to splitting and breaking. For main crop and overwintering. (EWK)
EWK SbS

Autumn King
A true winter carrot: robust vegetable, producing a heavy carrot which is, however, fairly smooth. It has a beautiful colour inside and outside. (Bakk)
Bakk Chil EWK Foth Howe John JWB MAS Mole OGC SbS

Autumn King 2
Long large roots. Fine deep rich red internal colour. Can be left in the ground for winter without splitting. Reliable heavy yielding main crop for eating fresh, winter storage or freezing, cropping late summer to autumn. (T&M)
Cart Dob T&M

Autumn King 2 Trophy
S&G

Autumn King 2 Vita Longa
A long stump-rooted variety. Heavy cropping, mostly red cored, and excellent keeper. Late harvesting type. (Brwn)
Brwn EWK John Mars Milt SbS Suff Tuck Unwi

Autumn King Gigantea
SbS

Autumn King Red Winter
SbS

Autumn King Viking
SbS

F1 Balin
Chil

F1 Bangor
Sutt

Banta
Sturdy, well coloured roots with high carotene content. Heavy top for good protection and easy lifting. (EWK)
SbS

Bercoro
RSlu

F1 Bergen
Bakk John

Berlicum
Beautiful, cylindrical, stump-rooted, red winter carrot. Narrow core. Fine flavour. (Bakk)
Bakk Howe John SbS

Berlicum 2 Berjo
A late maincrop with outstanding colour and especially high in vitamin A. Cylindrical shape. (Suff)
John Mars Mole SbS Suff Toze

Berlicum 2 Oranza
Maincrop tupe of good core and flesh colour. Roots are almost cylindrical and of very high quality. Suitable for harvest from August to Christmas. Mid season. (Brwn)
Brwn SbS

Berlicum 2 Zino
Has appeared in the Guiness Book of Records as the world's largest carrot. Huge well shaped roots with exceptionally high juice yield. Very large main crop. Excellent quality fresh, stored or juice. Cropping late summer and autumn. (T&M)
T&M

Berlicum Special
SbS

F1 Berlina
SbS

F1 Bertan
SbS T&M

F1 Bertop
T&M VanH

F1 Bolero
SbS

F1 Boston
John

Bridge
SbS

F1 Buror
Toze

Camberley
A high quality half-long maincrop. Tapered roots are usually 7-9in. (17-23cm) long with a deep orange colour and a smooth skin. Used for overwintering, particularly in heavy soils, and recommended for both commercial and garden use. (OGC)
>Toze

F1 Camden
>Toze

Campestra
An exceptionally good Autumn King type of appetising deep orange-red. The roots from 6-8in. long, are strong shouldered, slightly tapered and cylindrical. For use during autumn and early winter. (Dob)
>SbS Toze

F1 Cardinal
>Dob SbS

F1 Carousel
>John

Chanson
>RSlu

Chantenay Babycan
Ideal for the production of baby carrots. Seed may be broadcast to provide up to 45 plants per square foot. Develops fast. Rich coloured with little core and great flavour. (Suff)
>SbS Suff

Chantenay Canners Favourite
>Yate

Chantenay Long
>SbS

Chantenay Model Red Cored
see Chantenay Red Cored

Chantenay Red Cored
A stump-rooted, early maincrop with small cored orange roots of fine texture. (Dob)
>Chil Dob EWK Foth Howe John JWB MAS Milt Mole OGC

Chantenay Red Cored 2
A very good carrot, early, with thick, blunt ended roots. Suitable for early and late sowings. Stores well. (Unwi)
>Cart Mars Unwi

Chantenay Red Cored 3 Supreme
A greatly improved stump rooted form, slightly larger with very smooth skin and a much better colour than the original, without losing any of its reliability. Early maincrop. Fresh eating, canning, freezing and winter storage. Exhibition. Repeat sowings spring/late summer. (T&M)
>SbS

Chantenay Red Cored Fenman
>SbS

Chantenay a Coeur Rouge
see Chantenay Red Cored

Chantenay royal
A stump rooted main crop variety excellent in any soil, ideal for clay. Rich coloured roots. Fine flavour. (Suff)
  EWK John S&G SbS Suff Tuck

Chantenay royal 2
A high quality selected stump rooted variety. Mid season. (Brwn)
  Brwn

Chantenay royal 2 Gold King
  SbS

F1 Cobba
  Dob Yate

Cordia
  SbS

F1 Corrie
  Toze

D'Amsterdam a Forcer
see Amsterdam Forcing 3

F1 Dakota
  SbS

Danvers 126
  SbS

Danvers Scarlet Intermediate
  SbS

De Colmar a Coeur Rouge
see Autumn King

Decora
Fast growing Nantes type with very smooth, heavy yielding roots. (EWK)
  EWK SbS

F1 Disco
  Yate

Douceur
Especialy useful for growing baby carrots, the latest fashion in supermarket veg., is this earliest variety producing auniform crop of cylindrical roots with a smooth skin and fine core. Of course, if you don't want them as babies, you can let them survive to infancy, childhood, or even adulthood. (Chil)
  Chil

F1 Dragon
  Toze

Duke
  SbS

Early French Frame
Quick-maturing round roots up to 50mm (about 2 in) in diameter. Ideal for forcing or for sowing in succession outdoors. (Sutt)
  JWB Sutt

Early French Frame Carpa
Early, round carrot for the beginning as well as the advanced vegetable grower. Carpa has an exceptionally good interior and exterior texture, a red core and little foliage. Atpresent, the number one among the round carrots. (Bakk)
  Bakk

Early Horn
For early use this medium sized short, stump rooted carrot is very reliable. RHS highly recommended. (Unwi)
   Brwn Foth John JWB SbS Unwi

Early Market
An early, stump-rooted variety of excellent quality, ideal for both early and late sowing. (John)
   EWK Tuck Wall

Early Market Horn
see Chantenay Red Cored

Early Nantes
see Nantes

Early Scarlet Horn
see Early Horn

F1 Ebro
   S&G

Fakkell Mix
   SbS

Fancy
   SbS

F1 Favor
   Toze

Favourite
One of the most popular stump-rooted maincrop varieties. Excellent quality and recommended for exhibition in "short" classes. (Sutt)
   Sutt

Fedora
One of the most productive late varieties we offer. The heavy, smooth-skinned roots are very large and conical with an excellent colour throughout. (Unwi)
   SbS Unwi

First Pull
see Amsterdam Forcing 3

F1 Flacino
   RSlu

Flak
Fly resistant. The most productive carrot suitable for practically any soils, for an early crop, sow during June/early July for harvesting October until March. An absolute cert for the show bench. Guiness Book of Record Holder 10lbs.4oz. (VanH)
   VanH

Flakkee
Maincrop variety, large roots, excellent for the show bench. (JWB)
   JWB SMM Tuck

F1 Flamant
   SbS

F1 Flex
   Bakk

F1 Fly Away
   T&M Toze

French Frame 4 Lisa
   Mars

F1 Gregory
Wall

F1 Gringo
Yate

Guerande
A very old variety, with broad shoulders, stump rooted and early with a fine flavour. (Suff)
SbS Suff

Imperator
SbS

F1 Ingot
Brwn EWK Foth Howe Milt SbS T&M Tuck Unwi

James Scarlet Intermediate
A good early maincrop variety, with symmetrical and well tapered roots. It is well coloured and is of a good texture, making it an ideal carrot for culinary purposes. (John)
Chil EWK Foth John JWB OGC SbS Tuck Unwi VanH Wall

F1 Jasper
Dob

Jaune du Doubs
A traditional French carrot which forms good-sized half longpointed carrots of an orange-yellow colour. Hardy with excellenteatring qualities. Rare. (Suff)
SbS

Juared
A medium-early to medium-late variety, so it is not a true winter carrot. Juared is sometimes called the "health carrot", asit has the highest carotene content. Extremely rich in vitamin A. (Bakk)
Bakk John SbS Suff T&M

F1 Junior
Brwn

Juwarot
see Juared

Karotan
Long, stump-ended roots of large size for maincrop use. Excellent flavour with high juice content. (RSlu)
RZ SbS Wall

Kundulus
Window boxes, difficult soils, frames, small gardens. Very fast growing. (T&M)
Cart

F1 Laranda
T&M

Laros
SbS

F1 Liberno
T&M

Lobbericher
A sweet, yellow fodder carrot for cattle and rabbits, goats etc. Can be stored in a pit. (Bakk)
Bakk

Long Red Surrey
see St Valery

F1 Major
Brwn Toze

Minicor
Excellent flavour and colours up early. Uniform 6-7 in. Very slender roots. Best for "baby carrots". A gourmet variety. (Suff)
Foth RSlu SbS Suff

F1 Mokum
Bakk Cart John T&M

F1 Nabora
Yate

F1 Nairobi
Brwn John

F1 Nanco
John JWB Mars SbS

F1 Nandor
Rob Toze

F1 Nansen
SbS

Nantaise 2 Michel
EWK SbS

F1 Nanten
SbS

Nantes
Half-long, stump ended roots. Strong grower of first class quality and flavour. (EWK)
EWK Howe John JWB MAS Mole SMM Suff T&M Tuck VanH

Nantes 2
Very early and deservedly popular, long stump rooted with little core. (Unwi)
Foth Mars Milt Unwi

Nantes 2 Ideal
Dob SbS

Nantes 2 Romosa
A half long stump rooted early, excellent for forcing or outside sowing. Has very little core. A really succulent variety. First early. (Brwn)
Brwn

Nantes 5
Cart Sutt

Nantes 5 Champion Scarlet Horn
A fast maturing carrot of uniform shape and quality. (Dob)
Sutt

Nantes Express
Early maincrop. Suitable for early sowing in frames. Some cavity spot resistance. (T&M)
Unwi

Nantes Fruhbund
It colours very early and is, therefore, suitable for sowing early. A carrot with a good colour in- and outside, and with a very agreeable flavour. Recommended selection from the well-known Nantes group. (Bakk)
Bakk

Nantes Half Long
A well-known variety, popular for its high yields and its agreeable, sweet flavour. Nantes is a real summer carrot! (Bakk)
Bakk

F1 Nanthya
S&G

F1 Nantucket
John Tuck

F1 Naomi
SbS

F1 Napoli
Bakk John VanH

F1 Narante
Bakk

F1 Narbonne
Howe John

F1 Narman
Howe John Mole SbS

F1 Narova
EWK

F1 Narvo
SbS

Natan
Wall

F1 Navarre
Foth John

F1 Nelson
Dob John Sutt

New Radiance
SbS

New Red Intermediate
see St Valery

Newman
VanH

F1 Newmarket
Foth

Norfolk Giant
see Autumn King

F1 Panther
Bakk S&G Unwi

Parabell
SbS

Paramex
SbS

Parisje Markt
see Early French Frame

Parmex
A unique round carrot, 1-1.5 in. in diameter. Matures extraearly and develops flavour and bright colour while still young. Perfect for growing in heavy soil. Superb with fresh green peas. (Suff)
  Dob Foth John Suff

F1 Presto
  John

F1 Primo
  Cart Mars SbS

F1 Puma
  S&G

F1 Punta
  Yate

F1 Rapier
  Toze

Red Intermediate Stump Rooted
see Chantenay Red Cored

F1 Red Rum
  Foth Tuck

Redca
A recent Chantenay introduction, stump rooted and very uniform. Excellent root colour with a nice smooth skin. (OGC)
  OGC

Regulus
  SbS

Rocket
A superb carrot of the Nantes type, very early maturing variety hence the name. The carrots produced are of high qualityand cylindrical in shape. High in vitamin A, the roots are a good orange in colour. Excellent picked young for use in salads,or grown on as an early maincrop. An ideal variety for the patioin growing bags or tubs. (Dob)
  Dob Toze

Romosa
  SbS SbS

Rondo
Produces almost round shaped roots. Very early, uniform and sweet tasting. Easy to clean and cook whole. (EWK)
  EWK OGC Wall

Rubin
An early, round carrot with a good inside colour and narrow core, contrary to most other ball-shaped carrots. A variety for the professional as well as for the amateur vegetable grower. (Bakk)
  SbS

Saint-Valery
see St Valery

Scarlet Nantes
  SbS

F1 Senior
  Brwn Unwi

F1 Sheila
  Yate

St Valery
A pre 1880 variety from France with sweet tender flesh. For best results grow this carrot in a rich deep soil where it can attain a size of 2-3 in x 12 in! (Suff)
   Brwn Chil Dob EWK Foth John Mars OGC SbS SMM Suff

St Valery Special Selection
Long tapered roots, very uniform and good colour. (Rob)
   Rob

F1 Stelio
   Yate

Suko
One of the earliest sweetest little carrots we know. Recommended where space is limited also shallow or heavy soils. (T&M)
   John T&M

Sytan
This Nantes type carrot is less susceptible to carrot fly maggot than other varieties. (Mars)
   Mars

F1 Tam-tam
   Yate

F1 Tamino
   John OGC SbS

F1 Tancar
   Toze

F1 Thames
   S&G

Thumbelina
   SbS

Tip Top
Nantes type, very good colour and quality. (JWB)
   Dob JWB OGC SbS

Top Score
   SbS

Touchon Ideal Red
An old French variety (pre 1880) with a fine texture and superb flavour at any size. Will grow to 8 ins (20 cms). The best juicy carrot. Special improved selection. Main crop. (Suff)
   Suff Toze

F1 Turbo
   Yate

F1 Valor
   Toze

Waltham Hicolour
   SbS

White Fodder
Don't be put off by the name. A superb mild tasting carrot very much appreciated in France. Very easy to grow and remains deliciously tender even when very large. This is a safe carrot to eat for those allergic to carotene. (Suff)
   SbS

F1 Yukon
   S&G

Cauliflower

AG 63
SbS

Ace Early
Over the last ten years many late winter/early spring heading cauliflower varieties have disappeared. Therefore we arepleased to offer such an outstanding variety as Ace Early. Firm, white, rounded heads of outstanding quality are ready for cuttingfrom mid-March to mid-April. Good leaf bract coverage provides excellent protection to the curd from winter frosts. (Dob)
Dob Howe SbS

Ace High
Howe SbS

Adams Early White
SbS

F1 Akita
Toze

Alban
Yate

F1 Alegros
RSlu

Alice Springs
SbS

All Seasons
see All The Year Round

All the Year Round
Can be sown in late autumn or spring to produce large, whiteheads. A favourite which is well-known for its accomodating performance. It is an excellent choice for successional sowing. (Foth)
Bloo Brwn Cart Chil Dob EWK Foth John JWB Mars

Alpha
Very popular for early work, June/July. (JWB)
JWB

Alpha 5
Sow outside in early April for August cutting. Sow under glass September/January to mature June/July. It is a very good doer. (Mars)
Mars

Alpha 7 Jubro
John SbS

Alpha Begum
John

Alverda
Excellent quality yellow-green curds with good flavour makesa nice change to the usual white varieties. Sow late May/June forautumn cropping. (OGC)
Howe John OGC RZ Suff

F1 Amarok
RSlu

Angers Early
see Angers No 2

Angers Extra Early
see Angers No 1

Angers Extra Late
see Angers No 5

Angers Half Early
see Angers No 3

Angers Late
see Angers No 4

Angers No 1
Specially recommended for Southern and Western regions. Unsuitable for cold or exposed areas. All have pure white, solid curds. Heads January-February. (Sutt)
  SbS

Angers No 2
see Angers No. 1. Matures February-March. (Sutt)

  Mars SbS Sutt Unwi

Angers No 3
  SbS

Angers No 4
  SbS

Angers No 5
  SbS

Aprilex
  John SbS

F1 Arbon
  John RSlu SbS Toze

F1 Arcade
  RSlu

F1 Ardego
  Howe

F1 Armetta
  Bakk RSlu

Arminda
  John Mole SbS

F1 Arven
  S&G Wall

Asmer Bostonian
see Walcheren Winter 5

Asmer Juno
Usually cuts into June, producing large heads of superb quality before the first early summer cauliflowers are ready. (Mars)
  Mars

Asmer Snowcap March
The earliest variety of the hardy English type. (Mars)
  Mars

F1 Aston Purple
  Brwn Yate

F1 Astral
  Yate

Atares
  SbS

Aubade
The compact, smooth, solid curd has excellent flavour, cooks beautifully and holds its colour. (Foth)
Foth

Autumn Giant
Large heads for cutting from October onwards. (EWK)
Chil EWK John JWB Mole SbS SMM VanH Wall

Autumn Giant 3
Beautiful white firm heads, thoroughly protected by the leaves. Excellent for cutting in November and December. (T&M)
SbS T&M

Autumn Giant 4
Large and solid white heads ready for cutting in October and November. (Dob)
Dob Sutt

Autumn Giant Late Supreme
Yate

Autumn Glory
An old favourite but still deservedly popular. Exceedingly large heads of the finest quality. (Unwi)
Unwi

F1 Aviso
John Toze

F1 Baco
John RSlu SbS Toze

F1 Balmoral
Brwn Yate

F1 Bambi
S&G SbS T&M

Barrier Reef
Compact habit, well-protected deep, white, solid curds. Matures late October. (Sutt)
Brwn Chil EWK John JWB Mars Milt Mole SbS Suff

Batsman
A very vigorous variety which produces excellent quality white curds which are well protected. (Foth)
Foth John Toze

F1 Beauty
RSlu

F1 Belot
EWK

Boston Prize Early
SbS

F1 Breven
S&G

Briac 30
Australian type with large heads and short growing habit. Sow mid-May for maturity to mid-November. (EWK)
Toze Yate

F1 Briten
S&G Wall

5th Edition

F1 Calan
John SbS Toze

Cambridge Early Giant
SbS

Cambridge Mid Giant
SbS

Canberra
Australian variety for November cutting. Large solid heads of excellent colour and quality. (EWK)
Mars

F1 Candid Charm
Bakk EWK OGC SbS Suff Tuck

Capella
SbS

Cappacio
T&M

Cargill
Specially chosen for mini-cauliflower use it is quick growing, vigorous and without a heavy foliage canopy and will not mature all at once. (T&M)
John T&M

F1 Carlos
John RSlu SbS Toze

F1 Carron
Yate

F1 Castlegrant
Brwn Unwi Yate Yate

Celesta
RZ

Centauras
SbS

F1 Ciren
S&G

F1 Commander
S&G

Corvilia
Large head size, rather smooth and slightly domed in shape. Late summer to late autumn. (EWK)
Yate

Danish Perfection
Howe

Dok Elgon
Matures about 13 weeks after planting. Excellent as an early and late autumn crop. Vigorous growing with well-covered, firm, round, snow-white heads. (Mars)
Brwn Dob EWK John JWB Mars Milt Mole OGC Rob SbS

Dominant
Grows well in dry conditions with strong broad foliage for good protection. Autumn heading. (EWK)
EWK John Mars Mole OGC SbS Wall

F1 Dova
Howe John Milt RSlu SbS Toze

F1 Dunkeld
Yate

Dutch May Heading 0581
see Walcheren Winter 5

Early Feltham
see Angers No 2

Early Snowball
John

F1 Elby
Dob RSlu SbS T&M Toze

English Winter
SbS

Erfurt Prima
see Snowball

F1 Esmeraldo
Yate

Ewk's Late June
Heading during June. (JWB)
EWK JWB SbS

Ewk's May Star
Heading during May. (JWB)
JWB

Extra Early Feltham
see Angers No 1

Extra Late Feltham
see Angers No 5

F1 Fargo
John T&M

Firstman
John

Fleurly
An excellent addition! Fleurly produces solid clear white heads of exceptionally high quality. Cut from mid-late April froma late-May sowing. (Dob)
Dob Mole SbS

Flora Blanca
Matures September and October. Deep, pure white heads of first-class quality. Excellent for exhibition. (Sutt)
Sutt

Florian 51
Exceptional solid white heads and a strong weather resistance. (Foth)
Toze Yate

F1 Forrest
RSlu

Fortuna
Mole SbS

F1 Fremont
RSlu

Garant
Quick growing mini cauliflower. (EWK)
EWK OGC Suff

F1 Gipsy
Toze

Goodman
VanH

Grandessa
Medium large heads of pure white for autumn cutting. Strong mid green foliage giving excellent protection. (EWK)
  Bakk

Grodan
Danish giant type. Well protected curds. Crop August untilOctober/November. (Bloo)
  Bloo John Mole SbS Wall

F1 Hawkesbury
  Yate

Herfstreuzen
see Autumn Giant

Idol
An early summer cropping variety, with small flavoursome white heads. The tasty curds can be eaten raw in salads or lightly steamed in the traditional way. Cauliflower Idol is particularly suitable for freezing. (Dob)
  Dob Sutt

Inca
April heading variety with excellent white heads. Strong leaf protection and very frost resistant. (EWK)
  EWK Howe John OGC SbS Suff Toze Wall

Janus
Roscoff type, vigorous, matures January. (JWB)
  JWB SbS

Jaudy 45
  Toze Yate

F1 Jerome
  John Mars

Kestel
  SbS Toze

King
Medium large heads of pure white for autumn cutting. Strong mid green foliage giving excellent protection. (EWK)
  Mole SbS Wall Yate

Late Adonis
see Walcheren Winter 7

Late Feltham
see Angers No 4

Late Queen
  SbS

Lateman
A versatile, medium sized variety with lovely deep white curds. Sow from March to May for cutting August to October. (Dob)
  Brwn Dob Foth Howe John VanH

Lawnya
  SbS

Leamington
  SbS

Lecerf
A fool-proof cropper of excellent quality, having large, deep white heads with dark green upright leaves. For summer use sow March/April; for autumn use May/June. (VanH)
  VanH

Lenton Monarch
  SbS

Limelight
A beautiful soft green autumn cauliflower which retains its colour after cooking. Easy from a May sowing. (Mars)
  Mars Unwi

Lincoln Early
  SbS

F1 Linday
  S&G

F1 Lindon
  S&G

F1 Lindurian
  S&G

F1 Linero
  S&G

F1 Linex
  S&G

F1 Linmont
  S&G

F1 Lintop
  S&G

F1 Logan
  John

F1 Lumen
  S&G

Macerata
  Toze

Majestic
  see Autumn Giant 3

F1 Malimba
  RSlu

F1 Marba
  Howe

Markanta
Extra high quality, with pure white, deep curds produced from early May onwards. (Mars)
  Brwn Foth

F1 Marmalade
  Dob Milt Yate

F1 Martian
  S&G

F1 Marvin
  S&G

F1 Maverick
  S&G

May Blossom
  SbS

Maya
Late May heading. Very hardy, produces well protected, high quality curds. Can be sown as late as June. (Tuck)
OGC SbS VanH Wall

F1 Mayfair
S&G

F1 Mayflower
Toze

Mechelse 3 Carillon
S&G SbS

Mechelse Lincoln Early
see Lincoln Early

Midsummer
SbS

Minaret
Lime green small pointed florets of excellent flavour for late autumn cropping. (Brwn)
Brwn Howe John Milt Mole RZ SbS Toze Wall

F1 Montano
Mars S&G

F1 Nautilus
Brwn Howe John Toze

Nevada
SbS

New Late Dutch
see Walcheren Winter 6

F1 Ondine
Toze

Oze
SbS

Pacific Charm
SbS

F1 Pamir
RSlu

Panda
Mechelse type for early summer production. Perfectly round snow-white heads that withstand high temperatures very well. (EWK)
SbS

F1 Paradiso
RSlu

F1 Penduick
Toze

Perfection
A very reliable variety for October or January sowings. (Brwn)
John Mole SbS Toze Wall Yate

F1 Plana
Mars RSlu T&M Tuck

Polaris
see Alpha

F1 Predial
Mole SbS Wall

Predominant
An easy to grow, mini-cauliflower, can be sown later for heads maturing in September/October. (T&M)
:   Toze

F1 Profil
:   Mole Wall

F1 Pulsar
:   EWK

Purple Cape
A hardy purple cauliflower cropping in February and March. The curd turns green when cooked and has a fine flavour. (Mars)
:   Chil Dob John JWB Mars Mole OGC SbS Suff Unwi Wall

Purple Queen
Vigorous grower and very uniform. Deep purple heads for early autumn maturity. (EWK)
:   EWK Suff

Revito
This is a variety for autumn cultivation, so it should be sown in summer. (Bakk)
:   Bakk Howe John SbS Toze Yate

Rosalind
A quick growing purple headed variety for autumn cutting. Sow late May and June. Well worth trying. (Suff)
:   Toze

Royal Oak
Very fine late variety, heads in May. (Barb)
:   SbS

Selsto
:   Howe

F1 Sergeant
:   S&G

Sernio
:   RSlu

F1 Serrano
:   S&G

F1 Siria
:   John

Snow Cap
:   see Snowcap

F1 Snow Crown
:   EWK JWB Mars SbS Unwi

F1 Snow February
:   SbS

F1 Snow King
:   SbS

F1 Snow Prince
:   EWK SbS

Snow's Winter White
Invaluable and popular mid-winter cauliflower. Cold tolerant and easier to grow than spring varieties. (T&M)
:   SbS

Snowball
Compact and very early with solid pure white heads of superb quality. Can be sown as early as January and also during autumn. (Dob)
  Cart Dob EWK Foth JWB Mole SbS SMM Suff Sutt Wall

F1 Snowbred
  Chil EWK JWB OGC SbS Tuck

Snowcap
Very late variety that can be cut over a long period. Ready in 22 weeks from an early June sowing. (EWK)
  EWK JWB Mole OGC SbS Tuck Wall Yate

Snowy River
  SbS

Solide
  Mole SbS Wall

St George
A later variety, ready for harvesting in April and May, giving solid pure white heads. (John)
  Chil John SbS

St Mark
  SbS

F1 Stella
  John Toze

F1 Taroke
  SbS

F1 Taymount
  Brwn Yate

Thanet
see Walcheren Winter 3

F1 Tico
  Howe

Triskel 22
Produces superb quality heads in the hotter months of the year when other varieties are often poor. Sow April to mature late August; early May for September. (Mars)
  Toze Yate

F1 Tucson
  RSlu

F1 Tulchan
  Sutt Yate

Tuxedo
  Yate

Uranus
  SbS

Valentine
As its name suggests this variety heads mid-February to early March. Very white, deep smooth, curds which are well protected from winter weather. Specially recommended for Southern and Western regions, some protection may be needed in cold exposed areas. (Dob)
  Dob

Veitch's Autumn Giant Early
  John

Veitch's Self Protecting
Strong growing, late autumn heading. Will stand into November without spoiling. (EWK)
>John SbS Wall

Vernon
>Mole SbS

F1 Vidoke
>SbS

Vilna
The latest maturing overwinter cauliflower. Maturing end of May to mid-June. Very hardy. (Brwn)
>Brwn Howe John Milt SbS Toze

F1 Violet Queen
>Howe John Milt OGC S&G SbS Sutt Wall

Vision
A sister variety to Vilna, with the same characteristics. Slightly earlier maturing, mid-end of May. (Brwn)
>Howe John Milt Toze

Walcheren Florissant
>SbS

Walcheren Winter
This excellent variety produces tasty, wide heads from April until June. (Tuck)
>Dob

Walcheren Winter 1 Armado April
Superb-quality extra white curds maturing mid-April onwards. An outstanding variety. (Mars)
>Brwn Foth Howe John JWB Milt Mole OGC RSlu SbS T&M

Walcheren Winter 2 Armado May
Recommded for any part of the UK. Exceptional curds and above all robust and reliable. (T&M)
>EWK Howe John Mole RSlu SbS Toze

Walcheren Winter 3
>Sutt

Walcheren Winter 3 Armado April
Superb quality heads of pure white and large size. Cutting late April. (EWK)
>EWK Mars

Walcheren Winter 3 Armado Tardo
Solid, crunchy, pure white curds that will provide you with garden-fresh florets in one of the few periods in the year when, until now, it wasn't so easy to find a good late spring/early summer variety. Crops late April/early May. (Unwi)
>Howe John Mole RSlu SbS Toze Unwi

Walcheren Winter 4 Markanta
>Mars

Walcheren Winter 5
SbS

Walcheren Winter 6
SbS

Walcheren Winter 7
SbS

Walcheren Winter 8 Maystar
Excellent English overwintering type with solid pure white heads for cutting from early May. (EWK)
  Bloo EWK Howe John OGC S&G SbS Tuck Yate

Walcheren Winter Aprilex
see Aprilex

Walcheren Winter Arminda
see Arminda

Walcheren Winter Markanta
see Markanta

Walcheren Winter Maya
see Maya

Wallaby
For heading late September-early October, this variety is outstanding for its top quality solid white curds. The well-protected heads are ideal for freezing. (Sutt)
  JWB Mole OGC SbS T&M Toze Tuck VanH Wall Yate

Westmarsh Early
see Angers No 2

White Ball
Very white, deep curd with good covering leaves. May be autumn sown without going blind. A relatively new variety but already very popular. (Foth)
  Foth

F1 White Dove
Yate

White Fox
Matures September/October. Fine curds, long standing ability. (JWB)
  John SbS

White Rock
White Rock produces plenty of outer and inner leaves which protect the curd, it is very adaptable and is grown for the mild-July to October period. (Brwn)
  Brwn Howe John JWB Mole S&G SbS Toze

White Summer
Produces firm, round heads of excellent quality for late summer and early autumn cutting. This variety has proved very reliable even under adverse weather conditions. (Unwi)
  S&G

F1 Whitney
RSlu

F1 Woomera
Toze Yate

F1 Yann 37
Toze Yate

Yopal
see Zara

Yuletide
Sutt

F1 Zara
SbS Toze

Zero
Howe

Celeriac

Alabaster
John SbS

Albaster
see Alabaster

Balder
The roots of this vegetable are delicious, having a pronounced celery flavour which adds greatly to the enjoyment of salads. Easily grown and requires no earthing up. Late in the season strip off the foliage, dry the roots carefully and store them in a dry shed. (OGC)
Bloo Chil EWK OGC SbS

Boule de Marbre
see Marble Ball

Brilliant
Productive variety produces smooth roots with beautiful white flesh which does not discolour as so many other varieties tend to. More commonly known as Turnip Rooted Celery. (Dob)
Dob

Cascade
RZ

F1 Cesar
Howe Milt

Giant Prague
Globe shaped roots for use in salads. Quick growing and verytasty. (EWK)
Brwn EWK JWB Mole SbS SMM Suff Tuck Wall

Iram
Very clean, medium-sized, globe-shaped roots with few side growths. Easy to store and the flesh remains white after cooking. (Unwi)
Unwi

Marble Ball
Turnip-shaped roots with the taste of celery and easier to grow. Keeps well all winter. (Foth)
Foth SbS

Mentor
T&M

Monarch
The most widely grown variety for its smooth skin and tenderflesh. (Bree)
S&G SbS Toze

Regent
A real professional variety with very large roots and extremely firm, white flesh, also when cooked. The roots do not tend to become hollow and are hardly prone to Celeriac virus. (Bakk)
Bakk

Snow White
Early, with very white flesh; large size. Superb nutty flavour. (Mars)
  Mars

Tellus
Quick-growing, round roots with firm white flesh. Does not discolour when boiled. (Sutt)
  Sutt

Tellus Mentor
  VanH

Celery

American Green
see Greensnap

Avonpearl
A mid-season self-blanching variety, clear white colour. (OGC)
  SbS

Brydon's Prize Red
see Giant Red

Brydon's Prize White
A popular strain of excellent quality. (JWB)
  JWB

Celebrity
Crisp, early and bolt resistant, with plenty of vigour. The sticks are heavier than Lathom and less stringy than any variety. Excellent for an autumn crop, but can also be grown earlier in a cool greenhouse or cold frame. (Mars)
  Brwn Dob Howe Mars Milt Mole SbS Tuck Yate

Chatteris
see Lathom Self Blanching

Chinese Celery
Wild celery from China is more delicately flavoured and smaller than native types. Very hardy but can also be grown underglass. (OGC)
  OGC

F1 Claudius
  Toze

Clayworth Pink
see Giant Pink

Clayworth Prize Pink
see Giant Pink

Fenlander
see Hopkins Fenlander

Galaxy
Outstanding quality and flavoured stems. Thicker, stays stringless longer than any other variety. Can be sown early without running to seed and stands ready to harvest a long time. (T&M)
  T&M VanH

Giant Pink
A fine crisp pink variety which blanches easily and quickly. (Suff)
  John JWB SbS Suff Sutt

Giant Red
Large, solid and of good quality - will usually stand well into the New Year. (Mars)
  Chil EWK John Mars Mole SbS Tuck Unwi Wall Yate

Giant Solid White
Mole

Giant White
Solid, crisp and of superior flavour. Unsurpassed for table use. (Dob)
Brwn Chil Dob EWK SbS Tuck Wall

Golden Self Blanching
see Golden Self Blanching 3

Golden Self Blanching 3
A delicious, self-blanching celery with sturdy stalks which can be used as a salad, in savouries and as an exclusive cooked vegetable. (Bakk)
Bloo Cart Chil EWK Foth John JWB Mole OGC SbS Sutt

Golden Spartan
SbS

Green
see Green Utah

Green Light
SbS

Green Utah
For a change, grow a green celery! This variety has excellent flavour, is very tender and crisp. (OGC)
EWK JWB OGC

Greenlet
RSlu

Greensleeves
SbS

Greensnap
SbS

Groene Pascal
see White Pascal

Harvest Moon
SbS

Hopkins Fenlander
Excellent, long stemmed, white, market growers' variety. Very bulky sticks, crisp and full of flavour. Slightly hardier than most sorts. (Mars)
Mars Milt SbS T&M Toze VanH

Ivory Tower
Long, white, fleshy stems which are smooth and not stringy. (Foth)
Foth Sutt Toze

Jason Self Blanching
see Lathom Self Blanching

Lathom Self Blanching
Outstanding, self-blanching celery with excellent flavour and high yield, coupled with reluctance to bolt. An excellent pre-pack variety for glasshouse and outdoor cropping. (Bree)
John Mole S&G SbS Suff Toze Unwi

Loret
RSlu

Mammoth Pink
Rob

Mammoth Pink
see Giant Pink

Mammoth White
Rob

Martine
Rob

Multipak
SbS

New Dwarf White
Toze

Pearly Queen
SbS

Red Claret
see Tall Utah 52/70

Selfire
SbS

Shamrock
SbS

Sioux
A green celery for autumn harvesting. Has good holding ability even late in the season. Replaces Tall Utah. (Bree)
SbS

Solid Pink
A fine variety which blanches fairly easily and quickly and will stand some late frosts. (OGC)
OGC

Solid White
The stems of this variety are crisp, solid and of good flavour. Excellent for table use or for exhibition. (OGC)
Bloo OGC Sutt

Soup Celery d'Amsterdam
An indispensable, very tasty leaf celery for flavouring soups. Highly aromatic and prolific. (Bakk)
Bakk John

Stardust
SbS

Tall Utah 52-70
The most cultivated growers' variety at present. Tall Utah gives an excellent production of heavy celery of A1 quality. (Bakk)
Howe Bakk RSlu SbS Toze

Tendercrisp
SbS

Triumph
Tall growing plants produce succulent green stems which are an excellent addition to salads, soup and stews. Maturing late summer, early autumn, cropping may be extended by covering with cloches. (Sutt)
John Sutt

Unrivalled Pink
see Giant Pink

Utah 52-70
see Tall Utah 52-70

F1 Victoria
   Brwn Dob Mars Mole SbS T&M Toze Wall

White Pascal
   Large, solid, white heads, best grown in trenches. (EWK)
   EWK John SbS

Chard see Spinach Beet

Chenopodium capitatum

Strawberry Spinach
   Foth

Chenopodium foliosum

Beetberry
   Futu

Cherry

Alba
   SKee

Amber
   SKee Bowe

Archduke
   SIgm

August Heart
   SKee

Belle D'Orleans
   Allg

Bigarreau
   Allg

Bigarreau Gaucher
   SKee CSco SFru Bowe

Black Eagle
   Allg SKee

Black Elton
   SKee

Black Glory
   SKee Bowe

Black Heart
   Allg Bowe

Black Tartarian
   Allg SKee

Bradbourne Black
   SKee SFru Bowe

Caroon
   SKee

Circassian Black
   SKee

Colney
   GTwe SFru Bowe Edws

Compact Stella
   A compact form of Stella. (Brog)
   SDea WHig SKee CSco GTwe SIgm Bowe

Early Rivers
(1872) Mid to late June. Large, round, slightly heart-shaped fruits. Dark crimson black. Melting flesh with a good flavour. A vigorous tree. (Brog)
Allg SKee CSco GTwe SFru Bowe Edws

Elmer
Bowe

Elton Heart
SKee

Emperor Francis
Allg SKee Bowe

Florence
SKee CSco Bowe

Frogmore Early
Allg CSco Bowe

Governor Wood
(1842) Early July. A medium sized roundish cherry. Bright red on a pale yellow ground colour. Juicy with a very good flavour. A vigorous, spreading tree. (Brog)
Allg SKee CSco GTwe Bowe

Hertford
SFru Edws

Inga
Bowe

Inspecteur Lohnis
Bowe

Ironsides
SKee

Kassins Freu Herz
SKee

Kelleris No 16
Bowe

Kent Bigarreau
CSco

Kentish Bush
SKee

Kentish Red
SKee CSco

Knight's Early Black
Allg

Knorpel
Bowe

Lapins (Cherokee)
(1965) Van x Stella. Self-fertile. Late July. Very large, round, attractive dark red to black fruits. Very firm flesh, juicy with good flavour. Resistant to splitting. (Brog)
SDea SFam WHig WJas SKee CSco GTwe Muir SFru LBuc Bowe Edws

May Duke
SKee Bowe

Merchant
SKee GTwe SFru Bowe

Merla
Bowe

Mermat
Allg GTwe Bowe

Merpet
Allg GTwe

Merton Beauty
Bowe

Merton Bigarreau
(1924) Knight's Early Black x Bigarreau Napoleon. Mid to late July. Large, flattened round, blackish crimson fruits. Firm flesh, juicy and sweet with a good flavour. A vigorous, spreading tree. A good cropper. (Brog)
   Allg SFam SKee CSco SFru Bowe Edws

Merton Bounty
CSco Bowe

Merton Crane
CSco

Merton Favourite
Allg SKee CSco Bowe

Merton Glory
(1931) Ursula Rivers x Noble. Early July. A large, plump, round-conical white cherry. Soft, very juicy and sweet with a good flavour. Fruits tend to bruise easily. A moderately vigorous tree. A good cropper. (Brog)
   Allg SFam SKee CSco GTwe SFru Bowe Edws

Merton Heart
SKee CSco Bowe

Merton Late
SKee CSco

Merton Marvel
SKee CSco

Merton Premier
SKee CSco Bowe

Merton Reward
SKee CSco

Montmorency
SKee SFru

Morello
A cooking cherry. Late July to August. A large round, shiny dark red cherry. Juicy and acid. A medium sized, drooping tree. Performs well on North facing walls. (Brog)
   Allg Cast SDea SFam WHig WJas SKee Rog CSco GTwe Muir SFru

Nabella
CSco Bowe

Napoleon
SKee

Napoleon Bigarreau
Late July. A large, long heart shaped, yellow cherry considerably mottled with dark red. Very firm flesh. Sweet and juicy with a good flavour. The fruit can crack badly in wet weather. A vigorous, upright-spreading tree. Susceptible to Bacterial Canker. (Brog)
   Allg SFam CSco GTwe SFru Bowe Edws

Newstar
SFru

Noble
SKee

Noir de Guben
SKee GTwe SFru Bowe

Nutberry Black
SKee Bowe

Old Black Heart
SKee

Pat
Bowe

Peter van Mansfield
Bowe

Ronalds Heart
SKee

Roundel
Early July. A very large, heart-shaped, dark red cherry. Juicy and sweet with a good flavour. A vigorous, upright-spreading tree. (Brog)
SFam SKee CSco SFru Bowe

Sasha
GTwe Bowe

Smoky Dun
SKee

Stark Hardy Giant
SKee

Stella
(1964) Lambert x JI 2420. Self-fertile. Late July. A large, heart-shaped to oval cherry. Dark crimson to mahogany in colour. Firm flesh, sweet, juicy and with a good flavour. A vigorous, fairly upright tree. (Brog)
Allg Cast SDea SFam WHig WJas SKee Rog CSco GTwe Muir SFru

Strawberry Heart
SKee

Summit
SFru Bowe

Sunburst
Self-fertile. Mid to late July. A large, round, dark purple-red cherry. Firm flesh, juicy with a good flavour. Resistant to splitting. A moderately vigorous, fairly upright tree. A good cropper. (Brog)
SDea SFam WHig WJas SKee CSco GTwe Muir SFru LBuc Bowe Edws

Turkish Black
SKee

Van
Empress Eugenie open pollinated. Mid to late July. A large, firm black cherry with a good sweet flavour. An upright-spreading tree. A good cropper. (Brog)
SKee CSco GTwe SFru SIgm Bowe

Vega
GTwe

Waterloo
SKee SFru

5th Edition

White Heart
SKee Bowe

Wye Morello
SKee

Chicory

Apollo
Much easier to grow than traditional varieties because the white chicons remain compact with a soil covering. Distinctive flavour. (Mars)
Mars

Brussels Witloof
see Witloof

Crystal Head
Excellent in autumn salads. Crisp, green lettuce-like leaves. Quick and easy to grow. (Foth)
Bakk Unwi

F1 Flash
Bakk T&M

Gradina
SbS

F1 Karveel
RZ

Mechelse Medium-early
For cultivation without soil on top. Easy to grow in not toowarm (up to 17-18°C), dark surroundings (under black plastic).
(Bakk)
Bakk

Pain de Sucre
see Sugar Loaf

Pan di Zucchero
see Sugar Loaf

Snowflake
Autumn and winter fresh salad vegetable. Easy to grow, no forcing or blanching needed. Grow just like lettuces, sowing in June/July for 2-3 lb. crisp, tight heads, like large Cos lettuces, in late autumn and winter. Can be stored in the fridge or a shed for up to 3 months. (T&M)
Bloo T&M

Sugar Loaf
A quick growing large headed variety for Winter salads. (D&D)
Brwn EWK JWB OGC SbS Suff Sutt Tuck Wall

Winter Fare
Rather like a large Cos lettuce in appearance, provides lotsof crunchy, creamy, green heads ready to eat during late autumn and early winter. (Dob)
Dob

Winter Fare
see Snowflake

Witloof
Mostly grown for Winter forcing to produce pale green chicons. (D&D)
Chil EWK John JWB Mole OGC SbS Suff Tuck Wall

F1 Zoom
Dob Suff

The Fruit and Veg Finder

Chicory Radicchio

A Grumolo Verde
Round-leaved rosette shaped plant in winter; leaves blade-shaped in summer. Sow broadcast or in rows June-October. Summer leaves for salads. Stop cutting in late summer and allow the plants to develop their beautiful green rosettes for cutting in spring. Extremely hardy. (Suff)
Suff

Alouette
Fast growing, uniform early radicchio type. Medium size heads are a good red and well protected by larger green outer leaves. (Foth)
Bloo Foth T&M

Augusta
John

Bianca di Milano
When mature forms crisp elongated head or white and green leaves, almost self blanching. Use as cut and come again crop (at 2 in.) or thin plants to 6 in. for maturing. Fairly hardy and will normally over-winter outdoors or in an unheated greenhouse, especially when treated as "cutting" crop. (Suff)
SbS Suff

Biondissima di Trieste
Green, smooth round-leaved chicory. Used mainly as cut and come again crop. Sow spring to summer. The plants make rapid regrowth. Can also be used in winter, when small heads form. Reasonably hardy. (Suff)
Suff

F1 Carla
Bakk

Cesare
A mid-late variety with medium round heads and green outer leaves. Sow in July. (Suff)
John Suff

Chioggia
see Alouette

Giulio
Early compact round red heads with good bolting tolerance. Sow in May. (Suff)
John Suff

F1 Jupiter
Toze

Late Rossa di Chioggia
Very resistant to frost is this variety producing large and heavy heads up to almost a pound in weight well protected by large and numerous white veined, deep red leaves. (Chil)
Chil

Magdeburg
A large rooted variety used for blending with coffee. Lift the roots in autumn, cut into small sections and dry. May then be ground. (Suff)
SbS Suff

F1 Medusa
Bakk

Palla di Fuoco
An excellent variety for summer and autumn heading. Sow from March onwards. Firm round red heads with white veining. Very decorative. (Suff)
Suff

Palla rossa
Red-leaved chicory for Winter salads. (D&D)
EWK SbS SMM Wall Yate

Palla rossa Zorzi precoce
Red-leaved chicory for Winter salads. (D&D)
Cart JWB Mars SbS Sutt Tuck Unwi Unwi

Poncho
John

Prima Rossa
Yate

Red Treviso
see Rossa di Treviso

Red Verona
see Rossa di Verona

Red devil
Large red heads produce colourful leaves with attractive white veining and a distinctive taste. Best sown in late June and July for autumn harvesting. Has good resistance to early frosts. (Dob)
Dob

Rossa di Treviso
Somewhat similar to White Chicory but it is less compact. Strong variety that will tolerate light frost well. (Bakk)
OGC SbS Suff

Rossa di Verona
Forms a loose head in autumn and will crop again the following spring provided it is protected from severe frost. (Bakk)
OGC SbS Suff

F1 Rubello
Toze VanH

Variegata di Castelfranco
A wonderfully decorative chicory with green leaves blotched red and forming an inner loose head of red and white in autumn. An ancient variety developed in the 18th century in the Castelfranco region of northern Italy. One of the best for eating quality. Best results requires forcing during winter like Witloof. (Suff)
Chil SbS Suff

Variegata di Chioggia
Foliage green in summer, becoming red and white variegated in the cold weather. Sow broadcast or in rows, July-Aug. For use primarily in late autumn and early winter. Most suitable for forcing. Use in salads or cooked. (Suff)
Suff

Variegata di Sottomarina Precoce
A really unusual and decorative chicory becoming red speckled with white when mature. Another old variety named afterthe coastal town just south of Venice. (Suff)
Suff

Chinese Artichoke

Chinese Artichoke
Poyn SMM

Crosnes
A culinary sensation. The peculiar tubers with the series ofrings are harvested in late autumn. The flavour resembles that ofartichoke bottoms. One tuber will yield at least 25 tubers. (Bakk)
Bakk

Chinese Broccoli

F1 Green Lance
Chil EWK OGC SbS SMM Tuck

Kailan
Not a variety name.
EWK SbS SMM Suff Yate

Kintsai
Vivid green and unique aroma when cooked. Summer sowing, ready after two months. (D&D)
EWK SbS SMM Suff

Chinese Chives

Broadleaf
Distinct, mild garlic-flavour, widely varying culinary uses,harvestable three-quarters of the year. (T&M)
Chil T&M

Chinese Chives
Also known as Garlic Chives or Chinese Leeks producing clumps of narrow, flat leaves of delicate mild garlic flavour. Easily grown, having star-like flowers in summer. Leaves, stems, flower buds and flowers are all edible. (Dob)
Dob Foth Futu Milt

Chinese Gooseberry (Kiwifruit)

Abbot
Bowe

Atlas
Bowe

Blake (Self-fertile)
LBuc

Bruno
Bowe

Hayward (Female)
Muir ERea Bowe

Matua
Bowe

Mini-Kiwi Issai (Self-fertile)
WHig ERea LBuc

Monty
Bowe

Tomuri (Male)
ERea Bowe

Un-named selection (Female)
SDea WHig

Un-named selection (Male)
SDea WHig

Choy Sum (Hybrid Flowering Rape)

F1 Bouquet
EWK OGC SbS SbS SMM Suff Tuck

Choy Sum (Purple Flowered)

Choy Sum (Purple Flowered)
OGC SMM Tuck

Hon Tsai Tai
Chil

Chrysanthemum Greens

Shungiku
Shungiku is the Japanese name for these members of the daisy family, which are also known as Chop Suey Greens and Japanese Greens. There are two basic types, those with small, serrated leaves and those with larger, broader leaves. Named varieties to not appear to be available in Europe.
Chil Dob EWK Foth Futu John Milt OGC SbS SMM Suff

Citrus Bitter Orange

Bouquet de Fleurs
ERea CGOG

Calamondin
CGOG

Chinotto
ERea CGOG

Naranja Amarga
CGOG

Seville
ERea

Citrus Citron

Buddha's Hand Citron
ERea

Etrog
ERea

Citrus Grapefruit

Foster's
ERea

Golden Special
ERea

Red Blush
CGOG

Wheeny
CGOG

Citrus Kumquat

Meiwa
ERea

Nagami
ERea CGOG

Un-named
WHig

Citrus Lemon

Eureka
CGOG

Fino
CGOG

Imperial
ERea

Lemonade
ERea

Lisbon
ERea CGOG

Meyer's Lemon
WHig ERea CGOG

Ponderosa
ERea

Quartre Saisons
ERea

Variegated Lemon
ERea

Verna Lemon
CGOG

Villa Franca
ERea CGOG

Citrus Lime

Indian Lime
ERea

La Valette
ERea

Lima Bears
CGOG

Rangpur
ERea

Tahiti
ERea

Citrus Limequat

Eustis
ERea CGOG

Lakeland
ERea

Tavares
ERea

Citrus Mandarin & Satsuma

Blida
ERea

Clementina Arrufatina
CGOG

Clementina Hernandina
CGOG

Clementina Tomatera
CGOG

Clementina de Nules
CGOG

Clementine
ERea

Encore
ERea

Fortune
CGOG

Nova
CGOG

Okitsu
CGOG

Owari
CGOG

Satsuma
ERea

Silver Hill
ERea

Citrus Species, Hybrids & Relatives

Calamondin Orange
ERea

Shaddock (Citrus maxima)
ERea

Tangelo - Minneola
CGOG

Tangelo - Ortanique
CGOG

Tangelo - Seminole
ERea

Tangelo - Ugli
ERea

Tangor - Sweet
ERea

Variegated Calamondin
ERea

Citrus Sweet Orange

Egg
ERea

Embiguo
ERea

Harwood Late
ERea

Jaffa
ERea

Malta Blood
ERea

Midknight
ERea

Moro Blood
ERea

Navelate
CGOG

Navelina
CGOG

Newhall
CGOG

Parson Brown
ERea

Prata
ERea

Ruby Blood
ERea

Salustiana
CGOG

Sanguinelli
ERea CGOG

Shamouti
ERea

St Michaels
ERea

Valencia Late
ERea CGOG

Washington Navel
ERea CGOG

Corn Salad

Cavallo
Keeps on producing a mass of fresh flavoured, deep green leaf. A late summer sowing will guarantee winter salads as it is very hardy too. (T&M)
T&M

Corn Salad
A hardy quick growing salad vegetable for winter use. Sow in autumn for winter use. (D&D)
Bloo EWK Futu JWB Mole Poyn SMM Tuck Wall

D'Olanda
see Grote Noordhollandse

Grote Noordhollandse
Also known by the much nicer name of Lambs Lettuce, this is used when young and crisp as a salad plant, particularly useful in winter and spring. Very hardy, it has the great advantage that it can be grown using the sow-and-forget technique. Harvest whole when the plant has grown three or four pairs of leaves. (Chil)
Bakk Chil Dob John OGC S&G SbS Suff Sutt

Jade
A robust variety which is resistant to mildew. Tasty salad ingredient for the Winter months. (Mars)
  Mars

Louviers
Fine-seeded, spoon-shaped corn salad. Beautiful, dark green colour. An extremely tasty, high-yielding corn salad variety. Very hardy. (Bakk)
  Bakk

Progres
  RZ

Verte de Cambrai
A traditional French variety. Sow in rows or broadcast. Harvest complete rosettes at 6 to 8 leaves and use whole in a salad. Very decorative and unusual. (Suff)
  OGC SbS Suff

Vit
The most vigorous variety for spring and autumn crops, and over wintering. Long glossy green leaves. Delicious tender mild minty flavour. (Suff)
  Futu Suff

Volhart
Fine-seeded. An old, well-tried variety, still highly valued by many people. Bright green colour. Much recommended variety for the expert leisure-time vegetable grower. (Bakk)
  Bakk

Cranberry

Cranberry C N
Treh CSim Bowe

Early Black
Treh CSim Bowe

Franklin
Treh CSim Bowe

McFarlin
Muir

Pilgrim
CSim

Un-named selection
GTwe

Vaccinium Oxycocoss
WHig Bowe

Cress

American Land
This is very like water cress both in taste and appearance but can be grown in ordinary garden soil. Excellent for salads and sandwiches. (Dob)
  Chil Dob EWK Futu John JWB Mars OGC Poyn SbS SMM

Armada
Ready 3 days earlier than other cress - at the same time as mustard. Leaves twice the size of the common varieties and a beautiful deep green. (Mars)
  Mars

Broad Leaved
John

Curled
The ordinary type often grown in pots on the window sill, but it can be grown in the garden without trouble. (D&D)
Chil Mars Sutt Wall

Extra Curled
All-the-year-round, nutritious salad crop. Grow outdoors in the summer and inside during the winter. (T&M)
T&M

Extra Double Curled
Popular for salads and garnishing. Use at once when full grown. (Dob)
Dob

Extra Fine Moss Curled
John

Fine Curled
Dwarf growing strain with fine very well curled leaves. (EWK)
Brwn Cart EWK Foth SbS Suff Unwi

Greek
A completely new addition for the mixed salad. Delicious peppery taste. A fast growing salad crop that can be broadcast insuccession and cut young. (Suff)
OGC SbS Suff

Plain
Large leafed type, quick growing and very productive. (EWK)
EWK John JWB Milt Mole SbS VanH Wall

Super Salad
A great improvement over the ordinary type of plain-leaved cress because of its stronger stems and larger leaves. (Dob)
Dob

Cucumber

F1 Anka
Bakk

F1 Avanti
EWK SbS Tuck

F1 Bella
Sutt

F1 Bronco
Yate

Chinese Long Green
Well-known variety, still very much in demand for cultivation in the open. Stays green and is disease-resistant. (Bakk)
Bakk

F1 Cordoba
Bakk SbS

F1 Crispy Salad
T&M

F1 Danimas
Dob T&M Yate

Delicatesse
A very famous variety, particularly suitable for pickling. Much used in salads. (Bakk)
Bakk

Delikatess
see Delicatesse

F1 Farbiola
Toze

Hoffmans Giganta
Very suitable for cultivation in the open as well as in a frame or along wires in a greenhouse. A healthy, high-yielding variety, producing heavy cucumbers. (Bakk)
Bakk

F1 Janeen
Yate

F1 Jazzer
T&M VanH

F1 Mistral
Dob

F1 Mustang
Yate

F1 Slice King
EWK OGC Suff

F1 Sweet Success
Bakk

F1 Uniflora
SbS VanH Wall

Cucumber Frame

F1 Aidas
T&M

F1 Aramon
Mole SbS Wall

F1 Athene
Mars

F1 Azuro
S&G

F1 Birgit
Bakk Brwn Dob EWK Foth Howe John Milt Mole SbS

F1 Brunex
Bloo Mole OGC SbS Sutt Yate

Butcher's Disease Resistant
SbS

F1 Carmen
Mole SbS T&M

Conqueror
Recommended for growing in unheated greenhouses or cold frames. Crops very well. (Dob)
Dob OGC

F1 Destiny
Yate

F1 Diana
EWK Unwi

F1 Euphya
Bakk Mole SbS Wall

F1 Fembaby
T&M

F1 Femdam
Brwn John SbS SMM

F1 Femspot
Foth Mole SbS Sutt Toze Tuck

F1 Fenumex
EWK OGC SbS Suff Tuck Wall

F1 Fitness
Yate

F1 Flair
Yate

F1 Flamingo
Foth

F1 Hana
SbS

F1 Jessica
RZ

F1 Kamaron
Mole SbS

King George
Rob

F1 Monique
Mole SbS

F1 Passandra
Wall

F1 Pepinex 69
Brwn Cart Dob Howe John JWB Mars S&G SbS Unwi Wall

F1 Petita
Brwn Dob EWK Foth John Milt Mole OGC SbS SMM Sutt

F1 Primio
Bakk

F1 Pyralis
Howe

Rollison's Telegraph
see Telegraph Improved

F1 Sandra
Howe John

F1 Superator
John Milt Mole SbS

F1 Sweet Alphee
Suff

Telegraph
A well known and reliable variety with smooth-skinned, good-sized fruits. (Dob)
Bloo Cart Dob EWK John JWB Mars OGC Sutt Toze Unwi

Telegraph Improved
A prolific cropper producing long fruits of excellent flavour. (D&D)
Brwn Foth Milt Mole SbS Suff Sutt Tuck VanH Wall

F1 Telstar
Brwn

F1 Tetila
RZ

F1 Topsy
Unwi

F1 Tyria
Mars Mole SbS Toze

Cucumber Gherkin

F1 Accordia
Milt Mole Wall

F1 Arena
John

Beit Alpha Ellam
SbS

F1 Bestal
Mars

Boston Green
SbS

F1 Conda
Unwi

De Vorgebirg
see Venlo Pickling

F1 Fanfare
Foth

Gherkin
Very quick growing and prolific in habit. Produces a mass of small prickly fruits for pickling. (EWK)
EWK Wall

F1 Harmonie
RZ

Hokus
A mixed-flowering gherkin variety, especially suitable for cultivation in the open ground. Perfect gherkin for pickling. Vigorous grower which is not prone to mosaic and gummnosis. (Bakk)
Bakk Dob SbS

F1 Ilonca
Bakk

F1 Liberty
T&M

National
Produces large quantities of small green fruit which should be gathered for pickling when immature. (OGC)
Chil OGC SbS

Parisian Pickling
Well known variety for pickling. (Bakk)
Bakk John SbS

Pointsett
SbS

Toret
SbS

Venlo Pickling
Well-known, still very popular growers' variety which is often used for pickling. Gives a heavy crop of beautiful gherkins. (Bakk)
Bakk JWB SbS Sutt

Vert Petit de Paris
see Parisian Pickling

Cucumber Ridge

Apple Shaped
The fruits are apple shaped and are thought to be more digestable than the ordinary varieties. Easily grown out of doors, a prolific cropper. (JWB)
JWB

Bedfordshire Prize
see Long Green Ridge

Bianco Lungo di Parigi
Interestingly different is this cucumber for outdoor cultivation producing medium-sized fruits of an attractive, do-they-taste-as-good-as-they-look, creamy-white colour. Another variety to give visual appeal to the dining table. (Chil)
Chil

Burpless
see Burpless Tasty Green

F1 Burpless Tasty Green
Brwn EWK Foth JWB Mars Milt Mole OGC SbS Suff Sutt

F1 Bush Champion
Bakk Brwn Cart Dob OGC Sutt T&M

F1 Bush Crop
Foth Mars

Crystal Apple
Delightful round shaped fruits of pale colouring. Quick growing and very prolific. Reputed to be more digestible than other varieties. (EWK)
Bloo Chil EWK Mole OGC SbS Suff Sutt Wall

Kyoto
Good-flavoured variety producing long fruits with few seeds. Best grown on a cane tripod. (D&D)
SbS

Long Green Ridge
A popular heavy cropper. (JWB)
Chil EWK John JWB SbS SMM Sutt

Long Prickly
see Long Green Ridge

Marketeer
see Marketer

Marketer
SbS

Marketmore
(Improved King of the Ridge). An outdoor slicing cucumber. Fruits up to 8 in. long. Resistant to powdery mildew and downy mildew. (Mars)
Foth Mars Toze

Masterpiece
Outdoor type with large fruits of excellent taste. Highly productive. (EWK)
EWK OGC SbS

F1 Paska
Chil

Perfection
Smaller, slightly stumpy ridge cues. Easy to grow. (Foth)
John Milt Mole SbS Wall

F1 Pioneer
Unwi

Stockwood
see Long Green Ridge

F1 Tokyo Slicer
Toze Unwi

Yamato
Improved Japanese types for indoor or outside growing. Long thin fruits of superb flavour. (EWK)
EWK OGC SbS SMM Suff

Cucumis metulliferus

Kiwano
Futu

Damson & Bullace

Blue Violet
SKee

Bradley's King
SKee CSco Bowe

Bullace - Black
SKee

Bullace - Golden
SKee

Bullace - Langley
Allg SKee CSco

Bullace - Shepherd's
SKee CSco

Bullace - Un-named
SDea Rog

Bullace - Yellow Apricot
SKee

Farleigh Damson
(1820) Culinary. Mid-late September. A very small, blue-black round-oval damson with bloom. Partially self-fertile. Used as a windbreak. (Brog)
Allg SDea SKee CSco GTwe SFru SIgm Bowe

Godshill Damson
SDea

Merryweather Damson
(1907) Culinary. Early September. A medium sized, oval, blue-black damson with bloom. Partially self-fertile. Can be used as a windbreak. (Brog)
Allg Cast SDea SFam WJas SKee Rog CSco GTwe Muir ERea SFru

Shropshire Prune (Prune Damson)
(1870) Culinary. Mid to late September. A small oval, blue-black damson with bloom. Partially self-fertile. (Brog)
Cast SDea SFam WHig SKee Rog CSco GTwe Muir SFru LBuc SIgm

The Fruit and Veg Finder

Dandelion

A Coeur Plein
Probably the most nutritious green there is. Very rich in minerals and vitamins. Blanching under a flowerpot will take the bitterness away, or it may be forced like Witloof Chicory. (Suff)
Suff

Broad Leaved
Excellent for salads, has valuable medicinal properties. Helps to keep everyone young. (JWB)
JWB SbS

Thick-leaved
Considering we spend our lives trying to eradicate the wild form from our gardens, it is most suprising to learn just how useful this cultivated strain is. The large, thick, dark green leaves are used as a green vegetable for boiling or in a salad. For salads, though, a far more succulent can be made by blanchingthe hearts either by earthing up or tying the leaves together. The roots can be used for forcing or as a substitute for coffee by roasting in an oven until crisp and then grinding. Easy, vigorous and quick to grow. (Chil)
Chil

Duck Potato

Duck Potato
(Sagittaria latifolia) An aquatic species similar to our native arrowhead, the Wapato was an important food of native Americans for many centuries. The small tubers are borne on the ends of long runners and are harvested in the autumn. As they float, when detatched from the parent plant, it is possible to scoop them offthe water's surface. Native women used to collect them by wadinginto the water up to their chests and loosening the tubers with their toes. They can be cooked in a similar way to potatoes and have a pleasant flavour. An excellent plant for filtering eutrophic waters, as it is one of the heaviest feeding water plants. One of the collection of aquaculture species with Reed Mace and Canadian Pondweed which make up a promising pig fodder system. Spreads from small plantings so is economical to establish. (Futu)
Futu

Earth Chestnut

Earth Chestnut
(Bunium bulbocastaneum) A vigorous perennial that produces small tuberous roots said to taste like chestnuts when boiled. The seeds can also be used as a condiment. A rare native of chalk grasslands, also known as pig-nut.
Futu

Endive

Atria
Yate

Batavian Broad Leaved
see No. 5 2

Batavian Green
see No. 5 2

Breedblad Volhart Winter
see Avant Garde Winter

Casco d'Oro
Beautiful, heavy plants with golden-yellow heart. Tender variety for summer and autumn cultivation. (Bakk)
 Bakk

Cornet De Bordeaux
A very fine old French variety which is very hardy. Provides constant cut and come again through Winter. Performs outstandingly with cold tunnel/frame culture over Winter. (Suff)
 Suff

De Ruffec
Sharp, crisp vegetable which will liven up any salad. Use with or instead of lettuce. (Foth)
 Foth SbS

Dolly
Bred in France where it is extremely popular. Good curl with blanched centre. Cropping period October-November. (Mole)
 Mole SbS

Dorana
Yate

Elodie
Very compact variety suitable for close spacing with a very finely divided leaf, slow bolting and easy to blanch. (Bree)
 S&G

Elysee
Yate

Eminence
This variety is suitable for both indoor and outdoor production. The densely formed centres are yellow with medium to long outer broad leaves. Resistant to basal rot and strong against tipburn. Sow March to August for cropping June to October. (Brwn)
 Brwn SbS

Fijne Krul Groen
see Green Curled

Fine Maraichere
A small and compact variety which is very frizzy and looks very decorative. Not hardy so should be grown in spring and summer. (Suff)
 Suff

Geante Maraichere Bossa
New in our range, A compact, vigorously growing endive for summer and autumn cultivation. It can also be sown under glass for early cultivation. Beautiful light green plants with a bright yellow heart. Very resistant to bolting. (Bakk)
  Bakk

Glory
  Yate

Green Curled
Another alternative salad crop for outdoor or glasshouse use. Compact with curled heads of dark green leaves. (EWK)
  Chil EWK John JWB OGC SbS SMM Sutt Toze Tuck Wall

Ione
For spring to early autumn crops. Very fine curled leaves. (Toze)
  Dob Howe Toze

Jeti
Very uniform, large heavy heads. Upright foliage with self-blanching habit. Excellent for both summer and autumn use. (EWK)
  EWK SbS

Limnos
This vigorously growing endive is a broad leafed variety with a well-filled yellow heart and upright leaves. Suitable for early summer, summer, autumn cultivation. Slow to bolt. (Bakk)
  Bakk

Markant
A large and extensively curled endive, the heart blanches upwell because of the long upright leaves. An ideal variety for late sowings, performing well in late autumn conditions. Sow August for cropping late Sept/Nov. (Brwn)
  Howe Milt

Minerva
  Yate

Moss Curled
see Green Curled

No. 5 2
A crisp and tender variety with large leaves for winter salads and excellent, too, as a cooked vegetable. (Dob)
  Dob John JWB OGC SbS Sutt

No. 5 Malan
  RSlu

No. 5 Sinco
Escarole or smooth leaved endive, with a large size but should not be grown wider than 30 cm. X 30 cm. in order to promote a good blanch in the hearts. (Bree)
  S&G

Nuance
  Howe

Oxalie
  Mole RZ Wall

President

A strong, curled endive for summer and early autumn cultivation, slow in running to seed. Stands bad weather very well. Top quality. (Bakk)
   Bakk

Riccia Pancalieri

Very curled leaves with rose tinted white midribs, voluminous white heart. Sow in rows from March to September, thinning to about 12 in. apart. For use in summer, autumn and winter. Self-blanching variety. (Suff)
   Bloo OGC Suff

Sally

Easy to grow, the plants produce tight hearts of cut, curledand crisped leaves, naturally blanched in the centre. (Mars)
   Cart Mars Mole SbS Yate

Sanda

Vigorous, strap-leaved with a frilled edge and large size, somewhat less susceptible to tipburn, to cold and to bolting than other types, suitable for glasshouse and open field culture. (Bree)
   S&G

Scarola Verde

Forms very large head with green and white leaves, curled atedges with tasty, tender white midribs. Can blanche a few days before use by tying leaves together or covering with a box or pot. Most suitable for use in spring or summer, though it may bolt in sudden heat. (Suff)
   Suff

St Laurent-Midori

Medium-sized, very full, finely curled endive. Recommended for early sowing; for summer and autumn harvest. Early maturing and quick-blanching. (Bakk)
   Bakk Howe

Tres Fine Maraichere Coquette

Appetizing, slender very fine cut curled leaf. A notable uniform selection of the superb French variety Tres Fine Maraichere. It is a good all rounder, excellent if it is your first try at growing it. (T&M)
   T&M

Wallonne

A special selection of this traditional French variety. Forms a large tightly packed head with self-blanching heart and finely cut leaves. Vigorous and hardy. Sow Aug-Sept for Nov-Jan harvest. Also for tunnel culture. (Suff)
   RSlu Suff

Madawaska Buckwheat

Fagopyrum sp

A native of the Himalayas, this variety was developed in North America by native people and French Canadians. It is more drought resistant and cold tolerant than normal buckwheat and grew well for us in 1993, despite neglect and poor soil. Seeds can be ground and made into flour and used to make pancakes. Young leaves can also be eaten as spinach. (Futu)
   Futu

Fennel

Argo
RZ

Atos
S&G

Bronze
A handsome variety. Use the leaves in soups, sauces and fishdishes. (Poyn)
Poyn SbS Sutt

Cantino
Developed for its resistance to bolting from early sowing. Bulbs ready from August. Can be cooked or used raw in salads. Refreshing celery/aniseed flavour. (Mars)
EWK Mars OGC SbS SMM Suff Tuck

F1 Carmo
Toze

Common
SbS

Di Firenze
This is best sown between May and July. Medium sized bulbs with delicate aniseed flavour. (OGC)
Chil EWK OGC SbS VanH

Fino
A bulb fennel for early crops. The variety has strong resistance to bolting. (Bree)
Bakk Bloo Brwn Dob Foth Milt Mole Poyn SbS Toze

Florence
see Di Firenze

Green
Poyn

Herald
Plump, sweet anise-flavour bulbs. In trials it has shown a marked improvement in bolt resistance over all other varieties. Recommended for earlier and successional sowings. (T&M)
T&M

Perfection
Sow from May to July. Fairly resistant to bolting and produces medium sized bulbs with delicate aniseed flavour. (Suff)
Suff

Sirio
An Italian bred variety which produces large white solid bulbs on compact plants. Very sweet flavour and quite aromatic. (Sutt)
Sutt

Sweet Florence
see Di Firenze

Tardo
A bulb fennel for early crops. Strong resistance to bolting. (Bree)
Toze

Zefa Fino
see Fino

Zefa Tardo
see Tardo

Fig

Angelique
ERea

Black Ischia
ERea

Black Mission
CSim

Bourjasotte Grise
ERea

Brown Turkey
August-September. Medium-large fruits. Very sweet with a delicious flavour. The most popular variety. Hardy and very prolific. (Brog)
  Allg Cast SDea SFam WHig SKee Rog CSco GTwe Muir ERea SFru

Brunswick
August. Very large fruits. Good flavour when fully ripe. Hardy and fairly prolific. (Brog)
  Allg SFam GTwe ERea CSim Bowe Edws

Castle Kennedy
ERea

Desert King
CSim

Fig d'Or
ERea

Goutte d'Or
ERea

Green Ischia
CSim

Gross Longe Verte
ERea

Grosse Grise
ERea

Lisa
ERea

Longue d'Aout
ERea

Malta
ERea

Monstreuse
CSim

Negro Largo
ERea CSim

Osborne's Prolific
ERea CSim

Panachee
ERea

Precoce Ronde de Bordeaux
ERea

Rouge de Bordeaux
ERea

San Pedro Miro
ERea

St Jean
ERea

St Johns
ERea

Sugar 12
ERea

Sultane
ERea

Violette Dauphine
ERea

Violette Sepor
ERea

White Adriatic
ERea

White Ischia
ERea

White Marseilles
August. Large fruited. Very sweet and rich. (Brog)
SDea SFam GTwe ERea CSim Bowe

French Bean Climbing

Algarve
An improvement in quality on the popular variety Kwintus. Producing straight, flat, mid-green pods, 26-28cms. (10-11inches)long and 25mm. (1inch) wide which are totally stringless and of distinctive flavour. Resistant to common bean mosaic virus. (Dob)
Dob Yate

Astera
RZ

Blue Lake
Requires sticks or a climbing frame. Very productive and suitable for home freezing with an excellent flavour. Pods can also be dried for use as haricot. (OGC)

Blue Lake White Seeded
Requires sticks or a climbing frame. Very productive and suitable for home freezing with an excellent flavour. Pods can also be dried for use as haricot. (OGC)
Brwn Chil Dob EWK Foth Howe John JWB Milt Mole OGC

Borlotto
Unusual and attractive, the 6in. flat and broad pods are pale green with red stripes. When young the pods are cut and eaten as a normal french bean, left they may be shelled and the seeds eaten. (Foth)
Foth

Borlotto Lingua di Fuoco
This is the original Fire Tongue strain from Italy. May be eaten as green pods but grown mainly for delicious semi-dry beansand dry beans. Spectacular green pods with red stripes make this very decorative. (Suff)
Suff

Burro d'Ingegnoli
Traditional Italian variety unknown in the UK. Large flat yellow pods of excellent fleshy and stringless quality. Sweet and deliecious. 78 days. (Suff)
  Suff

Coco de Prague
Clearly recognizable by the red-coloured pods. The dried beans are decoratively spotted in red and have a marbled appearance. Vigorous grower! (Bakk)
  Bakk

Corona d'Oro
A climbing bean giving heavy yields of golden-yellow pods, round in section and succulent and tender in texture. Regular picking will encourage further pod formation of this useful and decorative variety. (John)
  EWK John Milt Tuck

Cristal
  Yate

Cunera
  RSlu

Femira
  RZ

Florint
  Mole

Goldmarie
  Sutt

Helda
  RSlu Toze

Hunter
Flat podded variety. Yields heavy crops of long straight, stringless pods. (Foth)
  Brwn EWK Foth John Mars Milt OGC Suff Sutt Tuck

Kentucky Blue
Excellent flavour and yields. Pods smooth and fleshy 16-17cm. (Bree)
  S&G Sutt T&M

Kingston Gold
  Rob

Kronos
  Mole S&G

Kwintus
Despite the seed bulges which tend to be produced, the 9-11in. pods are tender, have a delicious distinctive flavour andare usually stringless. (Dob)
  Mole Wall

Largo
A smashing variety growing tall like a runner bean but producing round, stringless delicious pods. (Foth)
  Brwn Mars

Marvel of Venice
see Or du Rhin

Mechelse Markt
Very much recommended to those who like a bean that is not too fleshy. Mechelse Markt produces clusters of so-called single beans which are unequalled as regards their fine flavour. Exceptionally heavy-cropping variety. (Bakk)
Bakk

Meraviglia di Venezia
see Or du Rhin

Musica
Wide, flat, stringless pods with a delicious true beany flavour. Sown early it crops weeks before outdoor crops. Can alsobe sown outdoors. (T&M)
Mole T&M

Musika
VanH

Neckargold
A real wax bean, producing an exceptionally high yield. Thelong, round-sectioned, deep yellow beans guarantee a tasty meal. Neckargold is a white-seeded variety, not stringy, and is resistant to mosaic virus. (Bakk)
Bakk Dob

Neckarkoenigin
A long thick bean which can be used for slicing as well as for breaking. It will give a high yield per plant. Very resistantto diseases. (Bakk)
Bakk

Or du Rhin
A very fine old variety with broad flat yellow pods. Delicious picked young and cooked whole, also used in minestrone and for fresh shelling beans. The crispest and tastiest bean we have tried. Black seeded. A late maincrop. (Suff)
Bakk OGC Suff

Pea Bean
The flat pods should be harvested young to eat whole, or shelled out like peas. Alternatively, leave to dry. Attractive bi-coloured seed. (OGC)
EWK OGC SbS SMM Suff

Purple Podded
see Purple Podded Climbing

Purple Podded Climbing
Decorative and delicious, ht. approx. 150cm. (5ft). (Sutt)
Sutt

Raadsheer
This variety is a considerable improvement of the older variety Rentmeester. It can be harvested ten days earlier. Veryprolific, stringless bean with long, broad pods. Raadsheer can also be grown in a greenhouse. (Bakk)
Bakk

Rakker
Unquestionably the highest yielding variety producing recordcrops! Early and extremely prolific. Thick, fleshy beans with a delicious flavour. Rakker is also suitable for cultivation in a greenhouse. (Bakk)
Bakk

Rheingold
see Or du Rhin

Robroy
A new climbing French bean, cream splashed with red. Very tender when cooked young. Good flavour and very attractive to grow. (CGar)
Rob

Robsplash
New climbing French bean, cream splashed purple, very tenderwhen cooked young. (CGar)
Rob

Romano
Long, fleshy, tender, meaty and stringless pods, liberally loaded with flavour. (T&M)
T&M

Terli
Improved type Neckarkönigin with long tender beans of approx. 28cm. Vigorous, open plants, easy to pick. (Bakk)
Bakk

Viola Cornetti
Typical Italian climbing bean with fine stringless purple podded beans. (OGC)
OGC Suff

Violet Podded Stringless
The pods are round, fleshy and tender with an excellent taste. Decorative dark purple pods change to green when boiled. (Foth)
Bakk Foth Tuck

Westlandia
A very richly bearing variety, producing beans in clusters of 4 to 6. The tasty beans are long and beautifully shaped. They have a dark green colour. An excellent, healthy vegetable. (Bakk)
Bakk

French Bean Dwarf

Admires
Excellent dwarf French bean (large podded) for slicing. Early and very prolific. Admires is very much in demand, especially because of its resistance to many diseases. A variety with a very fine flavour. (Bakk)
Bakk

Allure
Dark green pod, long and slender; very productive. Resistantto most occurring bean diseases. (Bakk)
Bakk

Annabel
Stringless, flavoursome, slim pods 4-5in. in length borne inprofusion. This compact item is ideal for the smaller garden and may also be grown in growing bags on the patio. (Dob)
Dob EWK Howe Tuck Wall

Aramis
Combines the high quality and flavour of the French "filet" types, with the high yield and concentrated podset of modern breeding. Very fine, round, stringless pods 14-15cm. in length. Pods are medium green colour with purple markings which disappear on cooking. (Bree)
S&G T&M Unwi

Arosa
RZ

Atlantica
Try this if you want high yields, a rich distinctive flavour and something a little different. Broad, flat juicy pods fleshy and stringless, a type much grown in the USA and Europe, delicious served sliced or whole. (T&M)
T&M

Bafin
This is like a true French haricot vert but stringless. It produces pencil slim, short beans ideal for freezing. (OGC)
OGC

Berggold
White-seeded, very healthy waxbean for bottling as well as for immediate use. A heavy crop of 12-13cm. long pods with a diameter of approx. 9mm. Can be harvested after approx. 55 days. (Bakk)
Bakk

Black Prince
SbS Wall

Brown Dutch
One of the best drying beans. Floury texture and an excellent flavour. Easy to grow, and easy to shell. (Suff)
OGC Suff

Canadian Wonder
Old established variety, producing very heavy crops of flat shaped pods. (EWK)
EWK John JWB MAS OGC SbS Wall

Capitole
With very thin 4 inch pods, resistance to bean mosaic virus and a number of fungi diseases, it is ideal for organic gardening. Pod type: fine pencil. (Brwn)
Brwn

Cascade
Howe John Mole Wall

Chevrier Vert
The classic French Flageolet dating from 1880. Tasty and tender greeny white fresh beans for classic French dishes. (Suff)
Bakk Suff

Contender
Very early and productive. Useful for both the private gardener and the commercial grower. Can also be used as a haricot. (OGC)
Bakk OGC SbS Shar

Coquette
OGC

Cropper Teepee
As Purple, except the round pods are slightly larger, and medium green and white seeded. An excellent variety with disease resistance. (Foth)
  Foth John OGC

Daisy
The long, stringless beans are held above the leaves so they are very easy to pick and are not splashed by soil. Excellent for freezing. (Mars)
  Mars T&M

Delinel
Ultra-fine deep green beans, with a unique texture and true French flavour. Heavy-cropping, it is one of the first of its type that is perfectly stringless. (Mars)
  Mars

Deuil Fin Precoce
Compact plants ideal for cloche work, produce a good crop of steely grey-green pods with unique delicacy of flavour. (OGC)
  OGC Suff

Dutch Princess
  VanH

Early Wax
see Earlybird

Earlybird
A golden yellow podded variety which produces straight, fleshy pods, 6in. in length. Wax or yellow podded varieties are gaining in popularity, not only for their novelty value but also because of their excellent flavour and succulent texture. (John)
  John

Fin de Bagnol
The old gourmet needle bean with delicious fine round pods which can be used as filet or snap beans. 52 days. (Suff)
  Suff

Flageolet Chevrier
see Chevrier Vert

Forum
High cold tolerance. High quality beans even in difficult conditions. Very useful in cold wet springs, resistance to halo blight CBMV and anthracnose. (T&M)
  S&G Wall

Golden Sands
Long pods which crop over a long period. Very good flavour. (EWK)
  EWK OGC Tuck

Gresham
  Mole

Groene Flageolet
see Chevrier Vert

Horsehead
Particulary suitable for growing in the UK. The dark red bean seeds are excellent for inclusion in soups, casseroles and chile con carne. Taken young pods can be eaten like conventional French beans. (OGC)
OGC

Irago
Toze Tuck

Keygold
This improved, yellow butter-bean is healthy and heavy-cropping. It produces beautiful, long beans. Keygold is fairly new on the market. It is greatly resistant to diseases.
Well worth to have a go at! (Bakk)
Bakk

Kinghorn Wax
Medium-size, stringless, round, yellow wax beans with a fineflavour. (Foth)
Sutt

Larma
Very long-podded bean, 20-25cm. A richly bearing variety, highly resistant to diseases. (Bakk)
Bakk

Lasso
An early maturing Kenyan fine bean, widely used by commercial growers in the UK and on the continent for the high yields of medium green, round crispy pods. Best eaten at approx. 4ins they can be cooked whole or sliced. Good plant vigour will give yields to October from late sowings. (Foth)
Foth

Laura
Toze Yate

Loch Ness
SbS

Masai
Flavour best of all. Ultra slim pods. Pick handfuls at a time of slim, extra fine, fillet beans a mere 0.25ins. wide, of superlative quality with distinctive, gourmet flavour. This is the variety grown in places like Kenya to supply the international restaurant trade. An excellent, sturdy, garden variety, early and high yielding, with good disease and cold tolerance. (T&M)
S&G T&M

Masterpiece
see St Andreas

Masterpiece Stringless
An improved, stringless development of Masterpiece for slicing. Very early. (Mars)
Cart EWK Howe Mars MAS Unwi

Maxidor
A marked improvement on the old yellow-fleshed varieties. Very rich-bearing dwarf French bean. Healthy variety. An excellent addition to the existing range. (Bakk)
Bakk

Milagrow
Yate

Minidor
Bakk

Mirage
Produces long, fine-seeded dark green beans. This delicious dwarf French bean is extremely disease-resistant. A guaranteed sure cropper. (Bakk)
Bakk

Mont d'Or
Probably the finest flavoured golden wax with stringless flat pods. A very old French variety. Seed black. (Suff)
JWB Mars Mole OGC SbS Suff Wall

Mont d'Or Golden Butter
see Mont d'Or

Montano
Round, dark green pods 15 cm. in length, stringless excellent for freezing. (Brwn)
Bakk Brwn John Milt Mole Yate

Narbonne
RSlu

Nassau
A flat podded French bean of the romano type. The pods are stringless and of very high quality with better flavour than mostsnap beans. (OGC)
Brwn John Milt OGC Shar Sutt Yate

Nerina
A unique and very special variety with very slim and stringless, well flavoured non-fading dark green pods which stay smooth longer and freeze well. Erect habit for easy picking and resistant to CBMV. (T&M)
John RSlu

Odessa
A very high yielding modern small podded variety ideal for the home gardener and for freezing and cooking whole. The pods are bright green in colour, rounded in section and have a maximumlength of 5in. Pod quality is excellent with slow seed development, the flavour is superb. (John)
John

Othello
An extremely fine-podded bean, also called "faux-filet". Othello is a needle bean, approx. 12cm. in length and with a cross-section of only approx 4-6mm. when picked young. First-class bean for gourmets. An impressive cropper. (Bakk)
Bakk

Primel
Mars

Processor
White seeded variety which can be used as a haricot bean when dried. (EWK)
Mole Wall

Pros
Excellent when picked regularly and eaten fresh, but also bred with the freezer in mind. Each plant bears quantities of round, sweet, juicy pods about 4-5in. long. When the first pods reach this size and can still be cleanly snapped between the fingers, the whole plant can be lifted, the beans removed and frozen whole, not sliced or chopped. (Dob)
Dob Mars Unwi

Provider
An early green round podded bean with delicious fleshy 5 in.long pods. Yield of the compact plants is good even in bad weather conditions. Pods remain fresh long after picking. One of the good reliable older varieties. (Suff)
Shar Suff

Purple King
EWK John

Purple Queen
One of the best flavours. A heavy yielder of glossy purple stringless beans. The round pods cook to an appetising dark green. (Foth)
Bakk Foth Milt SMM Sutt Unwi Wall

Purple Teepee
Fine flavoured, stringless pods are held high, for easy picking, turning rich green in boiling water. Very productive, quick to mature making it suitable for late, catching up sowings. (T&M)
Dob Foth Suff T&M

Radar
A new, slim podded variety of the type favoured by gourmet restaurants because the young pods are tender, full of flavour and quite stringless. A multipodded type which can be picked in bunches at the 4in. stage and cooked without slicing. (T&M)
T&M

Record
A fairly early double dwarf French bean which will tolerate some cold. Well-known variety, still very much in demand. (Bakk)
Bakk

Rido
Have you ever wanted to grow those super little French beansyou can now buy practically the year round at your local friendlysupermarket ever so neatly arranged in their plastic trays? Now's your chance as this is just such a variety. 'Rido' will produce a generous amount of dark green pods 4-5inches long but less than a quarter of an inch thick of connoisseur flavour; and just think, they'll be over 4,000 miles younger when you pick them in your own garden! Of much comfort in these Islands is thatit will produce an acceptable crop under an indifferent, let's-get-away-from-it, English summer. (Chil)
   Chil Dob

Rocquencourt
Lovely dark yellow long round/oval pods contrasting with dark green foliage. This variety is especially resistant to coldgrowing conditions. 64 days. (Suff)
   Suff

Roma II
One of the most widely grown beans in the business. Medium large fleshy pods that are traditionally cut in USA and Europe but can be served sliced or whole. (Bree)
   S&G

Royalty
Distinctive purple pods which turn green when cooked. Heavy crops of stringless beans with excellent flavour. (OGC)
   Chil EWK JWB Mars OGC Suff Tuck

Safari
Sutt

Saxa
A strong, early variety that can be picked very early. Saxagives a high yield of 12-13cm. long, round-oval sectioned pods. Extremely resistant to bad weather conditions. (Bakk)
   Bakk

Sirio
S&G

Slenderette
Really outstanding for its heavy crop of thick fleshy stringless pods. Strong-growing variety which crops over a long period. (Sutt)
   Shar

Sonate
One of the newest varieties. This exceptionally fine bean, which has a dark green colour, can bne picked early. It is a heavy cropper with a delicious flavour. (Bakk)
   Bakk

Sprite
Dark green, pencil shaped pods. Very suitable for freezing. (EWK)
   EWK SbS Sutt

St Andreas
Dob John JWB Mole SbS Sutt

Sunray
A highly appreciated variety for Market Growers as well as for Home Gardeners. Dark green pods which are excellent for deep freezing, stringless. (Brwn)
  Bakk Brwn John Milt

Tavera
RSlu

Tendercrop
Long round pods, stringless, crisp and fleshy. They remain in good condition on the plants for a long time. (Unwi)
  Unwi

Tendergreen
Fleshy, meaty pods which are stringless and fibreless with an excellent flavour. (T&M)
  Brwn Cart EWK Foth Howe John JWB Mole OGC SbS SMM

The Prince
Long slim pods with a magnificent flavour. Excellent for freezing and one of the most widely grown varieties. (T&M)
  Brwn Cart Chil EWK Foth John JWB Mars Mole OGC SbS

Torrina
Large round podded type 16cms in length. Quick to mature andpods are set high on plants for easy picking. (EWK)
  EWK

Triomphe de Farcy
An early variety gourmet bean with distinctive purple streaks on the pods. Another real old variety improved to use asfilet or snap bean. 49 days. (Suff)
  Bakk Suff

Valja
John

Vilbel
Very versatile with a long period of harvest. High yields oflong slender, stringless fillet, or fine, gourmet beans of excellent quality and flavour. (T&M)
  T&M

Wachs Goldperle
A juicy, succulent bean, attractive in appearance and highlyesteemed by Continental cooks. The productive plants carry clusters of golden-yellow, round fleshy pods about 5in. long. These remain tender for a good length of time. Both seeds and flowers are white. (Dob)
  Dob

Xera
RSlu

Garlic

Cristo
A long dormancy variety which I have grown for four years with outstanding results. Each bulb has about 10 to 15 cloves with 5 to 6 bulbs to the lb. A creamy colour and a very consistant shape. (Bir)
  Bir

Garlic

The sections, or cloves of each bulb should be separated and planted just below the soil surface during February/April. Space row 6-8 in. apart and allow 4 in. between cloves. Lift the crop in July-August. Store like Shallots. (Dob)
Bakk Brwn Dob Foth Poyn Suff Sutt T&M

Germidour
A short dormancy variety which must be planted before the end of the year. Produces large purple bulbs (almost as large asThermidrome but more attractive) each with 10 to 15 cloves. A very early cropper. (Bir)
Bir

Long Keeper
Well adapted to the British climate. Each clove planted should produce one garlic bulb. (Mars)
Mars

Pink
Plant from November to March in light free draining soil in a sunny position. Approximately 10-12 cloves per bulb. (Tuck)
Tuck

Printanor
OGC

Red Bulbed
SMM

Rocambole
Smaller red bulbed variety with a curled stem bearing bulbils. (Poyn)
Poyn

Thermidrome
A short dormancy variety which must be planted before the end of the year. Produces large white bulbs (about 4 to the lb.) each with 10 cloves. (Bir)
Bir

Good King Henry

Good King Henry
Perennial, 5 ft., ancient vegetable. Use young leaves like spinach, or force shoots in spring and use like asparagus. (D&D)
Chil Futu John JWB Poyn SbS SMM Suff Unwi

Lincolnshire Spinach
see Good King Henry

Mercury
see Good King Henry

Gooseberry

Achilles
GTwe Roug Bowe

Admiral Beattie
Rog GTwe Roug

Ajax
Roug

Alma
Rog Roug

Angler
Roug

Annelii
A red variety. Hardy.
SDea

Antagonist
Roug

Ashton Red
Rog Roug

Australia
Rog GTwe Roug

Beauty
Roug

Beauty Red
Roug

Bedford Red
Rog GTwe Roug

Bedford Yellow
GTwe Roug

Beech Tree Nestling
GTwe Roug

Belle de Meaux
Roug

Bellona
Rog Roug

Berry's Early Giant
Roug

Black Seedling
Roug

Blucher
Rog Roug

Bobby
Roug

Bobby Green
Roug

Bright Venus
GTwe Roug

British Oak
Roug

Broom Girl
Rog GTwe Roug Bowe

Brown's Red
Roug

Captivator
SDea GTwe Roug

Careless
Mid July. Culinary. A large, oval, pale green, smooth skinned berry. Good flavour. A moderately vigorous, spreading bush. A popular variety. (Brog)
  Allg Cast SDea SKee Rog CSco GTwe Muir Roug Bowe Edws

Catherina
Roug

Catherine
A variety offered in European markets. Dual purpose and prolific. Green to yellow.
SDea

Champagne
Allg

Champagne Red
GTwe

Champagne Yellow
Rog GTwe Roug

Champion
Roug

Clayton
Rog Roug

Coiners
Roug

Colossal
Roug

Conquering Hero
Roug

Cook's Eagle
GTwe Roug

Cousen's Seedling
GTwe

Criterion
Rog GTwe Roug

Crown Bob
Rog GTwe Roug Bowe

Dan's Mistake
Rog Roug

Drill
GTwe Roug

Early Green Hairy
Roug

Early Sulphur
Late June. Culinary and dessert. A medium sized yellow berry with good flavour. Hairy. A heavy cropper. A moderately vigorous, upright bush. (Brog)
SDea Rog SKee GTwe Roug Bowe

Echo
Roug

Edith Cavell
GTwe Roug

Emerald
Roug

Faithfull
Roug

Fascination
Roug

Firbob
Rog GTwe Roug

Forester
GTwe Roug

Forever Amber
Roug

Freedom
Rog GTwe Roug

Gautrey's Earliest
Roug

Gem
Roug

Gipsy Queen
GTwe Roug

Glencarse Muscat
Roug

Glenton Green
GTwe Roug

Globe Yellow
Roug

Golden Ball
SDea Roug

Golden Drop
Allg GTwe Roug Bowe

Golden Lion
Roug

Green Gascoigne
Roug

Green Gem
Rog GTwe Roug Bowe

Green Ocean
Rog GTwe Roug

Green Overall
Roug

Green Walnut
Roug

** Greenfinch
SDea GTwe Muir LBuc

Greengage (Pitmaston)
Rog Roug

Gretna Green
GTwe Roug

Grune Flaschen Beere
Roug

Grune Kugel
Roug

Grune Reisen
Roug

Guido
Rog GTwe Roug

Gunner
Mid to late July. Dessert. Large, oval, olive-green, hairy berries with good flavour. A vigorous, spreading bush. (Brog)
Allg Rog GTwe Roug Bowe

Guy's Seedling
Roug

Hamamekii
A red European variety. Extremely hardy. Used in Scandinavia. Resistant to mildew. A useful plant. (SDea)
SDea

5th Edition

Hearts of Oak
Rog GTwe Roug

Hedgehog
GTwe Roug Bowe

Helgrune Samtbeere
Roug

Hepburn's Prolific
GTwe Roug

Hero of the Nile
Rog GTwe Roug

High Sherriff
Rog GTwe Roug

Highlander
Roug

Hino Red
Bowe

Hino Yellow
Bowe

Honing's Fruheste
Roug

Hot Gossip
Roug

Hough's Supreme
Roug

Howard's Lancer
Mid to late July. Culinary and dessert. A medium sized, greenish white berry with very good flavour. Hairless but downy. A heavy cropper. A vigorous, upright becoming spreading bush. (Brog)
   SDea SKee Rog GTwe Roug Bowe

Hue and Cry
Roug

Improved Mistake
Roug

Independence
Roug

Ingall's Prolific
Roug

** Invicta
Late July. Culinary. Large, oval, pale green berries. Smoothskinned. A very heavy cropper. A vigorous, spreading and very spiny bush. Resistant to American gooseberry mildew. (Brog)
   Allg Cast SDea WHig SKee CSco GTwe Muir LBuc Bowe Edws

Ironmonger
Allg GTwe

Jenny Lind
Roug

Jolly Angler
Roug

Jolly Potter
Roug

Jubilee
Mid July. Culinary and dessert. A heavier cropping, virus-tested selection of 'Careless'. (Brog)
SKee Rog CSco Roug LBuc Bowe

Katherina Ohlenburg
Roug

Kathryn Harley
Roug

Keen's Seedling
GTwe Roug

Keepsake
Early July. Culinary. A medium to large, oval, greenish-white berry with good flavour. Slightly hairy. A vigorous, rather spreading bush. Susceptible to American gooseberrry mildew and frost damage. (Brog)
Allg SDea Rog GTwe Roug Bowe

King of Trumps
Rog GTwe Roug

Lady Delamare
Roug

Lady Haughton
Roug

Lady Leicester
Roug

Lancashire Lad
Late July. Culinary and dessert. A medium to large, oblong-oval, deep red berry with fair flavour. Hairy. A moderately vigorous bush. Fairly resistant to American gooseberrymildew. (Brog)
Allg Rog GTwe Roug Bowe

Langley Gage
Allg Rog GTwe Roug

Langley Green
Roug

Lauffener Glebe
Roug

Laxton's Amber
GTwe Roug

Leader
Roug

Leveller
Late July. Culinary and dessert. A very large, oblong-oval, greenish yellow berry with excellent flavour. Almost hairless. A moderately vigorous, spreading bush although rather weak on poor soils. A very popular dessert variety. (Brog)
Allg Cast SDea SKee Rog CSco GTwe Muir Roug LBuc Bowe Edws

Lily of the Valley
Roug

Lloyd George
Roug

London
Allg Rog GTwe Roug

Lord Audley
Roug

Lord Derby
Rog GTwe Roug Bowe

Lord Elcho
Roug

Lord Kitchener
Rog Roug

Macherauch's Seedling
Rog Roug

Major Hibbert
Roug

Marigold
Rog Roug

Marmorierte Gold Kugel
Roug

Matchless
Roug

Maurer's Seedling
Roug

May Duke
Early July. Culinary and dessert. A medium to large, round-oblong, green berry ripening to a dark red. Good flavour. A moderately vigorous, upright bush. (Brog)
SDea Rog GTwe Roug Bowe

Mertensis
Roug

Mischief
Roug

Mitre
GTwe Roug

Monarch
Roug

Montgomery
Roug

Mrs Westham
Roug

Muttons
Roug

Nailer
Roug

Napoleon le Grand
Roug

Norden Hero
Roug

Ostrich
Roug

Peru
Rog Roug

Pitmaston
GTwe Roug

Pixwell
Roug

Plain Long Green
Roug

Plunder
Rog Roug

Postman
Roug

Pottage
Roug

Preston Seedling
Roug

Prince Charles
GTwe Roug

Profit
Roug

Queen of Hearts
Rog Roug

Queen of Trumps
Rog GTwe Roug

Railway
Roug

Rearguard
Roug

Riese von Kothen
Roug

Rifleman
GTwe Roug

Roaring Lion
Roug

Robustenda
Roug

Rokula
GTwe

Roseberry
GTwe Roug

Rushwick Seedling
Roug

Scotch Red Rough
GTwe Roug

Scottish Chieftain
GTwe Roug

Sensation
Roug

Shiner
Roug

Sir G Brouse
Rog Roug

Sir John Brown
Roug

Slap Bang
Roug

Smaragbeere
Roug

Smiling Beauty
Roug

Snow
Roug

Snow Drop
GTwe Roug

Souter Johnny
Rog Roug

Speedwell
Rog Roug

Spinefree
GTwe Roug

Stockwell
Roug

Sulphur
Allg Roug

Sultan Juror
Rog Roug

Surprise
Allg Rog GTwe Roug

Talford
Roug

Telegraph
GTwe Roug

Thatcher
Roug

The Leader
Rog Roug

Thumper
Roug

Tom Joiner
GTwe Roug

Trumpeter
Rog Roug

Victoria
Rog GTwe Roug

Viper
Roug

Warrington
GTwe Roug

Weisse Riesen
Roug

Weisse Volltrissen
Roug

Werdersche Fruhemarkt
Roug

Whinham's Industry
Late July. Culinary and dessert. A medium to large, oval, dark red berry with very good flavour. Hairy. A vigorous, fairly upright bush. Very susceptible to American gooseberry mildew. (Brog)
 Allg Cast SDea WHig SKee Rog CSco GTwe Muir Roug LBuc Bowe

White Eagle
Rog Roug

White Fig
Roug

White Lion
Rog GTwe Roug Bowe

White Swan
Roug

White Transparent
GTwe Roug

Whitesmith
Late July. Culinary and dessert. A fairly large, oval, pale greenish-white, berry with a very good flavour. A good cropper. Avigorous, upright becoming spreading bush. (Brog)
Allg Cast SDea WHig SKee Rog CSco GTwe Roug Bowe

Woodpecker
Rog GTwe Roug

Gooseberry Hybrid

Black Velvet
Worcesterberry X Champagne Red Gooseberry. Entirely free of mildew. Fruit smallish, dark red.
CSco Bowe

Grape Greenhouse

Alicante
GTwe ERea Bowe

Angers Frontignan
ERea

Appley Towers
ERea

Ascot Citronelle
ERea

Black Corinth
ERea

Black Hamburgh
Early. A fairly large, black dessert grape. Juicy, firm and sweet. Easy to grow. Moderately vigorous. (Brog)
Allg SDea WHig SKee Rog CSco GTwe Muir ERea LBuc Bowe

Black Monukka
ERea

Black Prince
ERea

Buckland Sweetwater
GTwe ERea Bowe

Cannon Hall Muscat
ERea

Cardinal
ERea

Chaouch
ERea

Chasselas Rose
ERea Bowe

Chasselas Vibert
ERea

Ciotat
ERea

Cote House Seedling
ERea

Espiran
ERea

Foster's Seedling
Early. A large white dessert grape. Juicy and sweet with good flavour. A good cropper. (Brog)
SDea SKee GTwe ERea Bowe

Golden Champion
Bowe

Golden Chasselas
SDea

Golden Queen
ERea

Grizzley Fontignan
ERea

Gros Colmar
ERea

Gros Maroc
ERea Bowe

Hamburg Muscat
CSco

King's Ruby
ERea

Lady Downe's Seedling
ERea

Lady Hastings
ERea

Lady Hutt
ERea

Madeleine Angevine
Bowe

Madeleine Royale
ERea

Madiera Frontignan
ERea

Madresfield Court
SKee GTwe ERea Bowe

Mireille
SDea GTwe

Mrs Pearson
ERea

Mrs Pince's Black Muscat
ERea

Muscat Champion
ERea

Muscat Hamburgh
Muir ERea

Muscat of Alexandria
Late. A large white grape with an excellent flavour. Requires warmth and hand pollination to set a good crop. (Brog)
Allg CSco Muir ERea Bowe

Muscat of Hungary
ERea

Perle de Czaba
ERea

Primavis Frontignan
ERea

Royal Muscadine
Allg ERea

St Laurent
ERea

Syrian
ERea

Thompson's Seedless
ERea

Trebbiano
ERea

West's St Peter's
ERea

Grape Outdoor

Baco 1
GTwe

Boscoop Glory
GTwe Bowe

Brandt
Mid October. Heavy crops of small, sweet black grapes. Oftengrown for its autumn colour. Vigorous - very useful for wall cover. Some resistance to mildew. (Brog)
SDea WHig Rog CSco GTwe ERea Bowe

Cabernet Sauvignon
SDea

Californica
ERea

Cardinal
ERea

Cascade (Siebel 13053)
Early October. Small bunches of dark purple berries with redacid juice. Very vigorous -excellent as wall cover. Resistant to mildew. (Brog)
SDea SKee CSco GTwe Muir ERea LBuc Bowe

Chardonnay
SDea

Chasselas Doree
CSco

Coignetiae
ERea

Concord
ERea

Early Van der Laan
Bowe

Excelsior
SDea

Fragola
Bowe

Gagarin Blue
SDea ERea

Gamay Hatif
ERea

Gewurtztraminer
SDea

Glory of Boskoop
SDea

Himrod Seedless
SDea GTwe ERea

Interlaken
ERea

Leon Millot
SDea SKee Muir ERea

Madeleine Angevine
SDea WHig GTwe ERea

Madeleine Sylvaner
September. A medium sized, pale white grape producing a goodquality wine. Can be used as a dessert. Moderately vigorous. (Brog)
   SDea SKee CSco GTwe Muir ERea LBuc Bowe

Millers Burgundy (Pinot Meunier)
CSco ERea

Muller Thurgau (Riesling Sylvaner)
Mid October. A small to medium sized white grape mainly usedfor wine. Produces a wine with a delicate, attractive bouquet. Vigorous. A heavy cropper but requires good weather during pollination. (Brog)
   SDea SKee CSco GTwe Muir ERea Bowe

Muscat Bleu
ERea

New York Muscat
ERea

Noir Hatif de Marseilles
ERea

Oliver Irsay
ERea

Parsley Leafed Chasselas
SDea

Perle de Czaba
ERea

Pirovano 14
SDea GTwe ERea

Precoce de Malingre
ERea Bowe

Reine Olga
ERea

Rembrandt
Bowe

Seyve-Villard (Seyval Blanc)
Mid to late October. A medium sized white wine grape. A heavy cropper and easy to grow. Moderately vigorous. Resistant tomildew. (Brog)
   SDea WHig CSco GTwe Muir ERea Bowe

Siegerrebe
SDea GTwe Muir ERea

Strawberry Grape
SDea GTwe ERea

Teinturier Grape
ERea

Tereshkova
SDea ERea

Triomphe D'Alsace
SDea WHig

Wrotham Pinot
SDea

Groundnut

American Groundnut
A hardy perennial vine that will climb to well over 10m. under ideal conditions. It produces strings of small ovoid edible tubers, which sometimes reach bantam egg size. Fine fritillary-like flowers. A native of Eastern North America this plant was once cultivated by native peoples for its tasty tubers, which are similar in taste and texture to normal potatoes and can be eaten in much the same way. The plants produce nitrogen fixing nodules and so help to increase soil fertility. Tubers are harvested after the foliage dies down and are joined together on long strings, making the job easier. They should be stored damp or left in the ground until needed. (Futu)
Futu

Horseradish

Horseradish
Sore

Horseradish Japanese

Matsumi
Poyn

Huckleberry

Garden Huckleberry
A high-yielding, easy to grow annual crop. Give the unusual half-hardy annual treatment, planting out late May or early June. The large berries are very freely produced and are delicious in pies and tarts but wait until they are really soft, black and juicy otherwise the taste is bitter. Excellent for making delicious jam. (Unwi)
Unwi

Mrs B's Garden Huckleberry
An annual up to 1m tall which bares large quantities of black berries 3-4cms across best used cooked in jams and pies. Although not of outstanding flavour, the plants are prolific, easy to grow. The flavour mixes well with other fruits. Often self-seeds. (Futu)
Futu

Jerusalem Artichoke

Boston Red
Large red skinned, knobbly. (Futu)
SMM

Common
A very easy winter vegetable. Plant tubers 4 in. deep and 12in. apart as soon as possible in spring on a sunny site. Lift as required during the winter. (Mars)
   Mars

Cream
Cream skin. (SMM)
   SMM

Dwarf Sunray
Tender enough that peeling of outer skin is not necessary. Dwarf and unique in that it flowers freely so can be dual purposein the flower border. (T&M)
   Futu T&M

Fuseau
The uniform long tubers of this variety, with a very smooth surface, are much easier to prepare in the kitchen. Delicious boiled or fried. (Mars)
   Mars SMM Sore

Garnet
A variety similar to Sugarball but with red skin.
   Futu

Jerusalem Artichoke
Its yellow flowers grow to a height of up to 3 metres. Potato-sized tubers grow under soil level. Delicious flavour, cooked as well as fried. An old-time vegetable. Harvest in November. (Bakk)
   Bakk Bloo John Rog Tuck

Sugarball
A smooth variety with round tubers.
   Futu

Jicama

Jicama
(Pachyrhizus tuberosus - Leguminosae) This is a Mexican vegetable that it would seem is gaining popularity in the USA. Grown for its tuberous roots (its seeds are reputed to be poisonous - the reverse of Runner Beans where the roots are poisonous!), it is fact a highly ornamental twiner with dense racemes of purple flowers (although when growing for the roots, you must be steel-willed and pluck them off). The roots look like Turnips but have a thirst-quenching, fresh-apple taste. They are sliced and sprinkled either with sugar or salt and/or lemon juice. Alternatively, they can be used as water chestnuts in oriental cooking. Grow as a half-hardy annual and give them the warmest, sunniest spot you can spare, or let them loose in your greenhouse. (Chil)
   Chil

Kale

F1 Arsis
   RSlu

F1 Bornick
   SbS

F1 Buffalo
   S&G SbS

Cottagers
   John

F1 Darkibor
   Brwn Dob Milt

Dwarf Green Curled
Dwarf habit with closely curled leaves. (Dob)
   Bloo Brwn Cart Dob EWK Foth Howe John JWB Mars

Dwarf Green Curled Afro
   SbS Toze

Dwarf Green Curled Scotch
see Dwarf Green Curled

F1 Fribor
   EWK John JWB Mole OGC SbS Toze VanH Wall

Half Tall
see Dwarf Green Curled

Hungry Gap
Latest hardy variety, matures March/April when other greens are scarce. Sow up to August where it is to mature. (Mars)
   Mars Tuck

F1 Kobolt
   S&G

F1 Moosbor
   Bakk John

Pentland Brig
Leaves with curled edges can be harvested throughout winter. Also produces succulent side shoots in early spring. (Tuck)
   EWK John JWB Mars OGC SbS SMM Suff Tuck Unwi

F1 Showbor
   Dob John Sutt

Spurt
Grow like spinach. Masses of tender deep green curly leaf for salads, steaming or boiling. Ready in 6 weeks. (T&M)
   Bloo T&M

Tall Green Curled
Similar to Dwarf Green Curled. Some tolerance to club root and cabbage root fly. (Mars)
   Howe John Mars Mole SbS Wall

Tall Scotch Curled
see Tall Green Curled

Thousand Head
Strong-growing, hardy and prolific variety, useful both as a vegetable and for stock feeding. (Dob)
   JWB MAS Suff Sutt Tuck

Westland Autumn
Late-curling selection that can be harvested from December until the middle of February. Taste at its best when touched by the frost. Will even stand quite some frost. (Bakk)
   Bakk Dob

Westlandse Herfst
see Westland Autumn

F1 Winterbor
   EWK John SbS Toze Yate

Kiwano

Kiwano
(Cucumis metuliferus) Horny Cucumber. We are told that you will either love or hate the fruit of this rarely offered plant, although occasionally they are often flown in and offered at extravagant West End stores at luxury prices. Although closely related to the Common Cucumber, it is in fact analmost xerophytic, quick-growing plant from southern Africa with spiney, 4in. long brilliant orange fruits, bright green inside with an almost jelly-like texture with a subtle flavour said to be somewhere between banana and lime. Grow it like the ordinary Cucumber with possibly less water and humidity. (Chil)
    Chil

Kohlrabi

Azur Star
This variety is by far the earliest and most beautiful kohlrabi for cultivation in the greenhouse as well as in the open. Very suitable for sowing early; hardly prone to bolting. Azur Star has a slightly flattish-round shape and a deep blue colour. (Bakk)
    Bakk

Delicacy Purple
One of the best-known kohlrabi varieties. Exceptionally fineflavour, extremely tender. Marked improvement of the so-called Vienna types. (Bakk)
    Bakk

Delikatess Blauer
see Delicacy Purple

F1 Express Forcer
Bakk John

Green Vienna
see White Vienna

F1 Kolpak
John

F1 Lanro
Bakk Dob Toze

Logo
Sutt

F1 Purple Danube
EWK

Purple Vienna
Produces a purple bulb. Can be sown up to August as they have some frost resistance. (D&D)
    Bloo Brwn Chil Dob EWK Foth John JWB Milt Mole OGC

F1 Rhein
RZ

Roblau
Purple-skinned version of Lanro F1 with good shape and excellent crisp flesh. (Toze)
    Toze

Rolano
Very fast maturing variety producing succulent swollen stems approximately 8 weeks from sowing. This flavoursome item makes an interesting addition to salads when finely grated. (Dob)
Bakk Dob Howe Milt

F1 Rowel
Mars Unwi

Superschmelz
A giant kohlrabi, soft like butter, for outdoor cultivation. Well fertilized, it can reach a weight of up to 10 kg. Stores well in a cool spot. (Bakk)
Bakk

F1 Trero
T&M

F1 White Danube
OGC

White Vienna
Slightly earlier than the purple strain. Flesh has fine even texture of excellent flavour. (EWK)
Bloo Brwn Chil EWK John JWB Mole OGC SbS SMM Sutt

Komatsuna

Green Boy
SMM

Komatsuna
Fast growing leaf cabbage with mild fresh taste. (Suff)
EWK Futu OGC SbS SMM Suff Tuck

Osome Komatsuna
Milt

Red Giant
Suff

Tendergreen
(Spinach mustard) Ready in just 20 days and regrows quickly. Excellent for freezing. Sow spring to late summer. Heat and cold tolerant. (T&M)
Chil

F1 Tora
Yate

Leaf Beet see Spinach Beet

Leaf Celery

Cutting Celery
Very easy to grow, with the same flavour as normal celery; but produces lots of leaf, instead of stems for blanching. Ideal for soups, salads, and seasoning. Winter hardy. Produces well flavoured seed, ideal for soups &c. (Suff)
Dob Suff Sutt

Leaf Celery
Celery flavoured leaves for salads and soup. Allow some to go to seed the following year to give stronger flavour in soups. (OGC)
OGC

Leek

Alaska
An extremely winter hardy leek with dark blue-green foliage and stems 20-25 cm. long. Shows strong regrowth in spring for harvest until May, and will not bolt readily during this period. (OGC)
John OGC SbS Tuck

Albinstar
Excellent variety for lifting late summer or early autumn. Long, slender shaft with light green foliage. Ideal for exhibition work. (EWK)
EWK JWB OGC SbS Sutt Wall

Ardea
Howe Mole SbS

Armor
Yate

Autumn Giant 2 Argenta
Performs outstandingly whether sown early or late and does well over a long season. Matures in October, yet stands ready for harvest right through to May, giving high quality, thick, very heavy stems, of excellent mild flavour and yield with few bolters. (T&M)
Cart Dob John OGC RSlu SbS T&M Tuck

Autumn Giant Rami
Sutt Toze Yate

Autumn Mammoth
see Goliath

Autumn Mammoth 2
SbS

Autumn Mammoth 2 Goliath
Toze

Autumn Mammoth 2 Governor
Toze

Autumn Mammoth 2 Majestic
Toze

Autumn Mammoth 2 Walton Mammoth
Large and bold, a good general purpose variety for autumn and winter. Stands winter weather conditions well. Good blanch. (Brwn)
Brwn Mars SbS Toze

Bastion
Mole SbS Wall

Berdina
S&G

Bleu de Solaise
Sel. St. Victor. A French winter variety with sturdy stems; very much in demand. It will tolerate some frost and can be harvested until spring. (Bakk)
Bakk OGC SbS Suff

Blizzard
One of the finest new leeks available. Very winter hardy producing medium sized shafts of a fine colour and flavour through the winter months. Harvest from December to April. Blizzard is tolerant to yellow stripe virus. (VanH)
   John Mole SbS VanH Wall

Blue Green Autumn
   SbS

Blue Green Autumn Ducal
   Bakk

Blue Green Autumn Romil
   Yate

Bluestar
see Giant Winter 3

Branta
   Howe

Carentan
Robust, late autumn and winter leek which, provided it is not harvested too late, will yield a heavy crop. Strong stem, 20-30 cm. long. (Bakk)
   OGC SbS Suff

Carina
Developed from our Catalina, it has a longer white shaft and is fit for use from Christmas onwards. Upright leaves do not collect dirt as much as older varieties. (Mars)
   Mars S&G

Castlestar
   SbS

Catalina
Very productive, giving large crops of long, heavy, non-bulbing leeks. (Foth)
   Dob SbS Unwi

Cobham Empire
see Yates Empire

Coloma
   SbS

Conora
   Yate

Cortina
Combining exceptional winter hardiness and long standing ability with sturdy medium length stems, a pure white shaft and dark green leaves. Probably the best late. Maturing January to April. (T&M)
   John S&G

Davina
   S&G

Derrick
Thick, medium length stem with dark, bluish-green foliage. Autumn to early winter use. (EWK)
   EWK Howe John Milt SbS VanH

Elephant
A true autumn leek, early-maturing. It has a short, thick stem which ensures an extremely high yield. Elephant will tolerate some frost without causing any problems. It is, however, advisable not to wait that long and to harvest before the frost sets in. (Bakk)
   Bakk SbS

Elina
SbS

Emperor
Toze

Farinto
Chil

Gavia
SbS

Gennevilliers Splendid
see Splendid

Giant Winter
see Giant Winter 3

Giant Winter 3
Excellent late variety with good length stems. Slow to bolt. (EWK)
Bakk EWK Mole OGC SbS SMM Wall

Giant Winter Granada
Toze

Gino
Howe

Glorina
S&G

Goldina
John

Goliath
A quality autumn maturing variety with a good blanch. (Brwn)
John JWB SbS SMM Tuck

Hannibal
SbS

Herfstreuzen
see Goliath

Highland Giant
Hardy variety for lifting in January. Long shanks of pure white and will reach a good size when sown late March/early April. (VanH)
VanH

Hiverbleu
see Libertas

Jolant
A very vigorous grower for autumn harvesting the shaft is very long with abundant green foliage. No bulbing at the base. Probably the largest and most popular one year growing leek on the market. (VanH)
Howe Milt Mole SbS VanH

Kajak
Long standing winter variety. Dark green foliage and very long white shaft. Has resistance to virus and leaf spot. (EWK)
EWK OGC SbS Suff

Kelvedon King
SbS

Kilima
RSlu

King Richard
Very early with extremely long shafts. For late summer and early autumn harvest, though will stand some frost. Maturity 75 days. (OGC)
   Bloo Dob John Mars OGC SbS Suff Sutt Sutt T&M Tuck

Krystina
S&G

Latina
S&G

Lavi
SbS Yate

Libertas
A heavy cropping variety that is extremely hardy. White stem. Can be harvested until spring. (Bakk)
   Bakk

Longbow
A good winter-hardy variety with dark green foliage and a long white shank. Ideal for autumn/winter cropping. (RHS HC) Harvest date: Oct - Mar. (Brwn)
   Brwn Toze

Longina
S&G Wall

Longstanton
see Odin

Lyon
Good all round variety for autumn use. (EWK)
   Brwn EWK Foth John JWB MAS OGC SbS SMM Sutt T&M

Malabar
SbS

Malabare
see Malabar

Mammoth Blanch
A superior exhibition variety with extra long blanch. Specimens grown by amateurs have attained over 5 lbs weight and 100 cu. ins. Exceptionally thick with broad flag. (Rob)
   JWB Rob

Mammoth Pot
A true Pot leek, very thick, with short blanch of approximately 5.5 ins. (13 cms) Bred for the exhibitor but yet retaining good flavour with tight flesh. One of the easiest leeks to grow, very frost hardy. (Rob)
   Rob

Marina
S&G

Monstuoso di Carentan
see Carentan

Musselburgh
(1822) Harvest December-April. A most reliable and versatile variety which has been justifiably popular for many years. (OGC)
   Bloo Brwn Cart Chil Dob EWK Foth John JWB Mars MAS

Noel
SbS

Odin Longstanton
SbS SbS

Pancho
Early maturing, yet will stand into mid-winter. Long, crisp, white blanched stems of excellent flavour. Ideal for slicing in late salads, or for conventional cooking. (Dob)
Dob SbS Toze

Paragon
RZ

Poribleu
Very dark, upright foliage with easy to peel long stems showing very little bulbing. Stands in good condition exceptionally well from October to March. Shows some rust tolerance, a common problem during most seasons. (Dob)
Dob

Poristo
Foth SbS

Porvana
SbS

Pot
A real exhibition strain. With careful attention will grow to an immense size. (EWK)
EWK JWB SbS

Prelina
S&G

Prenora
EWK SbS Yate

Prizetaker
see Lyon

Profina
S&G

Senora
Yate

Siegfried Frost
Yate

Snowstar
First class to eat and to exhibit. Thick, sturdy white stems will hold in excellent condition all winter. A superb strain. (Foth)
Dob Foth John SbS Toze

Snowstar B
Mole SbS

Splendid
An excellent autumn and early winter leek that does not bulbat the base. It produces uniform blanched shafts about 12 cm. (5 in.) long, 2.5 cm. (1 in.) diameter. (Unwi)
John SbS Suff Toze Unwi

St Victor
see Blue Solaise

Startrack
A fairly long, slender variety, recommended for early autumncultivation. Of all Autumn Giant selections Startrack has the darkest leaves. (Bakk)
Brwn Howe John Toze

Sterna
This is an early variety suitable for lifting August/September. A Blue Green Autumn type with strong erect leaves and white stem. 22-24 cm. (Brwn)
Brwn Howe

Swiss Giant Tilna
Toze

Tadorna
Howe Mole SbS

The Lyon
see Lyon

Thor
Early type with very long shafts and medium green foliage. (EWK)
SbS

Tilina
S&G

Titan
An early summer leek, forming long stems. However, Titan does not tolerate frost. This variety has a very agreeable, aromatic flavour. (Bakk)
SbS

Toledo
A significant improvement in late leeks, the stem is almost twice the length of some varieties. An excellent cropper with winter hardiness for cropping from late December through to May. (T&M)
T&M Toze

Tropita
Late summer and early autumn variety. Extremely long shanks. (EWK)
EWK SbS

Varna
RSlu

Verina
Autumn Mammoth type. Strong resistance to rust disease, suited to organic methods. Produces medium length, very straight leeks with dark green leaves. (Unwi)
S&G Unwi

Walton Mammoth
see Autumn Mammoth 2

Wila
An extremely hardy leek with dark blue-green leaves. Stems straight and thick, increasing in weight in late winter and remaining in condition until May. (Mars)
Mars

Winora
Yate

Winter
A fine growing trench leek, very dark green leaves, frost hardy. (Rob)
Rob

Winter Crop
Outstanding late-maturing, extra-hardy variety with large white stems and very dark foliage. Stands well for use until April. (Sutt)
Sutt

Winterreuzen
see Giant Winter 3

Wintra
Excellent late winter type for maturity into March. Dark green, strong foliage and long, white stems. (Suff)
  EWK Howe Milt SbS Suff

Yates Empire
A very good leek with thick stems. Matures late, standing well into April. (Unwi)
  SbS Unwi

Zorba
  SbS

Lettuce

Action
First class butterhead lettuces which are quick to heart with thick, succulent light green leaves. Bred for resistance to all known races of lettuce mildew and tolerance of mosaic virus, making it the ideal choice for organic and inorganic gardeners alike. For early crops, seeds can be sown indoors January - March. (Foth)
  Foth Wall

Ambassador
  SbS

Bambi
A small cos type, very like Little Gem but with more compact darker green leaves forming a very uniform head approx. 6ins. across. Can also be sown under glass for early crops. (Foth)
  Foth

Bastion
A new crisp head variety for greenhouse production during the winter months. Forms large firm hearts which are welcome as an additional fresh vegetable for Christmas salads. (John)
  John Milt

Bastogne
  Bakk

Batavia Blonde
see Favourite

Besson
  Bakk

Black Seeded Simpson
  Bakk

Blonde de Paris
see Favourite

Carmen
New in our range! Reddish-green Batavia lettuce with a tender, large, heavy head. Carmen tolerates heat very well and is very slow to bolt. Hardly prone to lettuce mosaic. Extremely tasty! (Bakk)
  Bakk

Clarisse
John

Cosmic
Toze

Diana
SbS Toze

Dynasty
An autumn sowing variety for harvesting up to November/December with uniform habit and attractive heads. Resistant to mosaic virus, downy mildew and a high tolerance of tip burn. (OGC)
EWK OGC SbS

Favourite
Bakk SbS

Feltham King
SbS

Gloire de Nantes
see Feltham King

Hudson
Mole SbS

Jackpot
SbS

Kelly's
A crisp variety with bright green leaves. Sow Oct/Nov for harvest in Mar/Apr. (OGC)
Bloo EWK John Mars Milt Mole OGC SbS Suff Tuck

Kim
Howe Toze

Lillian
SbS

Marbello
A tasty crisp lettuce for sowing from Aug to Feb to produce succulent hearts in an unheated greenhouse or frame from Nov to May — a time when salad crops are typically scarce and expensice. (Dob)
Dob

Mayfair
May King type. (Brwn)
Toze

Novita
EWK Milt OGC SbS Suff Tuck

Pascal
For autumn, winter and spring cutting. Quick growing, thick leaves. Performed among the best in many international trials. Resistant to Bremia races 1, 2, 3, 4, 5 and 6. (Brwn)
Mole

Pavane
A little Gem or "Sucrine" type. Pavane forms a small cos-like head with a dense heart. Slightly darker than Little Gem, Pavane is a very uniform variety with added LMV resistance. (Bree)
S&G

Perlane
SbS

Premier Great Lakes
SbS

Prestine
SbS

Rave
SbS

Ravel
Emerald green heads for glasshouse use from October to earlyMay. (EWK)
EWK Mole SbS Tuck

Renania
Forms a robust, tender head which is very slow to run to seed. A true summer lettuce, deservedly called "the pride of every good gardener". (Bakk)
Bakk

Rossalita
Suff

Sangria
Sutt

Sioux
A new breeding development brings this superb, colourful item to our summer salads. It has deep red outer leaves, but a firm crunchy, blanched heart. Tolerates hot conditions particularly well. (Dob)
Dob

Sumian
One of the newest varieties for the professional amateur. It has a light green colour and is very healthy. Suitable for spring, summer, and autumn cultivation. (Bakk)
Bakk

White Self-closing
Bakk

Zodiac
Cart John Mole SbS

Lettuce Cos

Angela
Just as sweet and tender as Little Gem but much easier to separate leaves for garnish, salads etc. Mildew resistant. Virus tolerant. (T&M)
S&G

Ballon
see Balloon

Balloon
A heavy weight cos, light green with a brown tinge to the leaves. (OGC)
EWK JWB OGC SbS

Blonde Maraichere
see Paris White

Bubbles
An excellent Little Gem type with very crinkly leaves which snap crisply and have the same superb flavour. Grow at high density. Small gardens. (T&M)
Dob Milt Mole T&M Toze

Carten
SbS

Corsair
Flat dark green leaves with strong flavour. (SMM)
Brwn Dob T&M Toze

Corsaro
RSlu

Craquerelle du Midi
see Winter Density

Dark Green Boston
SbS

Dark Green Cos
Darker green and slower growing than Lobjoits, it is outstanding in later summer crops and is very resistant to tipburn and bolting. LMV tolerant. (Bree)
  JWB S&G SbS

Grise Maraichere
see Lobjoits Green Cos

Jewel
Solid dark heart like a larger Little Gem. Very sweet flavour. Sow spring or autumn. (Mars)
  Brwn SbS Sutt Toze

Little Gem
A cross between cos and cabbage lettuce with some of the benefits of both. Can be sown in the open throughout the growing season and lends itself well to being sown in the early autumn and cloched during the winter. (OGC)
  Bloo Brwn Cart Dob EWK Foth John JWB Mars Milt

Little Gem Delight
Howe

Little Leprechaun
A striking red-leaved semi-cos type. Very compact with good tolerance to heat and bolting. (OGC)
  EWK OGC SbS Suff

Lobjoits Green Cos
Tall, deep green hearts, very crisp. Self-folding. (Mars)
  Bloo EWK Foth John JWB Mars Mole OGC S&G SbS Suff

Manavert
Howe

Paris Island cos
SbS

Paris White
Much improved cos type with medium large compact heads. Willstand for a long time when ready to cut. (EWK)
  Cart Chil EWK JWB SbS Wall

Sucrine
see Little Gem

Toledo
Half way between Little Gem and a standard cos. Dark green leaves give a very sweet flavour and no bitterness. Mini cos. Reliable. Virus tolerant. (T&M)
  Mars RSlu VanH

Val d'Orge
see Valdor

Valdor
Overwinter greenhouse type. This can also be sown outside. Attractive light green heads with good resistance to bolting. Sow in Aug/Sep. (OGC)
Cart Dob EWK JWB Mole OGC SbS Sutt Tuck Wall

Valmaine
A cos type used for cut and come again, giving two crops from one sowing. Very productive and the individual leaves are deliciously crisp. Resistant to some races of mildew and particularly useful for summer/autumn use. (OGC)
EWK John JWB Mole OGC SbS Toze

Vaux's Self Folding
John OGC

Winter Density
Larger than Little Gem; a very good crisp variety, much used for autumn sowing. (OGC)
Brwn Chil Dob EWK Foth John JWB Mars Mole OGC SbS

Lettuce Head

All the Year Round
The heads of pale green leaves with crisp compact white hearts are slow to bolt and have a long cropping period. Sow: Mar - Aug. Harvest: 10-12 wks. (Brwn)
Brwn Cart Chil Dob EWK Foth John JWB Mars OGC SbS

Animo
John

Arctic King
Very hardy variety for autumn sowing outside to cut early spring. (EWK)
EWK John JWB MAS SbS Sutt Tuck VanH Wall

Attraction
see Unrivalled

Aubade
John

Avoncrisp
A crisp head type for autumn harvest. It can also be used for "cut-and-come-again" cropping. (OGC)
EWK JWB Mars Mole OGC SbS Tuck Wall Yate

Avondefiance
Dark green in colour. Useful for summer sowing due to its high resistance to mildew. Popular with commercial growers, and successful in warm climates. (OGC)
Dob EWK John JWB Mars Milt Mole OGC SbS Suff Sutt

Baltic
The largest, most solid iceberg, providing crisp, succulent salads from June onwards. In our trials it proved more resistant to cool spring weather than Saladin, which it replaces. (Mars)
Mars RSlu

Beatrice
A new generation of lettuce. Early, easy to grow with excellent mildew and root aphid resistance, superb vigour and fast crop growth. Ideal as an early Iceberg, with bright green solid crunchy heads and short internal stalk. (T&M)
  Mole OGC SbS T&M

Becky
  S&G

Berlo
  Toze

Bikini
  Yate

Blonde a Bord Rouge
see Iceberg

Borough Wonder
Excellent summer variety for a regular sowing. Large, pale green, tender heads. (EWK)
  EWK John Wall

Bristol
  John

British Hilde
see Hilde II

Bruna di Germania
Small red/brown hardy lettuce for overwintering, growing to 8 in. Does better with some protection, i. e. a cold frame, or tunnel. (Suff)
  Suff

Burgundy Boston
  SbS SMM

Buttercrunch
Dark green with compact heads which stands well. The centralleaves are very crisp and it is resistant to hot weather. One of the best garden lettuces. (OGC)
  Bloo Dob EWK John JWB OGC SbS Suff T&M Unwi VanH

Calgary
  RSlu

Carlton
  John

Challenge
  S&G

Chaperon
This slow-bolting butterhead type is suitable for spring, summer and early autumn crops. Has a nice heart with yellow-green leaves, strongly tinged with red outer leaves. Large heads. (Brwn)
  John

Cindy
  Mole Wall

Claret
  John

Clarion
Thick leaved variety cropping throughout the summer. Bremia resistant. (EWK)
  Bakk Brwn EWK Howe John Milt Mole SbS Toze

Cobham Green
Similar to New Market, but dark green colour. (JWB)
John JWB Mole SbS Toze Wall

Columbus
Greenhouse type. Fast growing. Bright green thick textured leaves. Sow late August to mid-February for late October-early May cropping. (Dob)
Cart Dob EWK SbS

Comanda
S&G

Constant Heart
see Hilde II

Continuity
Only suitable for sowing in the spring and summer, it is very long standing. Distinct reddish brown in colour, it improves the appearance of a mixed salad. It is claimed that the colour deters pigeons. (OGC)
EWK John JWB OGC SbS Tuck Wall

Cortina
John

Crestana
Crisp dense heads, like supermarket icebergs but much greener. Tolerates wide range of conditions. Very reliable. Mildew resistant. Virus tolerant. (T&M)
S&G T&M

Crispino
Small light green hearts with green hearts with a crisp texture and fine flavour are perfect throughout summer. They can be cropped to give individual leaves. (Foth)
Foth RSlu

Cynthia
A crisp, tasty butterhead type that is a little later to harvest than Kwiek. (Foth)
SbS Unwi

Daphne
Howe Mole SbS Toze Wall Yate

De Verrieres
see Imperial Winter

Debby
Extremely versatile. It can be sown indoors from January, outdoors from March to late July, to crop from May until early November. It is noted for producing full, firm heads in mid-summer, when many other varieties bolt easily. Resistance to lettuce root aphid, mildew and lettuce mosaic virus. (Mars)
Mars Tuck Unwi

Delta
SbS

Dorado
Howe

El Toro
Hard, dense, crisp, crunchy head. Very quick growing, yet mature heads stand till October. (T&M)
John T&M

Fivia
Firm, crisp, heavy heads with an attractive pink tinge. Sow mid-September to mid-January, harvest early November to late March. (T&M)
T&M

Fortune
see Hilde II

Gaby
Howe

Geneva
Toze

Glice
S&G

Grande
RSlu

Great Lakes
see Great Lakes 659

Great Lakes 659
The well-known American crisphead lettuce which forms a real"cabbage" that is not prone to bolt. Can be kept in the refrigerator for quite some time. (Bakk)
Bakk Brwn EWK John JWB Mars MAS Mole OGC SbS SMM

Great Lakes 659 Mesa
SbS

Greenway
Yate

Hilde II
Is at present considered one of the most cultivated varieties. Produces solid, healthy heads, tender and with a very fine flavour. Recommended! (Bakk)
Bakk Cart Mars SbS Sutt Unwi VanH

Iceball
RSlu

Iceberg
This is essentially a summer lettuce with pale green leaves,slightly red tinged with large crisp white hearts. (OGC)
Bloo EWK John JWB Mole OGC SbS SMM Suff T&M Tuck

Impala
Impala is a short day lettuce, producing high quality heads with a well closed base. Suggested sowing period September to November. Optimum harvest period December-April. Bremia resistance. (RSlu)
John

Imperial Winter
A hardy outdoor variety for autumn sowing and cutting in thespring. (OGC)
Bakk EWK John OGC SbS Wall

Ithaca
A crisp variety, slow bolting, resistant against mildew and tipburn. (Mole)
Mole SbS Toze

Jaguar
Large headed, very uniform and well shaped variety. Particularly suited to early sowings, poorer soils and cooler regions. (Brwn)
Brwn

Jasmin
Quick-growing crisphead lettuce with compact head. Very suitable for early outdoor cultivation, so it can be sown in the open in early March. Jasmine is resistant to mildew. This variety keeps well in the fridge. (Bakk)
Bakk

Kagraner Sommer
see Standwell

Kelvin
John Mole RSlu SbS Wall

King Crown
Superb thick, dark green leaves and large solid heads. Suitable for spring, late summer and autumn sowing and does well in all soils. (EWK)
EWK SbS

Kloek
A butterhead type for overwintering. Sow Oct/Nov for harvestin Mar/Apr. (OGC)
EWK OGC SbS Wall

Krizet
RZ

Kwiek
A butterhead variety for cutting in Nov/Dec. Sow in late August. (OGC)
Bloo EWK John OGC SbS Suff Sutt Wall

Kylie
S&G

Lake Nyah
A very uniform bright green crisp lettuce of good quality, especially recommended for July and August cutting when well developed medium-sized hearts will be produced. Stands well and is a fine variety of the Iceberg type. (Sutt)
SbS

Lakeland
The best iceberg lettuce for spring, summer or autumn. It comes into cut earlier than most and is ideal for spring croppingin frames as well as outdoor. It is resistant to mildew and lettuce root aphid. (Mars)
Brwn Dob Foth Mars Milt Toze Unwi VanH

Leopard
A top quality lettuce which is compact and fast maturing. Resistant to bolting, with very good standing ability. (Brwn)
Brwn

Lilian
Firm, well-wrapped heads of bright green with generous hearts of crisp-sweet taste. Ideal for successional sowings either in the open or under cloches. (Dob)
Dob Toze

Lollo Rosso Loros
Howe

Maikonig
see May King

Malika
Outdoor crisp lettuce valued for its earliness, unlike some other early varieties, "coning" in Malika is virtually unknown. Performs very well from early production under polythene as well as from unprotected crops. LMV tolerant. (Bree)
John S&G SbS

Marmer
Very firm, crisp, heavy heads. Sow Aug/Sep, harvest January. Sow Nov/Jan, harvest April on. Grows best in cool conditions. (T&M)
SbS

Massa
SbS

May King
An autumn planting lettuce, it can be equally successful when planted in the spring or summer. Mid-green, slightly tinged with red, early and hardy, it is first class for frame, cold greenhouse or outdoor growing. (OGC)
Bakk Dob EWK JWB OGC SbS

May Queen
see May King

Meraviglia delle Quattro Stagioni
see Merveille des Quatre Saisons

Merveille d'Hiver
see Imperial Winter

Merveille des Quatre Saisons
John Mole OGC SbS SMM Suff Toze Wall

Milva
EWK

Minetto
SbS

Minigreen
T&M VanH

Mirian
S&G

Musette
An excellent mid-green variety for summer and autumn, Musette is uniform with a large head. It shows resistance to downy mildew and mosaic virus. (OGC)
John Mole OGC SbS Sutt Tuck

Nancy
Mole SbS

Neckarriesen
Produces tender, large, bright green heads. A top quality lettuce with an excellent flavour, suitable for spring and summer cultivation. The seed is virus-free, so it will give an extremely high yield. (Bakk)
Bakk

New Market
see Unrivalled

New York
see Webbs Wonderful

Novita
Curly lettuce with a very well-filled head. Crispy texture and special flavour. Easier to grow than other varieties because of its resistance to tipburn. For sowing from September to mid-February. (Mars)
  Mars

Ovation
  VanH

Oxford
  John

Panama
  S&G

Pandorian
  S&G

Pansoma
  S&G

Pantra
  S&G

Parella
One of the hardiest winter lettuces grown in the mountainousregion of Northern Italy. Survived -15 degrees C in a cold winter. Broadcast autumn or spring and thin to 4-6 in. apart. Very tiny neat lettuce forming small heart or rosette. Cut and come again or harvest whole plant. (Suff)
  Suff

Parella Red
A decorative red version of the compact and hardy Parella Green. When left to bolt it makes a most decorative plant good enough for the flower garden. (Suff)
  Suff

Paulette
  John

Pedro
  Yate

Pennlake
Crinkly leaved, maturing just after Avoncrisp. A first class market variety. (Brwn)
  John Mole SbS

Plena
see Hilde II

Plevanos
  SbS

Polana
  Yate

Poulton Market
see Hilde II

Prillice
  RSlu

Prior
  John

Rachel
A semi-thick leaved variety with fresh green leaves, the heart is open and well filled, with a strong flat base. Sow August-December to cut throughout the winter. (Brwn)
Howe John Milt Mole Yate

Rebecca
John Mole Wall

Red Fire
Highly frilled dard red leaves. Heads have good uniformity and excellent flavour. Cropping from summer to autumn. Slow to bolt. (EWK)
EWK SbS T&M

Red Valeria
The most intense red with a uniform mound of fine serrated loose leaves. The centre can become slightly green/blonde. Looks so attractive and tastes quite exceptional. (Foth)
Foth

Regina dei Ghiacci
Crisphead lettuce for summer use; slow to run to seed. Sow March to July, thinning to 8-10 ins apart. Attractive foliage. (Suff)
Suff

Resi
Howe

Reskia
The variety for all season cropping from spring to autumn. Butterhead type with firm, large mid-green heads. (EWK)
EWK John JWB Mole SbS Wall

Ricardo
Short day cultivar for unheated or heated greenhouse. Thick leaved butterhead setting new standards for this type of lettuce. (Tuck)
EWK John SbS

Rolex
Howe

Rosana
John Mole Toze

Rossa Fruilana
Forms an attractive frilly leaved red tinged heart. Most decorative in summer salads. Like many lettuce varieties it will resprout from its base if cut young. (Suff)
Suff

Rossimo
This is between a crisp and a butterhead variety, lightly savoyed with curled margins, round to flat crisp leaves. Perfect for modern salad bowls. (Foth)
Foth

Rouge Grenobloise
Crisp, heavy lettuce with a very pleasant flavour. Hardly ornot at all bolting and, therefore, very suitable for sowing in summer. (Bakk)
Bakk

Rougette du Midi
A most attractive small reddish leaved lettuce. Sow in autumn for winter and spring lettuce. Very crisp and tasty. (Suff)
Suff

5th Edition

Roxette
RZ

Ruth
This variety has a glossy dark green leaf with slightly upright growth and good heart filling with clean flat base. Bremia NL 1-15 resistant. Sow August-December to cut throughout the winter. (Brwn)
John

Sabrina
An excellent addition to your choice of lettuce for the winter months. Inspire your salad bowl with the mouth watering, fresh green leaves and crisp heart. It grows fast, autumn to spring, in a slightly heated or unheated greenhouse. Good diseaseresistance. (Foth)
Foth Mole Toze

Saladin
An excellent crisphead variety, producing solid iceberg typeheads, light green in colour. Slow to bolt in hot weather and useful throughout the spring and summer. (OGC)
Bakk Brwn Chil Dob EWK Foth Howe John JWB Milt

Saladin Supreme
SbS

Salina
Mid green butterhead variety for summer production or protected cropping under polythene/glass. (CGar)
Mole SbS

Samba
EWK

Sano
Yate

Sesam
RZ

Sigmaball
Large, round, mid-green hearts of slightly crisp texture andfine flavour. Stands in condition over a long period, and is resistant to tipburn and root aphid. Sow outdoors April-June in succession. (Sutt)
Sutt

Sitonia
For harvesting late spring, summer and autumn. Excellent resistance to tipburn and bolting. Resistant to Bremia. (Brwn)
Mole SbS

Soraya
Top quality lettuce! Large, bright green heads. For many home gardeners the top lettuce from spring until autumn. A sure cropper and resistant to many diseases. We warmly recommend thisvariety! (Bakk)
Bakk John RZ

Standwell
Bakk

Supermarket
see Hilde II

The Fruit and Veg Finder

Suzan
Soft butterhead type with good compact heads. Quick maturity for early summer use. (EWK)
Brwn EWK John JWB Mole SbS Sutt Wall

Tanja
John

Tannex
Howe

Target
Sutt Yate

Tiger
Distinctive in the garden and on the plate. The deep red outer leaves surround pale green tender hearts, which are extremely heavy. Their flavour was better than all other icebergs. (Mars)
Mars

Timo
Howe

Titania
Howe John Mole Toze Wall Yate

Tom Thumb
An early dwarf variety which deserves greater popularity. It hearts quickly and is compact and long standing, thus cutting down on wastage. (OGC)
Bloo Brwn Cart Chil Dob EWK Foth John JWB Mars

Trocadero Improved
see Unrivalled

Unrivalled
Medium-sized hearts. Sow outdoors in spring and summer. Also excellent for January-February sowing under glass for transplanting outdoors. (Sutt)
Chil EWK John JWB Mole OGC SbS Suff Sutt Wall

Vicky
John Mole Toze

Warpath
Bred in England. A cross between a cos and an Iceberg with eating qualities from both and the crunchy leaves form a small heart. Faster to mature than an Iceberg it can be sown at up to twice the density. It has good bolt resistance. (Foth)
Milt Sutt

Webbs Wonderful
One of the most popular of all lettuces, crisp, solid, large, long standing and of excellent quality. (OGC)
Bloo Cart Chil Dob EWK Foth John JWB Mars Mole OGC

Windermere
An outstanding quality crisphead. Medium sized heads, very uniform growth. (OGC)
SbS Sutt

Winter Crop
see Imperial Winter

Winter Marvel
see Imperial Winter

Lettuce Leaf

Americana Bruna
Bakk

Biscia Rossa
A very pretty lettuce with red tinged leaves from Italy. Maybe used for cut and come again or allowed to grow on. (Suff)
Suff

Canasta
John S&G

Catalogna
(Radichetta) Something quite new from Italy. A cut and come again lettuce for all seasons. Leaves are elongated and deeply lobed, light green with tender crunchy ribs. Very fast regrowing. (Suff)
Suff

Cocarde
A large red oakleaf of the arrowhead type from France. Heads are trumpet shaped and leaves dark green with a red overlay. Superb salad quality. Slow bolting. 49 Days. (Suff)
Suff

Doree de Printemps
see Bataser

Everest
John

Grand Rapids
SbS

Lollo Bianda Casablanca
RSlu

Lollo Bionda
The fresh green cousin of Lollo Rossa. (Mars)
Dob EWK Mars Mole S&G SbS Toze Wall Yate

Lollo Bionda Lobi
Bakk Howe

Lollo Green
OGC Suff

Lollo Mixed
A delightful and attractive mixture of the popular Italian Lollo type lettuce, including the bright green Lollo Verde, with Rossa for extra colour in salads and garnishes. (Unwi)
Unwi

Lollo Red
see Lollo Rosso

Lollo Rossa
A deliciously crips lettuce with frilly leaves tinged with red. Decorative enough to include in the flower garden! (OGC)
Bakk Bloo Brwn Cart Chil Dob EWK Foth John JWB

Lollo Rossa Astina
John RSlu

Lollo Rossa Lovina
Yate

Lumina
Lumina produces loose, open-leaved plants that allow you to either cut the whole plant for use in one go, or to pick the outer leaves and return for more as you need them. The rich red and green leaves protect the paler green, crispy heart. (Unwi)
Unwi

Pablo
Provides a real lift to salads. The medium heads have thick, smooth leaves with true iceberg crispness, flavour and an attractive outer red sheen. (Foth)
John RSlu

Raisa
Two for the price of one. The young plants provide deep red oak leaves for garnish; more mature plants have a densly filled centre, tender and juicy, for the salad bowl. Each sowing will give you a supply for weeks. (Mars)
Mars RZ

Red Sails
Distinct All-American Selection winner. Highly recommended and nutritional, it is a loose leaf type and, with a greater leafarea exposed to the sun, has six times the vitamin A than of other crisp head varieties. The bronzy-red leaves greatly enhancea salad. (John)
Bakk John

Red Salad Bowl
A pretty form of Salad Bowl Green. Ideal for small gardens, will last throughout the summer if picked regularly. (Suff)
Bakk Bloo Brwn Dob EWK John JWB Milt Mole OGC SbS

Red Salad Bowl Kamino
Similar plant type to Salad Bowl, with indented oak leaf butwith strong red coloration. Suitable for outdoor cropping in spring, summer and autumn. (Bree)
S&G

Red Salad Bowl Rebosa
RSlu

Red Salad Bowl Selma
Yate

Riccia a folglia di Quercia
Oak leaved lettuce for cutting. Use for cut and come again crop. Sow broadcast from spring to autumn. Cut young leaves when about 2 in. high, leaving plant to resprout. (Suff)
Suff

Rosa Pablo
Provides a real 'lift' to salads. Medium heads have thick, smooth leaves with true iceberg crispness, flavour, and an attractive outer red sheen. (Foth)
Foth

Rusty
Toze

Salad Bowl
A very useful lettuce quite different from other varieties, as it has no heart, and a few leaves can be taken without uprooting the whole plant. (OGC)
   Bakk Bloo Brwn Cart Dob EWK John JWB Mars OGC SbS

Salad Bowl Mixed
Both the colours of oak-leaf lettuce together, with this crisp and tender non-hearting variety. Leaves can be picked a few at a time. Hardly ever bolts. (Foth)
   Foth Unwi

Salvo
   Yate

Sigla
A very attractive frilled leaf type with intense deep red colour. Low nitrate content. For spring, summer and early autumn cropping, also highly recommended for glasshouse crops. (Brwn)
   Mole

Soprane
   Yate

Valeria
This versatile variety, is a counterpart of Lollo Rossa and Lollo Bionda, producing intensive red leaf colour when grown during the winter months in a frost-free greenhouse or frame. Also superb when grown outdoors during spring and summer. (Dob)
   Dob

Lettuce Stem

Celtuce
Halfway between celery and lettuce, the stems and leaves are excellent alternatives and very tasty. (Foth). Celtuce is not a cross, but a type of lettuce grown primarily for its swollen stem.
   Bloo Chil EWK JWB OGC SbS SMM T&M Wall

Woh Sun
Grown for centuries in China. The leaves are used as lettuce, or in stir-fry and the stem for Shanghai pickles. Try the heart of the stem in salads. Has a faint lettuce flavour and an unusually juicy and crisp texture. (Suff)
   Suff

Lettuce Thai

Thai Lettuce
   OGC Suff

Loquat

Erybotryus japonica
   SDea CSim

Mangel

Prizewinner
Large golden orange roots which are ideal for wine making. Can also be used for feeding to goats. Very easy to grow. (EWK)
   EWK OGC Suff Wall

Wintergold
Yellow tankard. Produces a very large yield of wet and dry matter per acre. Fed to cattle, sheep, and pigs. (MAS)
  MAS SbS

Marrow

F1 Acceste
  RSlu

All Green Bush
Popular and reliable. A heavy cropper if kept picked. Do not allow the fruit to grow beyond 6 in. (D&D)
  Bloo Chil EWK John JWB Mole OGC SbS SMM VanH Wall

F1 Altea
  S&G

F1 Ambassador
  Bakk Brwn Dob Foth Howe John Mars Milt Mole OGC

F1 Arlesa
  S&G

F1 Badger Cross
  Mars Toze

F1 Bambino
  Toze

Bianco Friulano
Rated top class. Produces a good crop of crook necked squash which are pale yellow in colour with a warty appearance. Delicious flavour and firm texture. Cook the same as zucchini. (Suff)
  OGC Suff

F1 Botna
  Chil

Brimmer
Rated the best open pollinated variety in National Trials. Pick regularly for lots of high quality, succulent and tasty courgettes. An off shoot of hybrid breeding, the colour may vary a little from fruit to fruit. (T&M)
  John SbS

Burpee Golden Zucchini
  RZ SbS Sutt

Bush Green
A popular variety for the small garden. (JWB)
  JWB

Clarella
A new type of courgette with a remarkable delicate and distinctive flavour. Really delicious. A courgette with a pale green skin and sometimes a slightly flask shaped. A very productive bush variety. Pick the fruits young or leave to grow to small marrow size. (Suff)
  OGC Suff

F1 Clarita
  Unwi

Cobham Green Bush
Medium length fruits, medium green in colour with cream yellow stripe. Produces very attractive tasty marrows, quite unlike an overgrown courgette. (Bree)
   SbS Toze

F1 Cobra
   SbS

F1 Cora
   Yate

Custard White
An attractive bush variety with round and flattened white fruits about 7 in. in diameter, which have scalloped edges. (Dob)
   EWK John JWB Mole OGC SbS Suff Tuck Wall

Custard Yellow
   SbS

De Nice a fruit rond
This original and round courgette is used extensively in Mediterranean cuisine. The tasty light grey-green fruits can be picked from golf-ball size up to a cricket-ball. The fruits can be eaten raw, stuffed or boiled. The flowers can also be lightlybattered and frie, or added as interest to salads. Courgettes like a sunny sheltered position and a rich soil. Sow outdoors inlate May-early June or, for an earlier crop, indoors during March/April. Harvest regularly from July to October to encouragea continuous crop. (Foth)
   Foth T&M

F1 Defender
   OGC Sutt T&M Toze

F1 Diamond
   Bakk Mole SbS

Early Gem
   see Storr's Green

F1 Elite
   EWK John SbS Toze

Emerald Cross
   see Greyzini

F1 Excalibur
   Yate

F1 Gold Rush
   Bakk Bloo Brwn Chil Dob Foth Howe John JWB Mars

Golden Zucchini
   see Burpee Golden

Green Bush
   see Long Green Bush

Green Bush F1 Hybrid
   see Storr's Green

Green Bush Improved
Very early-maturing plants producing small, dark green, tender fruits in abundance. (Sutt)
   Sutt

Green Gem
   SbS

Green Trailing
see Long Green Trailing

F1 Greyzini
EWK Mole RSlu SbS Toze Wall Yate

F1 Jackpot
SbS

F1 Jemmer
EWK

F1 Jemmy
OGC

F1 Leprachaun
Toze

Long Green Bush
Probably the most popular - the compact, bushy habit is ideal for the smaller garden. (Foth)
Chil EWK Foth Howe John Milt OGC S&G SbS T&M Tuck

Long Green Bush 2
Dark green marrows with prominent cream stripes. (Mars)
Cart Dob Unwi

Long Green Bush 3 Smallpak
Similar to Green Bush improved, but fruits are shorter. Excellent for exhibition. (Sutt)
Sutt

Long Green Bush 4
Fruit rather smaller than the trailing type, dark green with lighter stripes. (Brwn)
Brwn Mars SbS

Long Green Bush Special
SbS

Long Green Striped
see Long Green Trailing

Long Green Trailing
Large fruits of dark green with paler stripes and a most delicious flesh. Stores well. (Foth)
Bloo Dob EWK Howe John JWB Mars Mole OGC SbS Suff

Long White Bush
Well-known variety, light green in colour and very tasty. If you do not let the fruit grow too large, you can harvest over a longer period. (Bakk)
Bakk Dob SbS

Long White Trailing
A very prolific variety with large white fruits. (Dob)
Dob SbS

Marco
see Ambassador

F1 Market King
SbS

Minipak
Green striped marrows grow to about 12 in. A very productive bush variety. Firm fruits of excellent quality. (Suff)
Chil EWK OGC SbS SMM Suff Wall

F1 Moreno
Foth John Mars SbS Yate

F1 Onyx
SbS

F1 Patriot
Toze Tuck

Prepak
SbS

F1 President
Howe John Mole SbS Yate

F1 Raven
Foth S&G

F1 Rebecca
S&G SbS

F1 Saracen
Brwn Toze

F1 Sardane
T&M

Spaghetti Pyjamas
A novel marrow with a green striped skin. The flesh, when cooked, looks like spaghetti but tastes like marrow. (Brwn)
Brwn

F1 Storr's Green
Cart Dob EWK Howe John JWB Mars Mole OGC RZ SbS

Superlative
see Blenheim Orange

F1 Supremo
Bakk Dob S&G T&M Wall

Table Dainty
Medium-sized fruits striped pale and dark green. Early maturing, and excellent for exhibition. (Sutt)
John SbS Sutt

F1 Tarmino
Unwi

Tender and True
Round, mottled green fruits from early maturing plants. Ideal for small gardens. (Sutt)
Sutt

F1 Tiger Cross
Foth Milt Mole OGC SbS Sutt T&M Toze Tuck Wall

Tondo di Nizza
Round courgette. Very productive, the fruit may be cut from 2-4 in. Ideal for stuffing. (Suff)
OGC Suff

Tromboncino
Unlike any zucchini you have ever seen. Fruits grow long and curved with a bell at the flower end. Harvest fruits at around 30 cm. long. Fruits will grow to a spectacular metre long and they are still good to eat. Plants are very vigorous climbers or can trail on the ground. (Suff)
OGC Suff

Vegetable Spaghetti
Trailing type which produces oval yellow/white fruit which can be stored in a frost-proof shed. The flesh is stringy, hence the name. (D&D)
Chil Dob EWK Foth John JWB OGC SbS SMM Suff T&M

F1 Zebra Cross
Bloo Brwn Mole SbS Toze Yate

F1 Zucchini
Brwn EWK Foth Suff Sutt Toze VanH

F1 Zucchini Blondy
T&M

Zucchini Dark Green
SbS

Zucchini F1
see Storr's Green

Zucchini True French
Deep green courgette. Constant cutting will ensure a heavy crop. Cook unpeeled, as they have tender skins, and allow to sizzle in butter. (T&M)
T&M

Mashua

Mashua
A close relative of the naturtium, mashua is cultivated in the Andes for its edible tubers. A climbing perennial up to 2 m. if given support, it will also grow across the ground, forming a dense mass of weed supressing foliage. Attractive orange-red trumpet shaped flowers are borne in the summer and autumn until a hard frost kills the plant. The tubers are about the size of small potatoes and have a yellow skin with numerous purple flecks. Eaten raw, they have a hot, mustardy flavour. This is lost on cooking and a strange, vanilla-like taste takes its place; definitely an acquirted taste. They can be boiled, baked or roasted. Tuberisation occurs as the days become shorter and in areas that have early frosts there may be insufficient time for tubers to develop properly. The plants are known to have nematocidal, bacteriocidal and insecticidal properties and in the Andes they are often intercropped with other tubers such as ocas and potatoes. (Futu)
Futu Poyn

Medlar

Breda Giant
GTwe Bowe

Dutch
SDea SKee CSco Bowe

Large Russian
SKee GTwe ERea

Monstrous
SDea GTwe

Nottingham
Small fruited but highly flavoured. The most popular variety. A good cropper. (Brog)
SDea SFam WHig WJas SKee CTho CSco GTwe ERea SFru LBuc Bowe

Royal
SFru

Un-named selection
Rog Muir CSim

Melon

F1 Amber Nectar
Bloo T&M

F1 Ananas
Bakk

Blenheim Orange
Good size fruits with scarlet flesh and lovely flavour. (OGC)
EWK JWB OGC SbS Sutt Wall

Charentais
Juicy, orange flesh from this canteloupe-type. Can be grown in the greenhouse, or under cloches or frames. (Foth)
Foth SbS Toze

Early Dawn
Hybrid musk melon with good yield and firm good flavoured orange flesh. (Toze)
Toze

F1 Early Sweet
Sutt

Emerald Gem
Rich green flesh of unusual thickness and excellent flavour. (Sutt)
Sutt

F1 Experimental TM/M01
T&M

F1 Fiesta
SbS

F1 Galia
Bakk Bloo SbS T&M Yate

F1 Geabel
Chil

Hero of Lockinge
Richly flavoured white flesh. For heated or cold greenhouse. (Sutt)
SbS

F1 Melina
RZ

Minnesota Midget
Takes up just 3 ft. of space. Each mini-vine grows many orange fleshed, tender to the rind, 4 in. melons with an exceptionally high sugar content and superb flavour. (T&M)
Bloo T&M

No Name

Juicy and aromatic amber-yellow flesh, full of superb flavour. Attractive green and yellow marbled skin. One of the best melons for cropping outdoors. Grow in either the cold greenhouse, frame or under cloches. (Unwi)
   Unwi

Ogen

Rather small, striped green fruits, 4-6 in. across, producedvery freely. Sweet, green flesh. (Mars)
   Bloo Brwn Dob EWK Howe John JWB Mars Milt Mole SbS

F1 Overgen Panogen
   S&G

F1 Romeo
   Mars

F1 Sweetheart
   Brwn Cart Dob EWK Foth Howe John JWB Mars Milt

Westlandia Sugar
see Honey Dew

Witte Suiker
see Honey Dew

Mesclun

Mixed Salad Leaf

The "green salad" of southern France. Traditionally it contains a minimum of 7 different leaves to which herbs and edible petals are added. (Foth)
   Foth

Mibuna Greens

Green Spray

Closely related to Mizuna greens, and is also a highly decorative plant, forming a dense clump of long narrow, deep green leaves. One oc the latest escapees from behind the bamboo curtain, Joy Larkcom uses it in winter salads and stir fries, and says that most people like the taste very much. Green Spray has a pleasant mild flavour, and is very versatile in use. Reasonably hardy.
   Suff

Miner's Lettuce

Miner's Lettuce

An excellent winter salad crop rich in vitamin C. Available from November to March from August sowing outdoors or in a cold greenhouse. Take a few leaves at a time on a "cut-and-come-again"basis. (OGC)
   Chil OGC Poyn SbS Suff Sutt

Mitsuba

Mitsuba

Like a cross between parsley and celery with a unique flavour for salads and soups. It can be blanched like celery. (OGC)
   Chil EWK Milt OGC Poyn SbS Suff Tuck

Mizuna Greens

Mizuna
Quick growing with dark green narrow leaves. Ready in 35 days from summer sowing and 60 days from winter sowing under cover. (D&D)
Chil EWK Futu OGC SbS SMM Suff Tuck Yate

Youzen
Decorative plant with glossy, dark green, deeply serrated leaves. Very versatile, and can be used at any stage from seedlings to maturity to flowering shoots. Mild flavoured, very hardy, and ornamental enough to grow in a flower bed. (Dob)
Dob

Mulberry

Illinois Everbearing
CSim

Large Black Mulberry (Morus nigra)
The only variety grown in this country for its fruit. Self-fertile. August-September. Large, raspberry-like fruits. Very slow to come into cropping. (Brog)
Cast SDea WHig SKee Rog CSco GTwe Muir LBuc Bowe

Morus alba 'Pendula'
GTwe ERea

Morus nigra 'Chelsea'
ERea

Multicaulis
ERea

Wellington
CSim

White mulberry (Morus alba)
SDea ERea LBuc Bowe

Mustard

Brown
Annual approx 85 days. (Suff)
Suff

Burgonde
Standard variety for producing French mustard and for hot brown and stoneground mustard. Small brown seed. May also be used as a green manure. (Suff)
Suff

Fine White
Grow as mustard and cress inside. If grown outside it makes an excellent cut and come again crop. (Suff)
Mars SbS Suff Unwi Wall

Giant Red
Yate

Kingston
EWK

Mustard
Fine strain and traditional companion to cress. To crop together, sow mustard four days later. (Foth)
Brwn Foth

Tilney
High grade quality shoots for salad use. (EWK)
Yate

White
The best variety to grow indoors for salads. Should be grown in the same way as cress. (Dob)
Cart Chil Dob John Sutt

Mustard Greens

Amsoi
Green Indian Mustard. Delicious tender green with a mustard tang for stir fry or salad use. Best sown from June to September for autumn crop. Sow September under cover for spring crop. In most winters should survive outside in seedling stage for early spring cuttings. (Suff)
Suff

Gai Choy
Many suppliers call this Green in Snow, but strictly Green in Snow is one group of Mustard Greens, and Gai Choy is just another name for Mustard Greens. We need more information if we are to make use of these excellent vegetables.
Bloo EWK Foth Futu John OGC SbS Suff Sutt Tuck

Kaai Tsoi
Just another spelling of Gai Choy.
Suff

Red Mustard
The large attractive reddish-green leaves and the stems may be eaten, the leaves being somewhat spicier. Inner leaves have a milder flavour. In addition to use in stir-frying, the leaves may also be steamed or used for pickling. Immature plants may be used in salads. (Dob)
Dob

Nectarine

Crimson Gold
SDea

Early Gem
SDea

Early Rivers
(1893) July. Large fruited. Greenish yellow, almost covered with brilliant scarlet flush and darker stripes. White to pale yellow flesh. Very tender and juicy with a rich flavour. (Brog)
Allg Cast Rog Muir ERea

Elruge
August. Medium sized fruits. Pale greenish white with a dark purplish red flush. White to pale yellow flesh. Melting flesh with a pleasant perfumed flavour. (Brog)
Allg SFam GTwe ERea SFru Bowe

Fantasia
SDea

Fire Gold
SDea

Humboldt
Cast GTwe SFru Bowe

John Rivers
Mid July. Medium to large fruits. Excellent flavour. (Brog)
Cast SFam GTwe ERea SFru Bowe

Kestrel
GTwe

Lord Napier
(1869) August. Large fruited. Pale yellow with a deep crimson brown flush covering most of the skin. White to pale yellow flesh. A delicious, rich flavour. (Brog)
Allg Cast SDea SFam WHig SKee CSco GTwe Muir ERea SFru LBuc

Nectared
SKee Bowe

Nectarella
WHig GTwe ERea Bowe

Pineapple
(1870) Early September. Fairly large fruits. Skin almost entirely covered with a rich crimson red flush on a yellow-green ground colour. Golden yellow flesh. Very melting with a deliciousflavour. (Brog)
Allg Cast SDea SFam WHig SKee CSco GTwe ERea SFru Bowe

Ruby Gold
SDea

Nuts Almond

Ingrid
CSim

Macrocarpa
CSim

Prunus dulcis
SDea SFam Muir Bowe

Nuts Cobnut & Filbert

Butler
SDea SKee ERea

Common Hazelnut
Cast Rog CSco ERea

Corylus avellana
SDea CSco

Corylus avellana 'Contorta'
The Corkscrew Hazel, also known as Harry Lauder's Walking Stick.
SDea CSco GTwe

Corylus x colurnoides (Trazel)
CSim

Cosford
(1816) A fairly vigorous, upright tree. Thin shell. Sweet with a good flavour. A fair cropper. (Brog)
Cast SDea WHig SKee Rog CSco GTwe Muir ERea LBuc CSim Bowe

Ennis
SDea SKee ERea

5th Edition

Fertile de Coutard
SKee ERea

Frizzled Filbert
ERea

Geant de Halle
Bowe

Gunslebert
SDea SKee ERea

Hall's Giant
SDea SKee GTwe ERea

Kentish Cob (Longue D'Espagne)
(1830) Very large fruits. A compact tree of medium vigour. Good flavour. A very popular variety. (Brog)
Cast SDea SFam WHig SKee Rog CSco GTwe Muir ERea LBuc CSim

Maxima
SDea GTwe

Pearson's Prolific (Nottingham Cob)
Medium sized fruits. Fairly thick shell. A spreading, vigorous tree. Good flavour. (Brog)
SDea CSco GTwe ERea LBuc CSim Bowe

Purple Leaved Filberrt
CSco LBuc Bowe

Red Filbert
Cast Rog ERea Bowe

Red Leaved Hazlenut
SKee

Tonne de Giffon
SKee

Webb's Prize
Large fruits. Resembles Kentish Cob in appearance. Good flavour. (Brog)
Cast SDea Rog ERea Bowe

White Filbert
Cast Rog CSco ERea

Nuts Sweet Chestnut

Castanea
SKee Rog

Castanea hybrid
CSim

Castanea sativa 'Bournette'
CSim

Marron de Lyon
CSim

Numbo
CSim

Un-named selection
SDea

Nuts Walnut

Juglans nigra (Black Walnut)
SDea SKee Rog GTwe CSim Bowe

Juglans regia (Common Walnut)
SDea SFam WHig SKee Rog CSco GTwe ERea LBuc CSim Bowe

White Walnut
CSim

Nuts Walnut Hybrid

Broadview
SDea SKee GTwe ERea Bowe

Buccaneer
SDea WHig GTwe Bowe

Franquette
SKee GTwe Bowe

Lara
SKee

Oca

Oca
From the Peruvian Andes this attractive yellow flowering herbaceous plant produces a tasty tuber that can be eaten fresh, boiled, stir-fried or used in stews. Grow like a potato. (Poyn)
Poyn

White Skinned
Futu

Okra

Clemson's Spineless
All America Winner. Probably the most popular variety, producing a heavy crop of high quality dark green lightly grooved spineless pods. Best picked when only 2-3 in. long. (T&M)
Bloo Chil EWK Foth John JWB Mole SbS SMM T&M Wall

Dwarf Green Longpod
SbS

Long Green
Grown for its ornamental seed pods, which provide a flavoursome addition to stews, sauces and soups. Sow in February/March and harvest when the pods are young and tender. For greenhouses or sheltered spots outside in warm areas. (Dob)
Dob Sutt

Okra
Milt

Pent Green
SbS

F1 Pure Luck
EWK Suff

Onion

A1
SbS

Agusta Rijnsburger
SbS

Ailsa Craig
An old, tried, tested and favourite variety, suitable for spring or autumn sowing, with large, globe-shaped, mild-flavouredbulbs with rich, straw-coloured skins. (Chil)
  Bakk Cart Chil Dob EWK Foth John JWB Mars MAS Milt

Ailsa Craig Crosslings Seedling
Giant onion used exclusively for exhibition work. Grows to an immense size weighing several pounds. To obtain best results start in greenhouse, or under glass, in January, plant out as soon as weather permits. Feed regularly and keep well watered. For exhibition onions sow by February 1. (VanH)
  SbS

Ailsa Craig Prizewinner
A good all round and well established variety which can holdits own on the show bench. Sow: Dec-Feb Harvest: Aug-onwards (Brwn)
  Brwn

F1 Albion
  Bakk Mars T&M VanH

Autumn Gold
Large, solid onions, half-round in shape. The attractive deep golden skins are really strong and the onions will keep until April or May from a September harvest. The crop is always huge and we have rarely known any bolters. (Mars)
  Mars

Autumn Queen
see Reliance

Balstora
Balstora produces a very heavy crop of beautiful globe-shaped onions with golden-brown skins. You should expect itto store at least until early May (Mars)
  Brwn Dob John Mars Mole SbS Toze Wall

F1 Barito
  RSlu

Barletta
Specially selected for pickling. Sow thickly in the rows in order to obtain beautiful, fine onions. One of the most popular silverskin onions. (Bakk)
  Bakk Mole SbS Suff

Beacon
  T&M

Bedfordshire Champion
Good-sized globe. Long keeper, improved strain. (Mars)
  Brwn Cart Chil Dob EWK Foth John JWB Mars MAS Milt

Best Of All
  SbS

F1 Brenda
  Howe

Brunswick
Flattish round, deep red onion with good keeping qualities. It has an excellent flavour and will give very high yields. (Bakk)
Bakk EWK Foth Milt Rog Sutt

Brunswick Red
see Brunswick

Brunswijker
see Brunswick

F1 Buffalo
Dob Foth Howe John JWB Mole SbS T&M Toze Tuck

F1 Caribo
John S&G T&M

F1 Centurion
Dob EWK Foth Rog Suff Unwi

Crosslings Seedling
see Ailsa Craig Crosslings Seedling

Daytona
VanH

F1 Dinaro
RSlu

F1 Django
Howe

Dobies' All Rounder
Round straw-coloured onions of fine flavour and of medium size—just right for the kitchen. Being quite thin necked, they
keep extremely well in winter storage, remaining in good condition until February and March. (Dob)
Dob

Downing Yellow Globe
SbS

Duraldo
Deep brown skinned, almost round shaped bulbs of fine eatingquality and exceptional keeping ability. (EWK)
EWK SbS

F1 Durco
S&G

Early Yellow Globe
SbS

Ebeneezer
SbS

F1 Express Harvest Yellow
EWK Mole OGC SbS Suff Wall

Express Yellow
see Express Harvest Yellow

Extra Early Kaizuka
Flattish bulb ripening to pale yellow. (Sutt)
John SbS

Giant Fen Globe
Produce a huge crop of perfectly shaped onions, often 50 lb or more from each bag planted. In our trials they give a higher yield than any other onion. They will usually keep until late May and have a fairly mild taste. (Mars)
Mars

Giant Rocca Brown
SbS

Giant Rocca Lemon
SbS

Giant Stuttgarter
see Stuttgart Giant

Giant Zittau
Produces excellent medium-sized pickles, pale brown in colour. Sow in March. (Mars)
EWK Mars OGC SbS Toze

Golden Ball
A most receptive onion set because it loves to be planted late. At this time the weather is warmer. Hence it avoids some of the pitfalls earlier sets face. It is a very rapid grower and planted 6 weeks later will be ready at approximately the same time as regular varieties and has comparable yield and long storage qualities. (T&M)
T&M

Golden Bear
see Norstar

F1 Goldito
RSlu

Gros
see White Lisbon

Guardsman
A cross between normal spring onion and a Japanese type, it will hold in good condition longer before the stems bulb and become stronger in flavour. You will be able to pull bunches of fine stems with deep green leaves and nice white bases over several weeks from one sowing. (Mars)
Dob Mars SbS Toze

F1 Hamlet
SbS

F1 Hi-keeper
Howe

Hikari Bunching
A modern type of spring or bunching onion, Hikari is a versatile performer. From a spring sowing, it can be harvested over a long period as it does not form bulbs. Begin pulling at pencil thickness and continue through to the size of a small carrot. Distinctive, delicious taste. (Dob)
Dob JWB Mole OGC RSlu SbS Suff Toze Tuck Wall Yate

F1 Hygro
Brwn Dob EWK John JWB Mars Milt Mole OGC SbS Toze

F1 Hyper
SbS

F1 Hyrate
SbS

F1 Hysam
John Mole SbS

F1 Hyton
John SbS VanH

Imai
see Imai Early Yellow

Imai Early Yellow
Semi-globe shape, maturing from late June. Yellow skin. (Mars)
Howe John Mars Mole SbS Yate

Imai Yellow
see Imai Early Yellow

Indared
Yate

Ishiko Straight Leaf
Yate

Ishikura
A new bunching onion: a cross between leek and coarse chives. Ishikura is a fast grower. It has beautiful, fairly long, white stems, and dark green leaves. An extremely prolific variety. (Bakk)
Bakk EWK Foth Howe John OGC SbS SMM Suff Sutt T&M

Ishikura Bunching
see Ishikura

Ishikuro
see Ishikura

Jagro
Mars

James Long Keeping
A good old variety with a very pleasant taste and first-class looks. The reddish brown, globe-shaped bulbs are excellent keepers. (Foth)
SbS Wall

Jumbo
It has a golden-brown skin, is a perfect ball shape, large, solid and very uniform. One of the heaviest croppers, with exceptionally good keeping qualities. (Unwi)
Dob SbS

F1 Keepwell
EWK John

Kelsae
see The Kelsae

Klabro
Sutt

Kujo Green
Chil

Kyoto Market
Although this is mild tasting, it makes a delicious additionto summer salads. Priming of the seed of this variety makes for far easier germination, especially from early sowings. Row length 20ft. (Dob)
Dob John S&G SbS

La Reine
see The Queen

Lancastrian
A giant globe shape variety ideal for exhibitions with sweet, crisp, white flesh and golden yellow skin. It is also excellent for cooking and storing. (Foth)
Dob Foth John T&M VanH

Laser
Yate

Long Red Florence
The traditional torpedo shaped red onion from Florence in Italy. Very reliable producing good sized bulbs with deep purple red colour. (Suff)
Suff

Long White Ishikura
see Ishikura

Long White Tokyo
A splendid plant with dark green leaves and the white succulent single stalks grow 16-19ins. long. Fairly resistant to both hot and cold weather, it is good for either a summer or winter crop. (Chil)
Chil

Malakoff
Toze

Mammoth
JWB Rob

Mammoth Improved
see Mammoth

Mammoth Red
Largest red onion in cultivation, has excellent keeping qualities with strong flavour. (CGar)
JWB Rob

F1 Maraton
Bakk Dob Howe John

F1 Markies
Howe John

F1 Maru
Howe

Monkston
Our new introduction which has been bred for exhibition use. Very large bulbs of superb shape and uniformity. (EWK)
EWK JWB SbS Wall

Monkston Exhibition
see Monkston

New Brown Pickling
Mole SbS

Nocera
SbS

Nordhollandse Bloedrode
see North Holland Blood Red

F1 Norstar
EWK OGC SbS Suff

North Holland Blood Red
Large red-skinned globe with crisp, pink flesh throughout. Stores very well. (Foth)
John

North Holland Blood Red Redmate
A novel red-skin that can be used as a spring or bulbing onion. The red colouration becomes more intense as the onions get larger though the flavour remains mild and the flesh crisp. Quick to mature. (Foth)
   Foth Sutt

North Holland Flat Yellow
   SbS

Oakey
see Reliance

Oporto
   SbS

Parade
   VanH

Paris
see Paris Silver Skin

Paris Silver Skin
Excellent "cocktail" pickler. Sow March to late June, lift when about marble size. (Mars)
   Brwn EWK Foth John JWB Mars Milt OGC SbS Sutt Tuck

Pompei
   SbS

Purplette
The first ever purple-red skinned mini onion. Decorative andvery tasty. The tiny bulbs turn a delicate pink when cooked or pickled. Can also be harvested very young as purple bunching onions. May also be left to harvest at normal size as mature
onions. (Suff)
   Mole OGC SbS SMM Suff

Radar
   Mars Mole SbS Wall

Red Baron
Early, prolific, flattish-round to round, deep red onion, suitable for eating fresh as well as for storing. Full-flavoured.Much in demand by the professional as well as by the amateur grower. (Bakk)
   Bakk Brwn Dob John JWB Mars OGC Rog T&M Tuck VanH

Red Brunswick
see Brunswick

Red Bunching Redbeard
A completely new bunching onion. Very decorative red stalks with colour extending in 2-4 layers. Extra decorative to use in salads. (Suff)
   OGC SbS Suff

Red Delicious
Red Delicious has a shiny deep red skin and crisp white flesh. Good crops of globe-shaped bulbs are produced with good keeping ability. (Dob)
   Dob

Red Italian
Chil SbS

Redmate
Yate

Reliance
A large, firm, flattish onion, it has a mild flavour and is a wonderful keeper. Recommended for spring sowing but can also beused for autumn sowings. (Unwi)
JWB OGC SbS Suff

Rijnsburger
A round onion with yellow skin and pure white flesh. Hard, long-keeping bulbs. (Sutt)
EWK John Wall

Rijnsburger 2 Sito
Very early with exceptionally high yields and storage ability for its type. In trials, it has even out-yielded early sets for August harvest. Globe-shaped bulbs with straw coloured skin of first class quality which will store until December. (Foth)
Foth

Rijnsburger 4
SbS Sutt

Rijnsburger Rocky
SbS Yate

Rinaldo
SbS

Robot
A very good onion for storing. Brownish-yellow colour. Extremely high-yielding variety. Robot can deservedly be called one of the best selections. (Bakk)
Bakk

Robusta
Very heavy cropper with outstanding globe shape, fine quality skin and extremely long keep ability. (EWK)
EWK John JWB Mole OGC SbS Toze

Rocardo
An excellent storing onion. Semi-globes with dark skins and a good flavour and texture. (Foth)
Sutt

F1 Romeo
Howe John

Rouge d'Italie
see Red Italian

F1 Royal Oak
Foth SbS Toze

SY300
A flavoursome, brown skinned pickling onion, with a uniform shape. (Brwn)
Brwn Dob Sutt Yate

Santa Claus
Forms long stalks which do not bulb. Will hold well in the grounds without going tough and from approximately 8 weeks will start to flush red from the base upwards. A good flavour. (Foth)
Foth T&M

F1 Saturn
RZ

Savel
Mars

Senshyu
see Senshyu Semi-Globe

Senshyu Semi-Globe
Like Imai Yellow, but maturing about 2 weeks later. Good sized solid bulbs. (Mars)
EWK Foth Howe John JWB Mars Milt Mole OGC SbS Sutt

Senshyu Yellow
see Senshyu Semi-Globe

Sentry
SbS Toze

F1 Shakespeare
Brwn Yate

F1 Sherpa
Brwn Howe Milt

Showmaster
Developed from a top exhibition strain of onion, this special variety will produce the largest onions from onion sets. (Mars)
Mars

F1 Sonic
John

Southport Red Globe
A blood-red onion which grows to a large size, very popular with exhibitors and a change for the cook. A good keeper whose ancestors were grown for 17th century sailors. (OGC)
EWK OGC SbS SMM Suff

Southport White Globe
SbS

Sturon
A considerable improvement of the Stuttgart: extremely prolific globe onion. An excellent variety. Very much recommended! (Bakk)
Bakk Brwn EWK Foth John Rog S&G Tuck Unwi

Stuttgart Giant
Flattish round onion which will keep for a fairly long time. However, the most important feature is that this variety can be harvested early. (Bakk)
Bakk EWK John Mars OGC Rog Tuck Unwi

Stuttgarter Riesen
see Stuttgart Giant

F1 Suntan
  SbS

F1 Super Bear
  EWK

F1 Sweet Sandwich
  T&M

  Tamrock
    Yate

  Tarzan
    SbS

  Terry
    Howe

The Kelsae
Without doubt one of the finest show onions, globe-shaped, makes lovely onion rings for frying. (JWB)
  JWB Wall

The Queen
True silver skin. Sow thickly and the resultant competition will prevent the bulbs from getting too large for pickling purposes. (Dob)
  Cart Dob

The Sutton Globe
  see Bedfordshire Champion

Toro
  Toze

Torpedo
Combining the flavour of a shallot with the sweetness of a Spanish onion is this most attractive-looking variety with smallish, red, torpedo-shaped bulbs. Thinly sliced, they add both savour and eye appeal to any salad. They can be sown in spring for a summer harvest or late summer for use the following year. (Chil)
  Chil

F1 Tough Ball
  Yate

F1 Toughball
  Howe

  Turbo
Exceptional onions which are vigorous, have high bolt resistance and store well. Very popular. (Foth)
    EWK OGC Rog S&G T&M Tuck

Unwin's Exhibition
Under average garden conditions, it will easily produce huge, top quality onions of about a pound in weight and, with a little bit of tender loving care, you will be able to go way beyond this figure. (Unwi)
  Unwi

White Knight
There are usually few salad onions in June, because the overwintered crop has ended and spring sowings are not ready. It is possible to raise a fine crop of White Knight in this period by sowing in Propapacks in early February, transplanting outdoors in early April. Can also be sown outdoors from March onwards. (Mars)
    Mars

White Lisbon
A very popular salad onion with a particularly fine flavour for using fresh in various dishes and in salads. Pull the small white onions and cut off the top ends, leaving approx 20-25 cm. of the hollow leaves. (Bakk)
    Bakk Brwn Brwn Cart Chil Dob EWK Foth Howe John

White Lisbon Winter Hardy
see Winter-over

White Portugal
    SbS

F1 White Spear
    Foth John SbS Yate

White Sweet Spanish
Grows to a good size and has a very mild flavour. (JWB)
    JWB SbS

Wigbo
    SbS

Winter Standing
see Winter-over

Winter White Bunching
Stiffer, stronger foliage than White Lisbon. Can be pulled in May from an August or September sowing. Slower to bulb than other over-wintering salad onions. (Mars)
    Mars SbS T&M Toze

Winter-over
Stands severe weather. Only suitable for autumn sowing. (Brwn)
    Dob EWK Foth Howe John Milt Mole OGC RSlu S&G SbS

Yellow Globe Danvers
    SbS

F1 Yellowstone (Topkeeper)
    Howe John

Zita
    Howe

Zittauer Gelbe
see Giant Zittau

Zur Robal
    S&G

Onion Other

Potato Onion
An onion that grows from offsets like shallots. Each bulb divides underground to form a clump of 6-8 mild flavoured onions that can be stored for several months. It is said to be very pest and disease resistant. (Futu)
    Futu

Red Welsh Onion
Use the green leaves like chives for flavouring, especially in the Winter. Has a milder flavour than the tree onion. (Poyn)
Poyn Suff

Tree Onion
An intriguing herb which bears clusters of small onions on the tips of its stems; delicious in salads or as pickles. The foliage may be cut throughout Winter. (Poyn)
Bloo Futu Poyn SMM

Welsh Onion
Perennial type, forming thickened and fleshy leaf bases instead of bulb. Useful for pulling as Spring Onions. Sow February-May where the plants are to grow. (Dob)
EWK Foth Futu Mars Poyn SbS SMM SMM

Orache

Green
The common variety with bright green leaves. (Futu)
Futu

Red
SbS

Pak Choi

F1 Autumn Poem
Chil

F1 Joi Choi
EWK John Mars OGC S&G SMM Suff Tuck Yate

F1 Kaneko Cross
Dob

F1 Mei Quing
Yate

Pak Choi
A novel Chinese vegetable of increasing popularity. Very versatile. The young central leaves may be used fresh in salads, the mature leaves have a mild flavour when cooked and the white leaf stalks are succulently tender. Tasty when boiled, steamed or stir-fried. Slow to bolt, should be sown in March-April and againin late summer. (Dob)
Chil Dob Milt SbS SMM Sutt

White Celery Mustard
A soup-spoon type, with thinner leaf stalks.
Chil EWK Foth OGC SbS SMM

Par-Cel

Par-Cel
Looks like parsley, tastes like celery. Instead of a parsleygarnish that is left on the side of the plate, Par-cel is the garnish with the real celery flavour that you can eat too. Fast becoming a basic salad ingredient it's plentiful, can be grown aseasily as radishes and gives a salad that wonderful warm celery flavour. (T&M)
Mars T&M

Parsley

Berliner
A tasty, fleshy vegetable. The highly aromatic, beautiful, smooth roots are very tender when cooked. Extraordinarily fine flavour. Roots can be stored. (Bakk)
  Bakk Unwi

Bravour
Really dark green finely curled leaves. Very hardy and stands for a long time. (EWK)
  Bakk Brwn EWK Howe John Mole SbS Toze Tuck Unwi

Calito
A vigorous and heavy yielding selection maintaining its colour well when overwintered in mild areas. Slightly looser curled than Bravour. (Yate)
  Yate

Champion
Parsley, as many gardeners know, can be difficult to germinate. Primed seed helps to overcome this. Champion is an improved selection from the popular Moss Curled variety. The plants produced are more attractively curled and fresher green incolour. Row length 25ft. (Dob)
  Dob

Champion Moss Curled
A highly selected strain, with curled intense green leaves. Stands much better than other varieties. (OGC)
  John Mole OGC SbS Toze Tuck VanH

Clivi
Dwarf, very neat and prolific. The only variety whose base leaves do not turn yellow and have to be wasted. (T&M)
  Howe Milt SbS T&M

Common
Has a stronger and more pungent flavour than the curled variety. Produces dark green sturdy plants with a great deal of bulk. Much used on the Continent. (OGC)
  Bakk EWK Mars Mole OGC Sutt T&M Unwi Wall

Consort
  SbS

Curled
Very sturdy in growth with good length stems and densely curled heads. (EWK)
  Poyn

Curlina
A very compact, short-stemmed variety with tightly curled leaves. (Mars)
  Cart Dob Foth Mars SbS Unwi

Darki
Really compact, dark green heads on long stems for easy cutting. Heavy yielding variety. (EWK)
  EWK Howe John SbS Yate

Envy
Dark green densely curled foliage. (Dob)
  Dob Sutt

Fakir
  VanH

Falco
RZ

French
Biennial, 18 in., rich soil. Stronger flavour than curled. (D&D)
Poyn SbS

Frison
Toze

Gigante di Napoli
see Italian Giant Leaved

Halblange
see Berliner

Hamburg Turnip Rooted
Grown mainly for its parsnip-like roots which, when lifted in the autumn, can be sliced or grated for added flavour on salads. (EWK)
EWK Foth Futu John JWB Mars OGC SbS SMM Suff Sutt

Hamburg Turnip Rooted Omega
An excellent dual purpose variety whose leaves can be used as ordinary parsley for garnishing or in soups or stew. White parsnip-shaped roots have a distinctive flavour and are deliciouswhen roasted. For sowing from March-May. Winter hardy. (Dob)
Dob

Italian Giant
Biennial, 2ft 6in in rich soil, vigorous. Strongest flavour. (D&D)
Poyn

Italian Plain Leaf
Yate

Korte
see Hamburg Turnip Rooted

Mooskrause
see Champion Moss Curled

Moss Curled
Very compact and has very finely curled leaves. Excellent for cutting, gives a distinctive flavour to soups, sauces and fish dishes. (Bakk)
Bakk EWK Foth JWB Wall

Moss Curled 2
Popular sort, dark green. Long standing. (Mars)
Brwn Cart Dob Mars Milt Sutt Toze

Moss Curled 2 Frisco
S&G

Moss Curled 2 Green Velvet
Beautiful, fully curled, piquantly flavoured variety with rich deep green appearance. (T&M)
T&M

Moss Curled 4 Afro
S&G T&M

Moss Curled Extra Triple Curled
EWK SbS SMM

Moss Curled Krausa
Widely used in Holland by the majority of housewifes. Moss Curled very uniform rich green leaves. Flavours many dishes in addition to its garnishing value. Outstanding Dutch herb. (VanH)
John

New Dark Green
SbS

Novas
Toze

Pagoda
VanH

Peerless
SbS

Plain
see Common

Plain Leaved
see Common

Regent
SbS

Robust
Toze

Sheeps
see Common

Spartacus
SbS

Thujade
Strong, curled, extremely dark green variety which, because of its dark colour, is preferred for use as a garnish. (Bakk)
Bakk

Triplex
RSlu

Verbo
Dark green colour with long stem. Highly productive with good standing. (Brwn)
Brwn John

Verdi
SbS

Parsnip

Alba
A refined prepacking variety of the same general shape as Cobham Improved Marrow but more slender, whiter and still less susceptible to canker. (Toze)
John SbS Toze

Arrow
Flavoursome, narrow shouldered parsnips with a smooth white skin. Suitable for harvesting as a mini or allowed to develop tofull size. Good tolerance to canker and powdery mildew. (Foth)
Foth

Avonresister
Small conical roots, resistant to canker. (Mars)
Brwn Cart EWK Foth Howe John
Mars MAS Milt Mole

Bayonet
Slender, length to 10 in. and modest 2.5 in. diameter shoulders. Very canker resistant. (Foth)
SbS Unwi

Bedford Monarch
SbS

Cambridge Improved Marrow
SbS

Cobham Improved Marrow
Selected for quality and resistance to canker, a very good medium-sized parsnip of tapering shape. The white roots are smooth-skinned and of fine flavour. (Dob)
Cart Dob Mars SbS Toze

Evesham
SbS

Exhibition Long
Extra long variety for the exhibitor, flavour and cooking quality is excellent. (Rob)
Dob JWB Rob Wall

F1 Gladiator
Brwn Foth John Milt OGC S&G Sutt T&M Toze

Harris Model
SbS

Hollow Crown
Large wide shouldered type with long tapering roots. (EWK)
Bakk Brwn Cart Chil EWK Foth John JWB Milt Mole

Hollow Crown Improved
An improved stock of this long-rooted type. (Dob)
Dob Unwi

Imperial Crown
Long, high quality roots of excellent flavour. Much smaller crown than usual in this type. (EWK)
EWK SbS Wall

Improved Marrow
Howe SbS Yate

F1 Javelin
Foth SbS Toze Tuck

Lancer
Mini-vegetable. A new Bayonet-type Parsnip, similar to those frequently seen in the larger supermarkets. Very smooth-skinned and its uniformly coloured flesh is superbly tasty. Very resistant to canker. (Dob)
Dob SbS Sutt Toze

Lisbonnais
A Soham Speciality. An excellent variety. (JWB)
Foth John JWB Mole SbS

New White Skin
A British bred variety with uniform wedge-shaped roots and a pure white skin which does not discolour after washing. Good canker resistance. (Sutt)
Dob SbS Sutt

Offenham
Half-long type with cream coloured flesh. Excellent quality and heavy cropper. (EWK)
   EWK JWB SbS Wall

Tender and True
Ideal for exhibition or kitchen. Long and smooth, very little core. (Mars)
   Brwn Dob EWK Foth John Mars MAS OGC SbS SMM Suff

The Student
Long slender roots of good size and flavour. (EWK)
   EWK OGC SbS SMM Wall

Viceroy
   SbS

White Diamond
   SbS

White Gem
Broad-shouldered smooth roots of good size with a fine whiteskin and considerable canker-tolerance. Excellent flavour. Very early and easy to lift. Superior to Offenham. (Mars)
   Brwn Howe John JWB Mars RSlu SbS Suff Sutt Tuck

White King
Very white flesh. Long tapering root. (D&D)
   EWK OGC SbS Wall

White Spear
An improvement in the White Gem type with greater uniformity. (Bree)
   John S&G SbS Toze

Yatesnip
   Yate

Pea

American Wonder
A sweet, early pea. This much-prized variety can be grown without wire netting or twiggy sticks on humus-rich soils. It produces a heavy crop of long pods with very tasty peas. Ht 45 cm. (Bakk)
   Bakk

Minnow
The first UK bred, true Petit Pois Pea. Produces massive crops of narrow stump pods containing approximately 8 small, mid-green tasty peas. Ht 2 ft. (Dob)
   Dob

Thomas Laxton
Early main crop, a good cropper with blunt-ended pods and sweet flavoured peas. Ht 3 ft. (OGC)
   SbS

Pea Round

Bountiful
A prolific, very early variety, highly valued by many, also by professional growers. This variety produces well-filled pods. Ht 140 cm. (Bakk)
   Bakk

Douce Provence
Sweeter than Feltham First and just as hardy. Ht 2 ft. (Mars)
   Foth John JWB Mars Mole SbS

Feltham Advance
SbS

Feltham First
An early, hardy variety with large, slightly curved painted pods. Ht 45 cm. (Bree)
Brwn Cart Dob EWK Foth Howe John JWB Mars Milt

Fortune
An early variety, slightly later than Feltham but a heavy cropper. 45 cm. (Brwn)
Brwn EWK John SbS

Meteor
Very dwarf habit, ht 14 in. (35 cm). Small well filled pods. First early. (EWK)
Bakk EWK Foth John JWB Mole OGC SbS Shar Suff Wall

Petit Provencal
see Meteor

Pilot
Very hardy variety for early spring or autumn sowing. Ht 36 in. (90 cm.). Long podded. First early. (EWK)
EWK John JWB OGC SbS

Premium
Tuck

Prince Albert
An early, vigorously growing variety. This selection can be sown early. It will produce a bumper crop of yellowish-green peas. Ht 1 m. (Bakk)
Bakk

Superb
SbS

Pea Sugar

Carouby de Maussane
Purple flowered mangetout type, with large flat pods up to 4.5in. long. Excellent flavour. (Brwn)
Brwn EWK Futu John OGC Shar Suff

De Grace
see Sugar Dwarf De Grace

Delikett
RSlu

Edula
It can be grown unsupported but we would advise short sticks or netting. The curved pods may be cooked whole when young; later the sweet, green peas can be shelled out. Height 90cms. (Unwi)
Unwi

Heraut
An early, heavy-cropping variety, very much in demand. It produces tender sugar peas, full of flavour. Should be trained upwards. Ht 140 cm. (Bakk)
RZ

Honey Pod
The earliest snap pea and indeed the sweetest. Producing smaller pods but many more of them than any other snap pea on a compact plant. They are also easier to harvest breaking cleanly without pulling the plant to pieces. (T&M)
  T&M

Nofila
An outstanding early Sugar Pea with broad fleshy pods. Nofila has been bred to produce heavy crops on dwarf growing plants, ideally suited to the lack of space in modern gardens. Harvest the young pods whole and serve raw in salads or lightly cooked in other dishes. Ht 15 in. (Dob)
  Dob

Norli
see Sugar Dwarf Sweet Green

Oregon Sugar Pod
Among the best of mange-tout with a particularly good flavour. Harvest while the pods are still flat and peas only just forming. (Foth)
  Brwn Cart EWK Foth Howe John JWB Mars S&G Shar

Pennine
  Shar

Reuzensuiker
Extra large, wide and fleshy pods, about 4 in. long, produced on compact plants which need little support. Begin harvesting the pods as soon as they are large enough to pull and finish when the seeds inside start to swell. Very sweet. Ht 3 ft. (Mars)
  John

Snowflake
More compact and later maturing variety than Oregon Sugar Pod with a similar medium long flat pod. (Bree)
  S&G

Sugar Ann
Very productive with big, fully edible pods on dwarf vines with juicy sweet flesh. Use fresh or cooked with or without the pods. (T&M)
  Foth John T&M Toze Tuck

Sugar Bon
An early maturing variety with medium length straw and medium-large pale green pods. Very easy to harvest. (Bree)
  Mars S&G Sutt

Sugar Dwarf De Grace
  Mole RSlu

Sugar Dwarf Sweet Green
Yields a fine crop of sweetly flavoured pods. White flowers. Ht 3 ft. (Dob)
  Bakk Brwn Chil Dob EWK Foth Howe John Milt Mole

Sugar Gem
Excellent quality, medium sized, sweet, crisp and succulent pods. Lightly cook, stir-fry or eat raw in salads or in the garden. They need good growing conditions and are not suited to wetter areas or seasons but otherwise, unlike other varieties, because of its mildew resistance, can be sown in succession through the summer to crop through the autumn. The first completely stringless and powdery mildew tolerant snap pea. (T&M)
S&G Sutt T&M

Sugar Rae
A late type to follow Sugar Lil with similar large dark green pods. (Bree)
Cart Dob EWK OGC

Sugar Snap
Very long season of use. The pods are thick and fleshy and can be eaten as well as the peas—served together or separately. When young, the pods are stringless. More mature pods can have the strings removed very easily. Very sweet. Ht 5 ft. (Mars)
Brwn Chil EWK Foth Howe John JWB Mars Milt OGC SbS

Sugar Tall White
Shar

Zuga
Mange tout, cooked whole when young. Ht 5 ft. (JWB)
John

Pea Wrinkled

Alderman
Tall growing variety which needs support. Very heavy crops of long, well filled pods. Late maincrop. (EWK)
Brwn Dob EWK John JWB Mars OGC SbS Shar Suff Unwi

Ambassador
OGC

Avola
A vigorous grower in almost all kinds of weather. The peas have a dark green colour. They have an excellent flavour and lendthemselves particularly well to deep-freezing. Ht 70 cm. (Bakk)
Toze

Banff
A very vigorous early variety suitable for picking fresh andfreezing. Three inch-long pods contain medium sized-peas of excellent flavour. Ht 2 ft. (OGC)
OGC

Bikini
The most widely grown semi-leafless type, with high yield and excellent processing quality, unique variety, semi-fasciated and highly concentrated pod set for maximum yield at freezing stage. (Bree)
John

Cavalier
A heavy cropping variety, producing masses of pods, mostly in pairs, each containing 10-11 sweet, small peas. Very good resistance to mildew making it ideal for June-July sowings, in addition to main season. Ht 60-75 cm. (2-2.5 ft). (Sutt)
    Brwn Mars Milt Sutt Toze

Chancelot
see Lord Chancellor

Cockpit
    S&G

Daisy
A short (2 ft) main crop producing a heavy yield of excellent quality peas, 8-10 peas per pod. (OGC)
    SbS

Darfon
Petit-pois. A new mid-late season variety producing a heavy pick of well filled pods giving an excellent yield of small dark-green peas. Its open habit helps to make picking easier. Ht 2-2.5 ft. (John)
    John

Daybreak
Exceptionally large, blunt pods hold approx. 8 sweet peas. A heavy yielder which can achieve a heigh of 2ft. A good recent introduction. (Foth)
    Foth S&G T&M

Early Onward
Heavy cropper, large blunt pods, ready 8-10 days ahead of Onward. Ht 60 cm. (Bree)
    Brwn Chil Dob EWK Howe John JWB Mars Mole OGC RSlu

Excellenz
    Yate

Gradus
(1890) A second early variety ready in late June from and early April sowing. Good sweet flavour. (OGC)
    EWK John JWB OGC SbS Tuck Wall

Holiday
    Shar Sutt

Hurst Beagle
Several days earlier than Kelvedon Wonder, this variety is truly sweet tasting. Blunt well-filled pods. Ht. 1.5 ft. (Mars)
    Brwn EWK Foth John JWB Mars Mole SbS Toze Unwi

Hurst Green Shaft
Carries a heavy crop of 4-4.5 in. pods of exhibition standard, which mature over a longer period than most varieties. Beautifully sweet peas. Ht 2.5 ft. (Mars)
    Brwn Cart Chil Dob EWK Foth Howe John JWB Mars

Johnson's Freezer
This wrinkled seeded, maincrop variety is in great demand with food processors, being an excellent freezing variety. It is an abundant cropper, giving peas of excellent quality and flavour, the pods being borne in pairs on dark green vines. Ht 2ft. Not suitable for autumn sowing. (John)
John

Kelvedon Monarch
see Victory Freezer

Kelvedon Triumph
SbS

Kelvedon Wonder
An early variety with narrow tapering pointed pods. Suitable for freezing. Ht 45 cm. (Bree)
Bakk Brwn Cart Chil Dob EWK Foth Howe John JWB

Kodiak
This mid season large podded pea has a high resistance to disease and is ideal for organic growing. 65 cm. (Brwn)
Shar

Laxton's Progress No. 9
see Progress No. 9

Lincoln
Very sweet flavoured peas. Heavy cropper, with dark green, curved pods. Ht 24 in. (60 cm). Maincrop. (EWK)
EWK John OGC SbS Shar Tuck

Little Marvel
A proven sort, one of the most popular varieties. Ht 1.5 ft. (Mars)
Dob EWK Foth John JWB Mars OGC SbS Shar Sutt T&M

Lord Chancellor
A later maturing pea. Very heavy crop of dark green pointed pods. Very reliable. Ht 90-120 cm. (3-4 ft). (Sutt)
SbS

Lynx
Petit pois type. A really sweet tasting and tender variety becoming increasingly popular for the home gardener looking for something different. 95 cm. (Brwn)
Brwn John

Markana
When grown in rows 6-12 in. apart the extra tendrils of this sort help the strong-growing plant to support themselves without sticks and the seedlings are not attacked so frequently by birds. The numerous 3.5-4 in. pods are held in pairs, each containing 8-9 medium-sized, deep green peas with a good flavour. Ht 2 ft. (Mars)
Bakk EWK John Mars OGC Tuck Wall Yate

Miracle
Good quality peas on medium tall plants 4.5 ft (135 cm.). Useful freezing variety. Second early. (EWK)
EWK JWB SbS

Multistar
Uniform in growth with dark green sweet tasting peas. For best results this variety should be sown thinly. Excellent for freezing. Maincrop. (EWK)
EWK Wall

Nova
Mars

Onward
The main pea. Easy to pick. Ht 2.5 ft. (Mars)
Brwn Cart Chil Dob EWK Foth Howe John JWB Mars

Progress No. 9
Long podded variety with heavy yields of dark green, pointedpods. Ht 18 in. (45 cm.). Early. (EWK)
Dob EWK John JWB Mole SbS Shar

Recette
SbS

Rondo
Shar

Senator
An exceptionally heavy cropper, ideal for the amateur gardener. The best main season variety. (Foth)
Bakk Foth Sutt

Show Perfection
Reliably produces an abundance of narrow pods about 6 in. long and packed with round, dark green peas. Excellent flavour. (Dob)
Brwn Dob JWB Rob

Somerset
S&G

Sparkle
S&G

Spring
Excellent variety for deep-freezing. Vigorous grower, also in fairly unfavourable weather conditions. Spring gives a high production of dark green peas with a very pleasing flavour. You should really try it! (Bakk)
Bakk

Telephone Nain
see Daisy

Top Pod
An excellent all rounder and a great improvement on Onward, it produces more pods containing nine to ten peas compared with Onward's six to seven. Resistant to fusarium and powdery mildew, which is a breakthrough for varieties of this type. (T&M)
S&G T&M VanH

Twiggy
An afila or leafless type, with large, easy to pick pods at the top of the plant. The leafless habit with intertwining tendrils means the plant stands up much better to the weather, making picking easier. Powdery mildew resistant. Ht 100 cm. (Bree)
T&M

Victory Freezer
SbS

Walton
Mole

Waverex
Produces a very heavy crop of blunt pods containing small, very sweet peas, sometimes called Petit Pois. Excellent for freezing. Ht 2.5 ft. (Mars)
    Chil EWK John JWB Mars Milt OGC SMM Suff Sutt Tuck

Peach

Alexandra Noblesse
Allg

Amsden June
(1868) Mid July. Medium sized fruits. Round, greenish-white with a red flush. Very melting flesh with a good flavour. Hardy. (Brog)
    Allg Cast SDea SFam GTwe ERea Bowe

Barrington
Allg

Belle Garde
(1732) Early to mid September. Large fruits. Golden yellow fruits almost entirely covered with dark crimson flush. Pale yellow melting flesh. Very rich flavour. A good cropper. (Brog)
    Allg Cast SDea SFam SKee GTwe ERea SFru Bowe

Bonanza
ERea Bowe

Breda
Bowe

Charles Ingouf
Bowe

Doctor Hogg
SDea

Duke of York
(1902) Mid July. Large, rich crimson fruits. Melting and refreshing flesh. (Brog)
    Allg Cast SDea SFam SKee CSco GTwe ERea SFru Bowe Edws

Dymond
GTwe ERea

Early Alexander
Allg GTwe Bowe

Early Rivers
(1864) Mid July. Fairly large, pale lemon yellow fruits with slight flush and stripes. White, melting flesh with a delicious flavour. (Brog)
    SDea SFam CSco GTwe ERea Bowe

Flat China
ERea

Francis
SKee

Garden Annie
ERea

Garden Lady
WHig GTwe ERea

Hales Early
(1850) August. Medium sized, pale lemon-yellow fruits with crimson flush and mottling. Melting flesh with a fair flavour. Hardy. (Brog)
Allg Cast SKee GTwe ERea Bowe

Hylands Peach
SDea

Miriam
SKee

Peregrine
(1906) Early August. Medium to fairly large, crimson red fruits. Firm, juicy flesh with a rich flavour. (Brog)
Allg Cast SDea SFam WHig WJas SKee Rog CSco GTwe Muir ERea

Red Haven
Mid August. Medium sized red fruits. Firm and juicy. A good cropper. (Brog)
Cast SDea SKee GTwe SIgm Bowe

Reliance
SDea

Robin Redbreast
SDea

Rochester
Mid to late August. Medium sized, yellow fruit, streaked with red. Firm and juicy. A good cropper. Ideal for growing outdoors. (Brog)
Allg Cast SDea SFam WHig SKee CSco GTwe Muir ERea SIgm Bowe

Royal George
Late August. Large, pale yellow fruits with a deep blood-red flush. Very melting flesh with a rich flavour. (Brog)
Cast SFam SKee Rog SFru Bowe

Saturn
Cast Bowe

South Coast
SKee

Springtime
SDea

Wassenberger
Bowe

Pear

Abbe Fetel
SKee

Admiral Gervais
SKee SFru

Alexandrina Bivort
CSco

Autumn Bergamot
SKee CTho

Baronne de Mello
SFam SKee CTho CSco

Belle Guerandais
SKee

Belle Julie
SKee

Bellissime d'Hiver
SKee SFru

Bergamotte Esperen
Allg SKee CSco

Beth
(1938) Dessert. Beurre Superfin x Williams Bon Chretien. Mid to late September. A pale yellow pear almost entirely covered with fine golden brown russet. Fine, juicy and melting flesh. A sweet, rich flavour. (Brog)
  Allg Cast SDea SFam WHig SKee Rog CSco GTwe Muir SFru LBuc

Beurre Alexandre Lucas
SKee CSco

Beurre Bedford
SKee CSco SIgm Bowe

Beurre Bosc
SKee CSco Bowe

Beurre Clairgeau
SKee

Beurre Diel
Allg

Beurre Dumont
SFam CSco SFru

Beurre Giffard
SFru

Beurre Hardy
(1820) Dessert. Mid to late October. A very vigorous tree. A large round conical russet bronze pear with faint red on cheek. Flesh is white with a faint pink tinge. Very tender and juicy with a rose water flavour. (Brog)
  Allg Cast SDea SFam SKee CTho Rog CSco GTwe ERea SFru LBuc

Beurre Jean Van Geert
SKee

Beurre Precoce
Bowe

Beurre Six
SKee

Beurre Superfin
(1844) Dessert. October. A moderately vigorous tree. A medium sized, round conical yellow pear with many patches of fine russet. Very melting, sweet flesh with a delicious perfumed flavour. (Brog)
  Allg SFam SKee CSco GTwe SFru Bowe

Beurre d'Amanlis
Allg SKee CSco

Beurre d'Arenberg
SFru

Beurre d'Avalon
CTho

Beurre de Jonghe
SKee

Beurre de Mortier
SKee

Beurre de Naghin
SKee

Bianchettone
SKee

Black Worcester
(1575) Culinary. Keeps till March. A moderately vigorous tree. A large, round Bergamotte pear, entirely covered with dark coppery brown russet. Crisp, rather gritty flesh. Little flavour. A good cooking pear. (Brog)
Cast WJas SKee CSco GTwe

Blickling
SKee

Bonne de Beugny
SKee

Bristol Cross
(1920) Dessert. Williams Bon Chretien x Conference. Late September to early October. Incompatible with Quince. A large, oval pyriform, yellowish green pear almost entirely covered with solid and mottled fawn russet. Soft, juicy, slightly gritty flesh. A slightly perfumed flavour. (Brog)
SKee CSco GTwe SIgm Bowe

Catillac
(1665) Culinary. December to April. A vigorous tree. A large Bergamotte shaped dull green pear with a brown red flush. One of the best stewing pears. Flesh becomes pink when cooked. (Brog)
Allg Cast SFam SKee CTho Rog CSco GTwe SFru Bowe

Chalk
SKee Bowe

Charneux
Bowe

Chaumontel
SKee

Clapps Favourite
Dessert. Early September. A vigorous, upright tree. A medium, pyriform pale yellow pear with a scarlet red flush and stripes. Melting, juicy and sweet with a fair flavour. (Brog)
Cast SKee Rog CSco GTwe SIgm Bowe

Colette
Bowe

Colmar d'Ete
CTho

Comte de Lamy
SFam SKee SFru

** Concorde
(1977) Dessert. Doyenne du Comice x Conference. November to December. A moderately vigorous, upright tree. Very similar in appearance to Conference. Melting, juicy flesh with a good flavour. A precocious, heavy cropping variety with good colour and skin finish. (Brog)
 Allg Cast SDea SFam WHig WJas SKee Rog CSco GTwe Muir SFru

Conference
(1885) Dessert. Leon Leclerc de Laval open pollinated. October to November. Self-fertile. A long pyriform, yellowish green pear with much solid and patchy russet. Firm, tender and juicy flesh with a sweet flavour. Tendency to produce misshapen parthenocarpic fruit. (Brog)
 Allg Cast SDea SFam WHig WJas SKee CTho Rog CSco GTwe Muir

Deacon's Pear
SDea

Devoe
SDea

Double de Guerre
SKee SFru

Doyenne Georges Boucher
SKee

Doyenne d'Ete
(c1700) Dessert. July to August. A weak, upright-spreading tree. A small, round conical, pale yellow pear with brownish-red flush. Melting, juicy flesh. Sweet. (Brog)
 SFam SKee CSco GTwe Bowe

Doyenne de Boussoch
SKee

Doyenne du Comice
(1849) Dessert. November to December. A moderately vigorous, upright-spreading tree. A large, oval pyriform, pale yellow pear, with very fine russet over most of the surface with an occasional brownish-red flush. Very melting, juicy flesh with a delicious flavour. One of the most popular varieties. (Brog)
 Allg Cast SDea SFam WHig WJas SKee CTho Rog CSco GTwe Muir

Dr Jules Guyot
SKee CSco Bowe

Duchesse d'Angouleme
SKee CSco Bowe

Duchesse de Bordeaux
SKee SFru

Durondeau
(1811) Dessert. October to November. A moderately vigorous, compact tree. A fairly large, almost calebash shaped golden yellow pear, almost entirely covered with reddish gold russet with slight red flush. Melting, sweet and juicy with a good flavour. (Brog)
 Allg Cast SFam SKee CTho Rog CSco GTwe SFru SIgm Bowe

Easter Beurre
CSco

Eldorado
Bowe

Emile d'Heyst
(1847) Dessert. October to November. A rather small tree. A medium sized, long oval pear. Pale yellow marbled with brown russet. Melting, juicy and very sweet with a rose water flavour. A good cropper. (Brog)
Allg SKee CTho CSco GTwe SIgm Bowe

Eva Baltet
SKee

Evening Doyenne
SKee

Fondante Thirriot
Allg

Fondante d'Automne
(1825) Dessert. September to October. A rather small, spreading tree. A medium sized, Bergamotte shaped pear. Greenish yellow partly covered with brownish russet. Melting, juicy and sweet with an aromatic flavour. (Brog)
Allg SKee CTho CSco GTwe SFru Bowe

Forelle
SKee

Gansells Bergamot
CTho

Glou Morceau
(1700s) Dessert. December to January. A moderately vigorous, rather spreading tree. A fairly large, oval pyriform, pea green pear becoming greenish yellow when ripe. Smooth, tender flesh with a rich and sugary flavour. Reasonably hardy and a good cropper. (Brog)
Allg Cast SDea SFam SKee CTho Rog CSco GTwe SFru SIgm Bowe

Glow Red Williams
SFam CSco

Gorham
(1910) Dessert. Bartlett x Josephine de Malines. Mid to late September. A moderately vigorous, fairly upright tree. A medium sized, pyriform pale yellow pear, almost entirely covered with a brownish golden russet. Juicy, melting flesh with a rich musky flavour. (Brog)
SFam SKee CTho CSco GTwe Bowe Edws

Gratiole de Jersey
CTho

Green Pear of Yair
SKee

Hacon's Incomparable
SKee

Harvest Queen
SDea

Hessle
(1827) Dessert. October. A fairly vigorous, upright-spreading tree. A small, round-conical pale yellow-brown pear, covered with small russet dots. Juicy and sweet. Hardy.
(Brog)
   Cast SDea SFam SKee Rog CSco GTwe Bowe

Highland
   SKee

Improved Fertility
Dessert. September to October. Tetraploid. Self-fertile. A large, conic to pyriform, yellow pear, almost entirely covered with solid fawn russet. Firm, coarse flesh. Juicy with a fair flavour. (Brog)
   SDea SKee CSco GTwe Bowe Edws

Jargonelle
(1600) Dessert. August. A medium sized, long conical, greenish yellow pear, with a faint brownish-red flush. Tender, juicy and sweet with a slight musky flavour. (Brog)
   Cast SDea SFam SKee Rog CSco GTwe SFru Bowe

Jeanne d'Arc
   Bowe

Josephine de Malines
(1830) Dessert. December to January. A moderately vigorous, rather weeping tree. A rather small, short conical, pale yellow pear, with some russet near stalk. Flesh very melting and sweet with a deliciously perfumed flavour. A good late pear. Fairly hardy. (Brog)
   Allg SDea SFam SKee CSco GTwe SFru SIgm Bowe Edws

Jules d'Airolles
   Bowe

Laxton's Foremost
   SKee CSco

Laxton's Satisfaction
   SFam CSco

Louise Bonne of Jersey
(1780) Dessert. October. A moderately vigorous, upright-spreading tree. A medium sized, long conical to oval pear. Yellowish-green with some red flush and prominent red spots. Very melting, sweet and with a delicious flavour. (Brog)
   Allg Cast SDea SFam SKee CTho Rog CSco GTwe SFru SIgm Bowe

Madame Treyve
   SFru

Magness
   Bowe

Marguerite Marillat
(1872) Dessert. September. A very upright tree. A very large, long calebasse golden yellow pear, with some red flush andslight russet. Very juicy but with little flavour. (Brog)
SDea SKee CSco GTwe Bowe

Marie Louise
Allg SKee CSco

Marie Louise d'Uccle
SKee

Martin Sec
SKee

Merton Pride
(1941) Dessert. Triploid. Glou Morceau x Double Williams (4X). September. A large, pyriform to conic, yellow pear, with solid fawn russet around the stalk and eye. Melting, juicy and sweet with a strong pear flavour. (Brog)
Allg Cast SDea SFam SKee CTho CSco GTwe SFru SIgm Bowe Edws

Merton Star
SKee Bowe

Moonglow
Cast Bowe

Morettini
SDea

Muirfield Egg
SKee

Nouveau Poiteau
(1843) Dessert. November. A rather large, oval pyriform, pale greenish yellow pear, almost entirely covered with russet and a slight red flush. Very melting and sweet. (Brog)
SKee CTho CSco GTwe SFru Bowe Edws

Novelle Fourvie
SKee

Olivier de Serres
SFam SKee CSco SFru

Onward
(1947) Dessert. Laxton's Superb x Doyenne du Comice. Late September. A large, short round pyriform to round conic, greenishyellow pear, flushed orange-red. Some russet over skin. Soft, melting, juicy and sweet with a good flavour. (Brog)
Cast SDea SFam SKee Rog CSco GTwe Muir SFru SIgm Bowe Edws

Ovid
CSco Bowe

Packham's Triumph
(1896) Dessert. Uvedale's Saint Germain x Williams Bon Chretien. October. A large, pyriform to conic, yellowish green pear covered with numerous golden dots. Melting, juicy and sweet with a good flavour. (Brog)
Allg Cast Rog CSco GTwe SFru Bowe Edws

Passe Colmar
CTho

Passe Crassane
SKee CTho CSco Bowe

Pear Apple
SDea

Pitmaston Duchesse
(1841) Culinary. Duchesse d'Angouleme x Glou Morceau. Late September to October. A fairly vigorous, upright-spreading tree. A very large, long pyriform pale yellow pear, marbled with brown russet. Melting, juicy flesh with a very pleasant flavour. (Brog)
  Allg SDea SKee CTho CSco GTwe SFru SIgm Bowe

Precoce de Trevoux
SKee Bowe

President Heron
Bowe

Pyrus Cordata
SKee

Red Comice
Cast SKee SIgm Bowe

Red Williams
SKee

Robin
Dessert. September to early October. A medium sized short pyriform to conic shaped pear. Greenish yellow with red flush. Juicy, sweet and rather coarse flesh with a slightly perfumed flavour. (Brog)
  SDea SKee CSco ERea Bowe

Roosevelt
SKee

Saint Remy
Bowe

Santa Claus
Dessert. December. A vigorous, upright tree. A medium sized, conical dull brown-red pear, almost entirely covered with russet. Melting flesh with a delicious flavour. (Brog)
  SDea SFam SKee CSco SFru Bowe

Satisfaction
SKee

Seckle
(1819) Dessert. October to November. A rather weak but upright tree. A small, round oval, dark brown-red pear covered with conspicuous white dots. Very sweet, tender flesh with a rich flavour. (Brog)
  SFam SKee CSco GTwe SFru SIgm Bowe

Sieger Wildeman
Bowe

Sierra
Bowe

Soleil d'Autumn
SKee

Souvenir du Congress
CSco

Swan's Egg
CTho

Thompson's

(1820) Dessert. October to November. A fairly large, oval pyriform, pale golden yellow pear with much russet marbling. Melting, buttery flesh with a very delicious flavour. (Brog)
SFam SKee CSco GTwe SFru SIgm Bowe

Triomphe de Vienne
SFam SKee Bowe

Triumph
SKee

Uvedale's St Germain
SKee CTho

Vicar of Winkfield
(1760) Culinary. December to January. A very vigorous tree. A very large, long calebasse, greenish-yellow pear. Rather firm, dry flesh. (Brog)
SDea SKee CSco GTwe Bowe

Warden
Bowe

Williams Bon Chretien
(1770) Dessert. September. Incompatible with Quince. A moderately vigorous tree. A fairly large, oval pyriform golden yellow pear, covered with extensive fine russet patches. Soft, tender and juicy with a sweet and strong musky flavour. Used for processing. (Brog)
Allg Cast SDea SFam WHig WJas SKee Rog CSco GTwe Muir ERea

Winter Nelis
(1818) Dessert. November to January. A medium sized, round-conical greenish yellow pear, almost entirely covered with thin dark brown russet, very juicy and sweet with a delicately perfumed flavour. (Brog)
Cast SDea SFam SKee CTho CSco GTwe SFru Bowe Edws

Perry Pear

Barland
CSco

Barnet
CTho CSco

Blakeney Red
SDea CTho CSco

Brandy
Cast SDea CTho CSco

Butt
CSco

Gin
CTho CSco Bowe

Green Horse
CTho CSco

Hellens Early (Sweet Huffcap)
CSco

Hendre Huffcap
CSco

Judge Amphlett
CSco

5th Edition

Moorcroft
CSco

Old Home
Cast

Oldfield
CSco Bowe

Parsonage
CSco

Red Pear
CSco

Taynton Squash
CSco Bowe

Thorn
Cast CTho CSco

Winnals Longden
CTho CSco

Yellow Huffcap
CSco

Pepper Hot

Anaheim
T&M

F1 Antler
Yate

F1 Apache
Brwn Dob John Milt Mole Sutt

Cayenne
Most useful in pickles, curries, sauces and on pizza. (Foth)
Foth JWB Mole SbS Unwi Wall

Cayenne Long Slim
The best-known hot Cayenne pepper, much used for flavouring exotic meat dishes and sauces. The flavour of these peppers tendsto get hotter when they are kept for a longer period of time. (Bakk)
Bakk John

Chili
Beware, they are very hot! For greenhouse production or indoors, this variety produces a mass of small pods, cropping over a long period. (OGC)
EWK OGC SMM Sutt

Crespin
An early and very high yielding semi-hot pepper. The conicalfruits grow to 3-4 in. in length and increase in heat and flavouras they go from green to red. A medium-tall plant. (Suff)
Suff

Ethiopian
This is an excellent variety of chilli pepper. Early prolific and firey hot. The long thin pods get hotter as they mature, and turn from green to red. A compact bushy plant. (Suff)
Suff

F1 Hero
T&M

The Fruit and Veg Finder

Hot Mexican
Bushy, compact plants carrying a profusion of 1-1.5 in. longchillis which turn red when ripe. (Mars)
Mars

F1 Jalapa
Yate

Jalapeno
"Pizza" peppers are most unusual and not for the faint-hearted. Hot! Pendant shaped, blunt ends and thick walls. The fruit size is 2.5 in. and is a medium green to red on maturity. (Foth)
Bakk Foth SbS Suff

Karlo
Yellow wax type Romanian cone shaped pepper up to 3 in. wide x 3-4 in. long. Colour changes to orange and then red when
mature. Impressive crop on short and compact plant. Flavour is mildly pungent for eating raw in salad or for cooking. (Suff)
Suff

Red Cherry
A novel, attractive variety bearing a heavy crop of large cherry sized, green fruits which ripen to red on maturity. Ideal for use in curries, pickles and sauces. (Sutt)
Sutt

Serrano Chili
Greenhouse or indoors only. Only 1.5 in. long, smothered in fruit and the hottest little devils you'll ever taste. A popular Mexican variety eaten fresh, either green or red or can be dried. (T&M)
Suff T&M

F1 Super Cayenne
Bloo T&M

Tabasco Habanero
A small fruited, very hot variety. Will really knock your socks off. (T&M)
T&M

Pepper Sweet

F1 Ace
Mars Unwi

F1 Actio
EWK

F1 Antaro
EWK

F1 Ariane
Bakk EWK Foth John Mole OGC SbS Toze Tuck

F1 Atlantic
Bakk

F1 Atol
Bakk

F1 Beauty Bell
EWK

Beauty Boy
Suff

F1 Bell Boy
Brwn Dob Howe John JWB Milt Mole OGC RSlu S&G SbS

F1 Bendigo
Howe John Mole Toze Wall

F1 Bianca
Mole

F1 Big Bertha
T&M

F1 Blondy
S&G

Bull Nose Red
SbS

California Wonder
Very pleasant mild flavour. (Mars) Chil Foth John Mars Mole SbS Unwi Wall

F1 Canape
Cart Dob T&M Unwi

F1 Carnival Mixed
Mars

F1 Cuby
S&G

F1 Delphin
Brwn Howe Mole VanH

F1 Duplo
Yate

F1 Eagle
Brwn

F1 Early Prolific
Mars

Golden Calwonder
SbS

F1 Gypsy
Foth Sutt T&M

Hungarian Wax
OGC SbS Suff

F1 Indalo
Yate

Jingle Bells
The earliest maturing pepper we know. Ideal for containers or where space is limited and a super cropper. Loads of miniature sweet bell peppers which turn red at maturity. Delicious in salads, stir-fries or stuffed. (T&M)
T&M

F1 Jumbo
T&M

F1 Kendo
John

F1 Kerala
RSlu

F1 Lambada
RZ

Long Red Marconi
Long thin, deep red pods of mild sweet flavour. Very productive. (EWK)
EWK

F1 Luteus
Bakk EWK Howe Milt Mole Suff Sutt Toze

Marconi
Large red fruits. Good cropper. (D&D)
SbS Suff

F1 Mavras
Bakk EWK Mole SbS Toze Wall

F1 New Ace
Bloo Foth John Mole OGC SbS Suff

F1 Orange Wonder
Yate

F1 Propa Rumba
Mole Wall

Purple Beauty
T&M

F1 Redskin
Bakk Brwn Dob EWK Foth John Milt Mole OGC Sutt T&M

F1 Ringo
Bloo Suff

F1 Rubens
Bloo Suff

Salad Festival
The bright mixture of fruit colours will add interest to your salads. Immature fruits of green, deep purple or cream turn red or gold as they ripen. All are of best greenhouse quality. (Unwi)
Unwi

F1 Salsa
RZ

F1 Sirono
RSlu

F1 Sirtaki
RZ

F1 Slim Pim
OGC SbS Suff

Sunnybrook
Sixty cm. tall plants. When they are red and ripe they can be used either raw or cooked in a great diversity of dishes such as salads and casseroles or stew. (Bakk)
Bakk

Sweet Chocolate
T&M

Sweet Green
SbS

Sweet Spanish Mixed
Yellow, red (and green) sweet peppers. Good cropper. (D&D)
SbS

F1 Tasty
S&G

F1 Tonika
RZ

Worldbeater
Fruits in abundance. Best grown under glass, but can be transplanted outdoors in June in warm, sheltered areas. (Sutt)
Sutt

Yolo Wonder
An open pollinated type, which has large square fruits and is pleasantly mild. (OGC)
OGC

Pepper-Tomato hybrid

Top Boy
Have proved themselves top favourites here in our trials. Fruit have the shape and size of Marmande tomatoes with thick walls. Seed core is very small and taste is like a very sweet and juicy pepper. Very productrive plants. Top Boy has red fruits and is the earliest to ripen. Ideal for growing in a greenhouse or polytunnel. (Suff)
SbS

Top Girl
Gold-yellow fruit. (Suff)
SbS

Plantago coronopus

Buckshorn Plantain
A common seaside plant, Buckshorn plantain can also be used as a salad ingredient. Young leaves are normally blanched for a few seconds in boiling water before use and are a common ingredient of the Italian mixed salad known as Misticanza. (Futu)
Futu

Plum & Gage

Allgrove's Superb
Allg

Angelina Burdett
Cast SKee Rog GTwe

Anna Spath
SKee CSco Bowe

Ariel
SDea SKee CSco Bowe

Autumn Compote
SKee

** **Avalon**
Dessert. Reeves Seedling Open Pollinated. Late August. A spreading and vigorous tree. Flowers early. Large, oval-oblong, red-yellow fruit. Golden-yellow juicy flesh with good flavour. Partial clingstone. Moderate resistance to Silver Leaf and Bacterial Canker. (Brog)
Cast WHig SKee GTwe SFru SIgm Bowe Edws

Belgian Purple
SKee

Belle de Louvain
(1845) Culinary. Mid to late August. A vigorous, upright tree. A large to very large, long oval dull purple-red plum. Moderately sweet and juicy with a rich flavour. Cooks well. Partially self-fertile. Used as a windbreak. (Brog)
Allg Cast SDea SKee CTho Rog CSco GTwe SFru Bowe

Black Prince
CSco Bowe

Blue Imperatrice
SKee

Bluetit
SKee Muir Bowe

Bonne de Bry
SKee CSco Bowe

Brandy Gage
SKee

Bryanston Gage
(1831) Dessert. Mid September. A large, spreading tree. A medium sized, round pale grreenish-yellow plum with a few small red dots. Fairly firm flesh with a delicious flavour. (Brog)
Allg SFam SKee CSco GTwe

Cambridge Gage
(1927) Dessert. Mid to late August. A vigorous, rather spreading tree. A medium sized, round greenish yellow plum, occasionally with some dull red flush and a little netted russet. Golden yellow, somewhat fibrous juicy flesh with a sweet, rich flavour, partially self-fertile. (Brog)
Allg Cast SDea SFam WHig SKee CTho Rog CSco GTwe Muir ERea

Carlsen Skiodt
CSco

Coe's Golden Drop
(1700s) Dessert. Green Gage x White Magnum Bonum. Mid to late September. A medium to large, oval, amber yellow plum flushed with some red spots. Firm yellow sweet flesh with a rich flavour. (Brog)
Allg Cast SDea SFam SKee CSco GTwe Muir SFru SIgm Bowe

Count Althann's Gage
(1850s) Dessert. Green Gage open pollinated. Mid September. A moderately vigorous, rather upright tree. A large, round, dark crimson-red plum, marked with large golden dots. Excellent flavour. (Brog)
Cast SDea SFam SKee Rog CSco GTwe SFru SIgm Bowe

Cox's Emperor
SKee CSco

Crimson Drop
SKee

Curlew
SDea

Czar
(1871) Culinary. Prince Englebert x Early Rivers. Early August. A moderately vigorous, upright, twiggy tree. A medium sized, roundish-oval, blue-black plum with moderate bloom. Self-fertile. Cooks well. (Brog)
  Allg Cast SDea SFam SKee Rog CSco GTwe Muir SFru LBuc SIgm

Delicious (Laxton)
Cast SKee Rog CSco

Denniston's Superb
(1790) Dessert. Green Gage open pollinated. Mid to late August. A fairly vigorous, upright-spreading tree. A medium sized, round-oval, greenish yellow plum with streaks of darker green. Good flavour. Self-fertile. (Brog)
  Allg Cast SDea SFam WHig SKee CSco GTwe Muir SFru LBuc SIgm

Diamond
SKee Bowe

Dittisham Ploughman
SKee CTho

Early Laxton
(1902) Dual purpose. Catalonia x Early Rivers. Late July to early August. A medium sized, oval-oblong, yellow plum with a pinkish-red flush. Juicy and sweet with a pleasant flavour. Partially self-fertile. (Brog)
  Cast SDea SFam SKee CSco GTwe Bowe Edws

Early Orleans
SKee Bowe

Early Prolific (Rivers)
(1830) Culinary. Precoce de Tours open pollinated. Late July. A small, round-oval blue-black plum with a strong bloom. Golden yellow firm flesh. Delicious flavour when cooked. (Brog)
  Allg Cast SDea SKee CTho Rog CSco GTwe SFru SIgm Bowe Edws

Early Transparent Gage
(1866) Dessert. Transparent Gage open pollinated. Mid August. A medium sized, round-oblong, pale apricot yellow plum dotted with crimson spots. Very sweet with a rich flavour. Self-fertile. (Brog)
  Allg Cast SDea SFam CSco GTwe Muir SFru SIgm Bowe

Early Victoria
SDea

Edwards
(1930) Dual purpose. Early to mid September. An upright tree. A very large, oval, blue-black plum with bloom. Sweet and juicy with an acceptable flavour. A good cropper. (Brog)
  Cast SDea SFam WHig SKee CSco GTwe SFru SIgm Bowe Edws

** Excalibur
Dessert. Reeves Seedling open pollinated. Early September. A fairly dense, vigorous, upright-spreading tree. Moderate resistance to Silver Leaf and Bacterial Canker. A large, oval-round, pink-yellow plum with a mauve flush. Moderately firm and juicy with a good flavour. (Brog)
    Cast GTwe SFru SIgm Bowe Edws

First
    CSco

Giant Prune
(1895) Culinary. D'Agen x Pond's Seedling. Mid to late September. A moderately vigorous tree. Can be subject to Bacterial Canker and Silver Leaf. A large, long-oval, red plum. Cooks well. Self-fertile. (Brog)
    Allg Cast SDea SKee Rog CSco GTwe Bowe Edws

Godshill Blue
    SDea

Golden Transparent Gage
(1890) Dessert. Transparent Gage open pollinated. Late September. A very large, oblong, golden yellow plum, dotted with red. Firm, sweet flesh with an excellent flavour. Self-fertile. (Brog)
    Allg Cast SFam Rog GTwe SFru Bowe

Goldfinch
(1906) Dessert. Early Transparent Gage x Jefferson. Mid to late August. A large, round-oblong, yellow plum. Very sweet and juicy with a rich flavour. (Brog)
    Cast SKee Rog CSco GTwe Bowe

Greengage (Old)
Dessert. Late August to early September. A small, round, green fruit with slight red flush or dots. Tender, delicious flesh. (Brog)
    Allg Cast SDea SFam WHig WJas SKee Rog CSco GTwe SFru SIgm

Grove's Late Victoria
    SKee CSco Bowe

Guthrie's Late Gage
    SKee

Herman
Dual-purpose. Czar x Ruth Gerstetter. Mid to late July. A moderately vigorous, somewhat spreading tree. A medium to large, oval-oblong blue-black plum with bloom. Self-fertile. (Brog)
    Allg Cast GTwe LBuc Edws

Heron
    GTwe

Imperial Epineuse
    SKee

Jefferson
(1825) Dessert. Early September. A medium sized, oval pale greenish-yellow plum, with a faint bloom; often with a slight redflush or dots. Rather fibrous, juicy flesh with a delicious flavour. (Brog)
   Allg Cast SDea SFam SKee Rog CSco GTwe SFru SIgm Bowe

Kea
   SKee

Kentish Bush
   SKee Bowe

Kirke's
Dessert. Early to mid September. A medium to large, round blue-black plum with a deep bloom. Greenish yellow flesh of good flavour. Freestone. (Brog)
   Allg Cast SDea SFam SKee CTho CSco GTwe SFru SIgm Bowe

Late Muscatel
   SKee

Late Transparent
   CSco

Laxton's Cropper
(1906) Culinary. Victoria x Aylesbury Prune. Early to mid September. A medium to large, oval, blue-black plum. Self-fertile. A good cropper. (Brog)
   Cast SKee Rog CSco GTwe Bowe

Laxton's Delight
   GTwe

Laxton's Gage
   Allg SDea SKee

Laxton's Supreme
   CSco

Magda Jensen
   CSco

Mann No 1
   Bowe

Marjories Seedling
(1912) Culinary. Late September to early October. A vigorous, upright tree. A large, oval-oblong, blue-black plum with bloom. Flesh is firm, juicy and moderately sweet. Cooks well. Partially self-fertile. (Brog)
   Allg Cast SDea SFam WHig WJas SKee CTho CSco GTwe Muir SFru

McLaughlin's Gage
   SKee

Merton Gem
(1923) Dual-purpose. Coe's Violet x Victoria. Early to mid September. A moderately vigorous tree with a spreading habit. A medium to large, oval-oblong golden plum with a pinkish-red flush. Slight bloom. Good eating quality. Self-fertile. (Brog)
   SKee CSco GTwe SFru Bowe

Mirabelle Petite
   CSco SFru

Mirabelle de Nancy
   SDea SKee CTho GTwe

Monarch
(1885) Culinary. Autumn Compote open pollinated. Mid to lateSeptember. A vigorous, upright tree. A large round-oval, blue-black plum with a thick bloom and russet patches. Little flavour. Cooks well. (Brog)
Allg SKee CSco GTwe Bowe

Monsieur Hatif
Bowe

Myrobalan (Cherry Plum)
(1600s) Culinary. Late July to early August. Widely used as a plum rootstock and for windbreaks and hedging. A small, round, shiny cherry red fruit. Good flavour when cooked. (Brog)
SKee Rog CSco SFru Bowe

Olympia
SKee

Ontario
SKee CSco GTwe Bowe

Opal
(1925) Dessert. Oullins Gage x Early Favourite. Early to midAugust. A medium sized, oval-oblong, reddish purple plum with bloom. Moderately firm golden flesh. A rich, sweet flavour. Partially self-fertile. Flowers are susceptible to bullfinch damage. (Brog)
Allg Cast SDea SFam WHig SKee CSco GTwe Muir LBuc SIgm Bowe

Orleans
SKee

Oullin's Golden Gage
(1860) Dessert and culinary. Mid August. A medium to large, round-oval, golden yellow plum with a slight bloom. Sweet with very little flavour. Partially self-fertile. Cooks well. (Brog)
Allg Cast SDea SFam SKee Rog CSco GTwe Muir ERea LBuc SIgm

Peach Plum
SKee

Pershore Yellow Egg
(1827) Culinary. Mid to late August. A medium to large, oval, golden yellow plum. Rather mealy flesh and poor flavour, but cooks well. Used as a rootstock. Self-fertile. (Brog)
Cast SDea SFam SKee CTho Rog CSco GTwe Bowe

Pond's Seedling
Allg SDea SKee Bowe

President
Allg SDea SKee GTwe

Prince Englebert
SKee

Priory Plum
SDea

Purple Pershore
(c1877) Culinary. Mid to late August. A medium to large, oval, blue-black plum with bloom. Self-fertile. (Brog)
Cast SDea SKee Rog CSco GTwe Bowe

Quetsche
SFam CSco

Quetsche d'Alsace
SKee

Red Cherry Plum
SDea CSco

Reeves Seedling
(1940) Dessert. Mid to late August. A fairly vigorous, spreading tree. A very large, round, purple-red plum covered with patches of russet. Very juicy and sweet with a good flavour. A good quality dessert plum. Partially self-fertile. (Brog)
Cast SKee CSco GTwe SFru SIgm Bowe

Reine-Claude Violette
SKee

Reine-Claude de Bavay
(c1832) Dessert. Green Gage open pollinated. Mid to late September. A medium sized, round-oval, greenish yellow plum with many red and white dots. Juicy with a very rich gage flavour. Self-fertile. (Brog)
Allg Cast SFam SKee Rog CSco GTwe Bowe

Royale de Vilvoorde
SKee

Ruth Gerstetter
SKee

Sanctus Hubertus
Dessert. Mater Dolorosa x Early Rivers. Early August. A moderately vigorous tree with a drooping habit. A large, oval, purple-blue plum with bloom. Moderate flavour. (Brog)
Cast SDea SKee CSco GTwe LBuc SIgm Bowe Edws

Severn Cross
SKee CSco GTwe Bowe

Shropshire Prune
Allg WJas Edws

Stint
SKee

Swan
GTwe

Thames Cross
CSco

Trailblazer
SKee

Transparent Gage
SKee SFru

Utility
SKee

Valor
Cast GTwe Bowe

Victoria

(1840) Dual purpose. Late August to early September. Rather subject to Silver Leaf and Bacterial Canker. A medium to large, oval, red plum speckled with darker dots. Firm, juicy and sweet with slight flavour. Self-fertile. A heavy, regular cropper. A good variety for bottling and jam.

Allg Cast SDea SFam WHig WJas SKee CTho Rog CSco GTwe Muir

Warwickshire Drooper

Culinary. Early to mid September. A medium to large, oval-oblong, yellow plum. Good flavour when cooked. (Brog)

Allg Cast SDea SFam SKee CTho CSco GTwe SFru Bowe Edws

Washington

SKee CTho CSco

White Magnum Bonum

SDea CTho

Willington Gage

Cast GTwe

Wyedale

CSco GTwe

Yellow Cherry Plum

SDea CSco

Potato

Accent

First Early. 1991. Lifting just after Dunluce, in first trials it has produced shallow-eyed tubers which have been notable for their eating quality, with an excellent new potato flavour. The flesh is pale cream, waxy and firm after boiling. Accent continues to bulk up to produce a heavy crop and mature tubers show no cracking, even under drought conditions. (Mars)

Mars Mart Tuck

Ailsa

Maincrop. 1894. Round oval, white, with cream-coloured flesh. Heavy yield of even tubers. Resistant to external damage, and highly resistant to blackleg. Susceptible to spraing and virus Y. (GPG)

McL Rog Tuck

Alcmaria

First Early. 1969. Oval, yellow. Heavy early yield. Resistant to golden eelworm and slugs. Some resistance to common scab. (GPG)

Mart

Alhambra

Maincrop. 1986. Long, red, with waxy texture. High yield. Resistant to golden eelworm. Susceptible to leaf roll virus. (GPG)

McL

Alwara
Second Early. Date unknown. Red oval. Close waxy texture. Eelworm resistant. (Webs)
McL

Aminca
First Early. 1974. High yielding. (GPG)
McL OGC Suff

Arkula
First Early. 1982. Oval, white. Very high yielding early. Resistant to spraing. Susceptible to foliage and tuber blight, also blackleg. (GPG)
Mart

Arran Banner
Maincrop. 1927. White, round, with deep eyes. Heavy yield, but irregular shape and often hollow hearted. Susceptible to slugs. (GPG)
Webs

Arran Comet
First Early. 1956. Oval, white, with waxy texture. High early yield. Some resistance to common scab. Susceptible to virus Y, spraing, and blight, but is usually lifted before blight attacks. (GPG)
Hend Tuck

Arran Consul
Webs

Arran Peak
McL

Arran Pilot
First Early. 1930. Heavy crop early but matures too large with uneven tubers. Liable to fail from cut seed tubers. Resistant to common scab, drought, and spraing. Susceptible to external damage and virus Y. (GPG)
Brwn Call Hend Mart McL Rog Tuck Webs

Arran Victory
Late Maincrop. 1918. Round, purple, with white, very floury flesh. Good cooking qualities. Heavy cropper that keeps well. Resistant to common scab. A favourite in Ireland where it thrives in the moist climate. (GPG)
McL Webs

Asterix
Medium-late variety which produces a heavy crop of oval, red-skinned potatoes. Easy to pre-germinate in order to advance the harvest. This variety, too, is firm when cooked and also suitable for making French fries. (Bakk)
Bakk

Atlantic
Webs

Aura
McL

Avalanche
Second Early. Date unknown. Round oval, white, with white flesh. Very uniform tubers. (GPG)
Webs

BF 15
McL

Baillie
Second Early. 1981. Round, white, with shallow eyes. Moderate to high yield of uniform tubers. Resistant to Blight. (GPG)
McL

Ballydoon
First Early. 1931. White, oval. (GPG)
McL

Balmoral
Rog Tuck Webs

Belle de Fontenay
Early. Date unknown. For the very first salad potatoes. An extremely old French variety, which is still grown because of itsexceptional culinary qualities. Small smooth kidney-shaped tuberswith deep yellow flesh. Compact foliage. (Mars)
Mars McL Tuck

Berber
Early Maincrop. Date unknown. White, round. High yield, stores well. A good all round variety, waxy. Eelworm resistant. (Webs)
McL

Berolina
McL

Bintje
Maincrop. 1910. Oval, white. Yellow flesh, high dry matter, resists drought, susceptible to blight and scab. Outclassed by Record, which is scab resisting. (GPG)
Bakk

Bishop
McL

Blue Catriona
Second Early. Date unknown. Long blue. Exhibition. (Webs)
McL

Bonnie Dundee
McL

British Queen
Second Early. 1894. Oval, white, with shallow eyes and white, floury flesh. Boils to mash if overcooked. Crops well. Resistant to slugs. Susceptible to blight and wart disease. (GPG)
McL Webs

Brodick
Webs

Bute Blue
McL

Cara
Late Maincrop. 1976. Oval, pink, with shallow eyes and floury, white flesh. Ideal for jacket baking. High yield of uniform tubers. Late foliage maturity. Like a better-tempered King Edward. Resistant to blight, golden eelworm and virus Y. Some resistance to blackleg. Susceptible to powdery scab, gangrene and slugs. (GPG)
Hend Mars Mart McL Rog Tuck

Cardinal
McL

Carlingford
Second Early. 1982. Round oval, white. (GPG)
McL Tuck

Catriona
Second Early. 1920. Long oval, purple, with white, floury flesh. Low growing foliage which can be good for windy sites. Heavy cropper, haulm dies down early enough to miss blight and belifted well before the worst slug attack. (GPG)
Call Call Hend Mart McL Rog Tuck Webs

Champion
McL

Charlotte
Second Early. Date unknown. Developed in France during the 1980s to give tubers 50% bigger than other salad varieties. The crop is very uniform, shallow-eyed, long-oval in shape. The tender creamy-yellow flesh remains very firm and does not blackenon cooking. The excellent flavour—perhaps not quite as fine as Ratte—coupled with ease of culture ensures Charlotte's place in the first rank of potatoes for the connoisseur. (Mars)
Mars McL

Civa
McL

Cleopatra
Tuck

Colmo
Tuck

Concorde
Very early giving a heavy crop of quite large, long-oval tubers with shallow eyes. Has quickly become a popular show potato. The pale yellow flesh is firm and waxy in texture with exceptional flavour. Suitable for all soil types and quite resistant to late frosts. (Mars)
Brwn Mars Mart Tuck

Corine
McL

Cornes de Bique
McL

Costella
Second Early. Date unknown. Round oval, white, with yellow flesh. A good all round variety produces a heavy crop. Eelworm resistant. (Webs)
McL Webs

Cromwell
McL

Cultra
Rog Webs

Desiree
Maincrop. 1962. Long oval, red, with pale yellow, waxy flesh. Good for chips and baking. High yields but can get misshapen tubers on heavy soils. Crops well in drought, better than any other variety, even in 1976. Resistant to virus Y. Susceptible to mild mosaic virus, and very susceptible to common scab. Save your first lawn-mowings to put in the trenches againstscab. (GPG)
Brwn Call Dob Hend Mart OGC Rog Suff Tuck

Di Vernon
First Early. 1922. Oval, white skin, purple eyes. A very heavy cropper and a good cooker, floury flesh. (GPG)
McL Webs

Diamant
Maincrop. 1982. Oval, white, with non-floury texture. Resistant to blight. (GPG)
McL

Diana
Maincrop. 1982. Round oval, red. Heavy yield of large, uniform tubers. Early foliage maturity. Some resistance to blackleg. Susceptible to external damage and bruising. (GPG)
Tuck

Doon Pearl
McL

Doon Star
Webs

Dr McIntosh
Maincrop. 1944. Long, white. Susceptible to blight and drought. Shallow eyes, slow in dry seasons, flavour only moderate. (GPG)
McL

Duke Of York
First Early. 1891. Oval, white, with yellow floury flesh. Good for baking. Moderate yields of small tubers but can be left to grow large for storing. Susceptible to blight, wart disease and drought. (GPG)
Bakk Call Hend Mart McL OGC Rog Tuck Webs

Dunbar Standard
Late Maincrop. 1936. Long oval, white, with shallow eyes. Good keeper and cooker, excellent for chips, but tendency to after-cooking blackening. Liable to fail if tubers are cut. Late maturing, the haulm goes down in October. (GPG)
McL Tuck Webs

Dunluce
First Early. 1976. Oval, white, with firm, cream flesh. Ideal for salad. Perhaps the earliest early of all, good for greenhouse forcing. Susceptible to blight and drought. (GPG)
Mars Tuck

Edgecote Purple
Cropping unknown. Date unknown. A smooth skinned purple kidney with shallow eyes. (Webs)
McL

Edzell Blue
Second Early. 1890. Round oval, purple blue, with white, floury flesh. Knobbly tubers, excellent roasted or steamed. (GPG)
McL Tuck Webs

Epicure
First Early. 1897. Round, white, with deep eyes. High early yield. Tends to fail from cut seed. Good frost resistance. Susceptible to blight and wart disease. (GPG)
Call Hend Mart McL Tuck Webs

Estima
Second Early. 1937. Oval, white, with yellow, slightly waxy flesh. Good cooking and keeping qualities. Heavy crop particularly at later lifts. Resistant to blight, slugs and drought. Very susceptible to blackleg. Susceptible to powdery scab, virus Y and spraing. (GPG)
Call Hend Mart Rog Tuck

Etoile Du Nord
McL

Fanfare
Early Maincrop. Date unknown. Round oval, pink. Exhibition. (Webs)
McL

Foremost
First Early. 1954. Oval, white with waxy, yellow flesh. Goodcooker. Moderate yield. Poor foliage cover. Some slug resistance. (GPG)
Call Hend Mars Mart Rog Sutt Tuck

Fortyfold
McL

Foxton
Maincrop. 1981. Oval, red-skin with light yellow flesh, firmfloury texture. Excellent for roasting but some disintegration on
boiling. (Seed)
McL

Fronika
Second Early. Date unknown. Round, red, waxy fleshed. Eelworm resistant. (Scot)
McL

Gladstone
McL

Glamis
Webs

Golden Wonder
Late Maincrop. 1906. Long, russet, with floury, yellow flesh. Good baker, tends to disintegrate on boiling. Low yield of small tubers and does not thrive on all soils, suits the humid Irish climate best. Resistant to common scab. Susceptible to slug damage and drought. (GPG)
Call Hend McL Rog Tuck Webs

Gracia
McL

Heather
Mars Tuck Webs

Home Guard
First Early. 1942. Oval, white, with waxy flesh. Prone to blackening after cooking. Sprouts fast and bulks early. Resistant to external damage. Susceptible to drought and blight. Picks up any taint such as BHC from the soil, an organic gardener's potato. (GPG)
Call Hend Mart Rog Tuck

Kepplestone Kidney
Early Maincrop. Date unknown. Round, pink. A top show variety in very short supply. (Webs)
McL

Kerr's Pink
Late Maincrop. 1917. Round, pink, with floury, cream flesh. Ideal for chips and does not blacken left cut up without water. Tendency to discolour and disintegrate with boiling. A late maturing, high yielder with a compact haulm that suppresses weeds. Quite susceptible to blight and scab. (GPG)
Call Hend McL OGC Rog Tuck Webs

Kestrel
Mars Mart McL Tuck Webs

King Edward
Maincrop. 1902. Long oval, pink and white, with floury, cream flesh. Good jacket potato. Famous for yield and quality, but only on soils it suits. Needs deep cultivation and was always a farm rather than a garden variety. Cut seed often fails. Susceptible to blight, wart disease, virus Y and drought. (GPG)
Call Hend Mart McL Rog Tuck Webs

King George
McL

Kingston
Late Maincrop. 1981. Oval, white, with floury texture. Good jacket-baked. High yielding. Golden eelworm resistant. Susceptible to blight. (GPG)
McL

Kipfler
McL

Kirsty
Maincrop. 1982. Round, white, with shallow eyes and creamy flesh. Excellent for jacket baking and creaming. High yield, medium sized tubers. Late foliage maturity. Some resistance to blackleg. Susceptible to spraing. HDRA members report that this variety can be very susceptible to slug damage. (GPG)
Mars

Kondor
Maincrop. 1984. Oval, red, with yellow, creamy flesh that stays firm when boiled. High yielding Dutch variety with very large tubers. Blight resistant. (GPG)
Brwn Mars Mart Tuck

Linzer Delikatess
Early. 1975. The soft yellow salad potato preferred by the Austrians. Bred in Linz in 1975, it has only just been registeredfor sale in Britain. It produces large numbers of medium-sized, long-oval potatoes, with superficial eyes. Delicious hot or cold. (Mars)
Mars Tuck

Lola
First Early. 1981. Long oval, white, with pale yellow waxy flesh. No discoloration. Earlier and heavier cropping than Maris Bard. Resistant to common scab and virus Y. Susceptible to tuber blight. (GPG)
Mars

Majestic
Call Hend Mart McL Rog Tuck Webs

Manna
First Early. 1977. Oval, white, with shallow eyes and waxy flesh. Heavy early crop. Susceptible to blight and blackleg. (GPG)
Tuck

Marfona
Second Early. 1977. Round, white. Dutch variety, excellent for baking. Heavy yield, large tubers, good foliage cover. Good on light soils. Good overall disease resistance, including some to blackleg. (GPG)
Brwn Mars Mart McL Rog Tuck Webs

Maris Bard
First Early. 1972. Long oval, white, with waxy flesh. Very early and high yielding, sprouts relatively late. Good forced under glass. Susceptible to powdery scab and blackleg. (GPG)
Brwn Call Dob Hend Mars Mart Rog Tuck Webs

Maris Peer
Second Early. 1962. Round oval, white, with waxy flesh. Moderate yield, plentiful small tubers, used for canned new potatoes. Early sprouter. Resistant to common scab and skin spot.Susceptible to drought. (GPG)
Call Hend Mart Rog Tuck Webs

Maris Piper
Maincrop. 1963. Oval, white, with floury flesh. Good baker. High yield, large number tubers per plant. Eelworm (golden) resistant and some resistance to blackleg. Susceptible to common and powdery scab, drought, and slugs. (GPG)
    Call Dob Hend Mart McL Rog Tuck Webs

Mauve Queen
McL

May Queen
McL

Mona Lisa
Germinates rapidly, which guarantees quick covering of the soil. It gives a good yield of yellow-skinned potatoes with yellow flesh as early as June. Firm when cooked, with a very
fine flavour. Does not discolour after cooking. (Bakk)
    Bakk McL Tuck Webs

Montana
McL

Morene
Second Early. 1983. Round, white. High yield, large tubers. Resistant to common scab and golden eelworm. Susceptible to wart disease, gangrene and virus Y. Very susceptible to blackleg. (GPG)
    McL

Nadine
The housewife's choice. Lots of uniform-sized round tubers, strongly resistant to eelworm. The skin is exceptionally smooth with shallow eyes, perfect for showing. The sweet white flesh remains firm and moist on cooking. (Mars)
    Call Dob Hend Mars Mart McL Rog Tuck Webs

Obelix
Tuck

Ostara
Tuck

Palma
McL

Penta
Second Early. 1983. Round, pink-eyed, with yellow flesh. High yield, large tubers. Resistant to external damage. Susceptible to leaf roll virus, powdery scab. (GPG)
    McL Webs

Pentland Crown
Maincrop. 1958. Oval, white, with waxy flesh. Tendency to blackening after cooking. Very high yielder. Can be rather tasteless, but improves after Christmas. A supermarket suppliers' favourite. Resistant to common scab, leaf roll virus, virus Y. Some resistance to blackleg. Susceptible to slugs, powdery scab, spraing. (GPG)
    Call Hend Mart Rog Tuck Webs

Pentland Dell
Late Maincrop. 1960. Long oval, white, with floury texture. Good for baking and roasting but tendency to blacken, and to disintegrate on boiling. High yielder. Very susceptible to tuber blight and spraing. (GPG)
Call Hend Rog Tuck Webs

Pentland Hawk
Maincrop. 1967. Oval, white, with waxy flesh. Good in salads. Moderate to high yields, long keeper. Susceptible to virus Y and spraing. (GPG)
Call Hend Rog

Pentland Javelin
First Early. 1968. Oval, white, with very white, waxy flesh. Slow sprouting, bulks late. Resistant to golden eelworm, virus Y and common scab. Susceptible to spraing. (GPG)
Call Hend Mart Rog Tuck Webs

Pentland Squire
Maincrop. 1970. Oval, white. High yield of large tubers if on fertile soil. Prone to hollow heart, so needs high seed rate to prevent tubers getting too big. Some resistance to blight and blackleg. (GPG)
Call Hend Rog Webs

Picasso
Webs

Pimpernel
McL

Pink Fir Apple
Late Maincrop. 1880. Long, pink, with yellow, waxy flesh. Salad potatoes, remaining firm when diced cold, appreciated in France where they make the real "French Fried". Low yield, unusual shaped tubers. (GPG)
Brwn Call Hend Mars Mart McL OGC Rog SMM Tuck Webs

Premier
Tuck Webs

Pride Of Bute
McL

Promesse
McL

Provost
First Early. 1981. Oval, white. Good foliage cover. (GPG)
McL

Ratte
Second Early. 1972. Long, white, with yellow, waxy flesh. Ideal for salad and boiling. Grown in France since 1972 as a higher yielding alternative to Pink Fir Apple. (GPG)
Mars McL Rog Webs

Record
Maincrop. 1944. Oval, white, with yellow floury flesh. The highest dry matter potato, mainly grown on contract for potato crisps. Moderate to low yield. Resists blight, spraing and commonscab. Susceptible to virus Y, blackleg, drought and internal bruising. (GPG)

   Hend McL Webs

Red Craigs Royal
Second Early. 1957. Oval, pink, with shallow eyes and flouryflesh. Excellent for potato salad, remaining firm when diced cold, as good as Pink Fir Apple, but a vastly greater yield. The only way to enjoy the old Craig's Royal flavour. Moderate yield, tubers large if left to grow. A good keeper. Resistant to powderyscab. Susceptible to external damage and hair cracking. (GPG)

   Webs

Red Duke of York
First Early. 1942. Oval, red, with floury flesh. Good for baking. The flavour, keeping and floury baking qualities of the old white skinned favourite, combined with good exhibition colour. (GPG)

   Call Hend Mart McL Tuck Webs

Red King Edward
Maincrop. 1916. Long oval, red, with floury texture. Good general cooking qualities. Moderate yield, large number of tubersper plant. Differs only in colour from the original. Resistant tocommon scab. Susceptible to wart disease, blight, virus Y and drought. (GPG)

   McL Webs

Red Pontiac
Maincrop. 1985. Round, red, with waxy flesh. Excellent jacket baked. An American variety. (Webs)

   Webs

Red Stormont 480
McL

Remarka
OGC Suff

Rocket
Just as early as Dunluce, it has pure white flesh, which is waxy and soft at first digging. Even sized tubers, a little larger than a hen's egg. (Mars)

   Brwn Hend Mars Mart McL Rog Tuck Webs

Rode Eerstelling
see Red Duke of York

Romano
Maincrop. 1978. Round oval, red. White flesh with a creamy texture. Stays firm on cooking. Moderate to high yields. Resistant to virus Y. Some resistance to blight and blackleg. Susceptible to leaf roll virus and drought. Like an earlier, lessscab likely Desiree. (GPG)
Hend Mars Mart Rog Tuck Webs

Royal Kidney
Second Early. 1899. Long oval, white, with yellow flesh. Keeps if left to grow large. Fine flavour. Susceptible to wart disease. (GPG)
McL

Russet Burbank
Webs

Russet Conference
McL

Ryecroft Purple
McL

Salad Blue
Second Early. Date unknown. Novelty blue flesh. (Webs)
McL

Salad Red
McL

Samba
Long and oval in shape, white skinned with a creamy flesh. (Tuck)
Mars Tuck

Sangre
Webs

Sante
Maincrop. 1983. Round oval, white, with shallow eyes and cream coloured, floury flesh. High yield of uniform tubers. Good all-round disease resistance, including resistance to golden eelworm, and partial resistance to pale eelworm. Some susceptibility to blackleg and gangrene. (GPG)
Mars OGC Tuck

Seaforde
McL

Sharpe's Express
First Early. 1901. Long, white, with yellow, floury flesh. Ideal baker, but goes to mash if overcooked. Moderate to low yield, large number of tubers per plant. Keeps well. Like Duke of York, grown as an early for scraping and a second early for keeping. Susceptible to tuber blight and wart disease. (GPG)
Call Hend Mart McL Rog Tuck Webs

Shula
Cropping unknown. Date unknown. Pink splashed oval white. Great for showing. Excellent long keeping firm fleshed variety. The best for baking or microwave use. (Scot)
Rog Tuck Webs

Stamina
Webs

Stemster
Maincrop. 1986. Long oval, pink, with light yellow flesh. High yield, large tubers. Golden eelworm and slug resistant. Excellent exhibition. (GPG)
Hend Mart Tuck Webs

Stormont Star
McL

Stroma
Second Early. Date unknown. Oval, light yellow, with pale yellow flesh. Some slug resistance. (GPG)
Hend Mart Sutt Tuck Webs

Sutton's Foremost
see Foremost

Swift
Mars McL Webs

Symphonia
Webs

Ukama
An excellent early potato for making French fries. This variety produces a very high yield of pure yellow-skinned potatoes which remain firm when cooked. Highly disease-resistant. (Bakk)
Bakk McL

Ulster Chieftain
First Early. 1938. Oval, white. An excellent early roaster. Has short haulm so does well on wind-swept sites and grows fast early, with a better crop than Arran Pilot by the end of June. Susceptible to blight, scab and frost damage. (GPG)
Hend Mart McL Rog Tuck Webs

Ulster Classic
McL

Ulster Prince
First Early. 1947. Long, white, with waxy flesh. Produces few tubers per plant. Emergence often slow and irregular. Forces well under glass. Resists drought. Susceptible to frost damage and very susceptible to spraing. (GPG)
Rog Tuck Webs

Ulster Sceptre
First Early. 1964. Long, white. High yielder on fertile soil. Very early and high yielding, sprouts rapidly. Drought resistant. Poor virus resistance. Seed susceptible to mechanical damage and gangrene. (GPG)
Rog Tuck Webs

Ulster Sovereign
McL

Up-to-Date
Late Maincrop. 1894. Oval, white. Moderate yields, good keeper. Drought resistant. Susceptible to blight, common scab and wart disease. (GPG)
McL

Urgenta
Early. Date unknown, pre 1981. Oval, red skin, yellow flesh, shallow eyes, heavy yields, excellent cooking quality and flavour. Dutch variety. (GSI)
McL

Valor
Mars Tuck Webs

Vanessa
Hend Mart McL Tuck

Verena
McL

Wilja
Second Early. 1972. Long, white with yellow, waxy flesh. Good for potato salads. High yield with large number of tubers per plant. Blight resistant, and some resistance to common scab and blackleg. Susceptible to virus Y. (GPG)
Brwn Call Dob Hend Mart Rog Tuck Webs

Winston
Mart Tuck Webs

Witchhill
McL

Purslane

Common
A succulent continental salad herb. Sow outside in spring, watering well at seeding stage. (Poyn)
Poyn

Golden
Attractive yellow leaves. Rather rare. (Suff)
Futu Suff

Green
Well flavoured and vigorous. Pick over a long season. (Suff)
Futu SbS Suff

Pink
Montia sibirica. An attractive annual with glossy green leaves and pretty pink flowers. A native of North America that is commonly naturalised, Pink Purslane grows well in moist and shady places. The pleasantly flavoured leaves can be eaten as a salad or cooked. (Futu)
Futu

Yellow
Is this a more prosaic Golden?
SbS

Quince

Champion
A large, apple-shaped, golden-yellow quince. (Brog)
Allg CSco GTwe SFru Bowe

Le Bourgeaut
GTwe Bowe

Lescovatz
Bowe

Ludovic
GTwe

Meech's Prolific
A fairly large, pyriform shaped bright golden yellow fruits. Smooth skinned. Growth - vigorous. (Brog)
  SDea SFam WHig SKee CSco GTwe Muir ERea SFru SIgm CSim Bowe

Pear-shaped
  Rog

Portugal
A large, oval-oblong, light orange quince. Early ripening. Growth - very vigorous. (Brog)
  Allg Rog CSco GTwe SIgm

Seibosa
  SKee

Vranja (Bereczki)
A very large, pear-shaped, golden-yellow quince. Very fragrant, tender flesh. Growth - very vigorous. (Brog)
  Allg SDea SFam WHig WJas SKee CTho Rog CSco GTwe ERea SFru

Quinoa

Faro
Has small white seeds, the most productive of 16 varieties. (Futu)
  Futu

Isluga Yellow
Medium sized yellow seed. Early maturing and high yielding. (Futu)
  Futu

Radish

18 Day
Fast "French Breakfast" which is crisp with a mild sweet flavour. Has long white tipped scarlet roots. (Suff)
  SbS Suff

Beacon
  SbS

Bison
  John

F1 Briljant
  Mole

Carvella
  SbS

Cello
  SbS

F1 Cherokee
  Dob John

Cherry Belle
Excellent variety for spring and summer cultivation outdoors. Beautiful colour. Flesh stays deliciously crisp. (Bakk)
  Bakk Brwn Dob EWK Howe John JWB Mars Milt Mole OGC

Crimson Giant
  SbS

Crystal Ball
Slow to go pithy. Roots remain firm and crisp when other varieties have gone pithy. (Toze)
  SbS Sutt Toze

F1 Cyros
EWK SbS

D'Avignon
Longest French variety with delicate crunchy flesh with a touch of fire. Very pretty too with intense rose colour and a white tip. Up to 3 in. long. (Suff)
SbS Suff

F1 Durabel
Bakk

Easter Egg
Round radish that comes in four different colours. Red, pink, purple and white. Ready to pick early and they stay crisp and mild even when large. Great fun for children to grow. Best grown in cool weather. (Suff)
SbS Suff

Fire Candle
Smooth skinned red variety grows up to 6 in. in length. Ideal for slicing with a strong flavour. Sow from July onwards. (OGC)
OGC

Flair
Mole RZ SbS

Flamboyant 2 Sabina
S&G SbS T&M Yate

F1 Fluo
Foth Tuck

F1 Flyer
SbS

Fota
SbS

French Breakfast
Mild flavoured, crisp and tender. Long-rooted, red with a white tip and tail. (Foth)
Bakk Chil EWK Foth Howe John JWB Mole OGC SbS SMM

French Breakfast 2 Lanquette
RSlu

French Breakfast 3
Solid, sweet, cylindrical crimson and white roots. (Sutt)
Brwn Cart Dob Milt SbS Sutt T&M Toze Unwi

French Breakfast Forcing
Mole SbS Toze

French Breakfast Fusilier
An early stock of this popular variety suitable for forcing. (Brwn)
John SbS

French Breakfast Large White Tipped
SbS

Gaudry
Suitable for sowing in the open as well as under glass. A delicious variety, much used for garnishing salads. One of the most widely grown Continental radish varieties. (Bakk)
Bakk

Helro
Very high quality round roots of intense red. Suitable for outdoor production and protected cropping. (Toze)
John SbS

Jaba
OGC Suff

F1 Juliette
T&M

Long White Icicle
Long-rooted, crisp, tender with a mild flavour and white tips. A change from usual reds. (Foth)
Bakk Dob EWK Foth John JWB Mars Milt Mole OGC SbS

F1 Mantanghong
John Sutt T&M

Misato Green
Similar to Misato Red but green all through. (OGC)
OGC

Misato Red
EWK OGC SbS SMM Wall

Novired
RSlu

Olivia
RZ

Parat
Can be left to grow to enormous size without going pithy or splitting. Roots are round, attractive carmine-red and have a mild flavour. (Foth)
Foth

Pegaso
Mole SbS

Pernot
A French Breakfast type with lovely flavour and an attractive white and pale-red colour. Sow:Mar-Aug Harvest; May-Nov (Brwn)
Brwn

Pink Beauty
Of unique colouring and subtle flavour. Attractive, pink, globe-shaped roots are very uniform in size and of first-rate quality. (Dob)
Dob John OGC Sutt

Poker
SbS

Primella
SbS

Prinz Rotin
Fine scarlet globe, which keeps crisp and does not go pithy when quite large, up to 1.5 in. across if sown thinly. (Mars)
Brwn EWK Foth Mars SbS T&M Unwi

Revosa
Small round scarlet roots which mature very rapidly. A popular variety which will stay solid for a long time. Very uniform and of excellent flavour. Not suitable for sowing under glass. (VanH)
VanH

Ribella
Very fast growing, for earliest crops of outdoor radish. Also for cold frames, cloches, etc. Beautiful, round, bright-red roots, slow to become pithy. Sow from February onwards. (Mars)
Mars

Riesenbutter
King-sized radish with flesh as soft as butter. Slow in getting spongy. Fast grower that can be grown successfully by every home gardener. (Bakk)
Bakk

Robino
Mars

F1 Rondar
S&G

Ronde Rode
see Round Red Forcing

Rota
Deep red radish which remains firm and crisp even when oversize. Excellent both for under glass and outside cropping. (OGC)
John Mole SbS

Round Red Forcing Real
SbS

Rudi
Yate

Saxa
Standard variety, guaranteed to give a high yield of bright red radishes. Advisable to sow Saxa in the open. (Bakk)
Bakk John JWB Mole SbS

Saxa 2 Nova
S&G

Scarlet Globe
Excellent shaped round roots, quick growing and very pungent. Can be sown early in cold frames. (EWK)
Cart Chil EWK Foth John Mole OGC SbS SMM Sutt Wall

Scharo
Mole SbS Wall

F1 Serrida
Bakk

Short Top Forcing
For sowing during October-February in a cold frame, greenhouse or under cloches. A fine round, bright scarlet radish which holds its colour and retains its quality when grown under protection. (Dob)
Dob SbS Sutt Toze

F1 Solar
S&G

Sparkler
Very uniform globe type with brighter red skin and white tip. (EWK)
EWK

Sparkler 3
Medium-sized, round red roots tipped with white. (Sutt)
Dob John JWB OGC SbS Sutt Wall

Summer Crunch
A brand new introduction of the French Breakfast type. Longstump ended roots of deep pink colour with very small white tip. Really crisp, sweet tasting white flesh. (Suff)
EWK SbS Suff

Summerred
RSlu

Volcano
Our new introduction of the semi-long type. Superb quality roots with scarlet skin and very small white tip. Crisp white pungent flesh for early forcing or maincrop production. (EWK)
EWK SbS

White Hailstone
SbS

White Turnip
SbS

Woods Frame
SbS

Radish Storage

F1 April Cross
Foth John Mars SbS T&M Toze Unwi Yate

Belrosa
RZ

Black Spanish Long
Long black roots with white flesh, spicy and hot. (OGC)
Chil EWK John OGC SbS Suff

Black Spanish Round
Very hardy with white flesh of good flavour. (Dob)
Brwn EWK Futu John JWB Mars OGC SbS Suff Sutt Tuck

China Rose
Good flavoured longer roots with white flesh. Sow in the autumn. (D&D)
EWK John JWB Mole OGC SbS Suff Sutt Tuck Wall

Mino Early
A large Japanese variety for use, thinly sliced, in autumn and winter salads. The roots, about 15 in. long and 2 in. in diameter are very mild in flavour. (Dob)
Dob John Sutt

F1 Minowase
EWK JWB OGC Suff Tuck Yate

F1 Minowase 2
John SbS Wall

Mooli

Not a variety name, but a general term for a long, white radish.
 EWK Milt

Munchen Bier

Grown for its tasty seed pods. Leave to grow and it will flower very quickly. Spicy pods for eating raw or lightly cooked. (EWK)
 EWK OGC SbS Suff T&M

Ostergruss rosa

Pungent and highly aromatic variety. Does not become spongy. Sow from April onwards. (Bakk)
 Bakk

Robino
 John SbS

F1 Silverstar
 Bakk

Rampion

Rampion

(Campanula rapunculus) We have again been able to obtain seeds of this very interesting salad plant. Grown both for it white, spindle- (or carrot-even) shaped, very firm and crisp roots, ready for use from October right through winter, and its numerous leaves. Both make an unusual addition to any salad. Mix the very fine seed with sand and sow in very shallow drills in May and June and thin out to 4ins. apart. (Chil)
 Chil

Rape

Broad Leaf Essex

May be used instead of mustard and cress and as a sprouting seed. Sown outside makes a good cut and come again crop. (Suff)
 Mole SbS Suff Wall

Emerald

Emerald is resistant to finger-and-toe disease. (MAS)
 MAS Yate

Giant English

Popular in salads in place of mustard, milder flavour. (JWB)
 JWB MAS

Salad Rape

The old traditional "Mustard and Cress". Quick growing with excellent flavour. Sow inside in containers or direct into open ground. Make frequent sowings for continuous cutting. Ready in 10days. (EWK)
 Chil EWK John OGC S&G

Raspberry

Allgold
 Cast

** Augusta
 Cast GTwe Muir Bowe

** Autumn Bliss
Mid August-October. A heavy yielding autumn fruiting raspberry. Large, medium to dark-red berries with good flavour. Fairly easy to plug. Short, sturdy canes - support may not be needed. Aphid resistant. (Brog)
   Cast SDea WHig SKee CSco GTwe Muir LBuc Bowe Edws

Blackie
   Bowe

Fallgold
   Allg CSco GTwe Bowe

** Glen Clova
Early July-late July. Medium sized fruits with fair flavour. A heavy cropper. Canes vigorous and abundant. Susceptible to virus. (Brog)
   Allg Cast SKee Rog CSco GTwe Bowe Edws

Glen Garry
   WHig

** Glen Lyon
   GTwe LBuc

** Glen Moy
Early July-late July. Large, pale-red, short conical firm fruits with a good, slightly aromatic flavour. Fruits are easy toplug and do not crumble. A heavy cropper. Canes are moderately tall, prolific and totally free of spines. Resistant to spur blight, botrytis and some aphids. (Brog)
   Cast SDea WHig SKee Rog CSco GTwe Muir LBuc Bowe

** Glen Prosen
Mid July-mid August. Medium sized, round, very firm fruits with good flavour. Produces only a moderate crop. Canes moderately vigorous, erect and spine-free. (Brog)
   Allg Cast SDea WHig SKee Rog CSco GTwe Muir LBuc Bowe Edws

** Glencoe
   Cast GTwe Bowe

Golden Everest
   Allg CSco Bowe

Haida
   Bowe

Heritage
   Allg CSco Bowe

** Leo
Late July-late August. Medium sized, roundish orange-red fruits which are firm and have a good flavour. Produces a moderate crop. Canes are very vigorous, although sparse and moderately spiny. Fairly resistant to spur blight, botrytis and some aphids. (Brog)
   Allg Cast WHig SKee CSco GTwe Muir Bowe Edws

Malling Admiral
Mid July-mid August. Large, conical, bright red fruits with an excellent flavour. A heavy cropper. Canes are vigorous, prolific and spine-free. Resistant to spur blight, botrytis and mildew. (Brog)
   Allg SKee Rog CSco GTwe Muir Bowe Edws

Malling Delight
Early July-late July. Very large, pale orange-red, rather crumbly fruits. Not recommended for freezing. A good cropper. Canes vigorous and prolific. Susceptible to botrytis and spur blight. (Brog)
Allg Cast WHig SKee Rog CSco GTwe Bowe Edws

Malling Jewel
Early July-late July. Medium to large, medium red fruits with a good, sweet flavour. A good cropper. Canes have a compact habit. Tolerant of virus infection. A popular variety. (Brog)
Allg Cast SDea WHig SKee CSco GTwe Muir LBuc Bowe Edws

Malling Joy
Bowe

Malling Orion
Allg CSco GTwe Bowe

Malling Promise
Allg CSco Bowe

Norfolk Giant
Bowe

Redsetter
Muir

Ruby
Muir

Sceptre
Bowe

September
Allg CSco Bowe

Starlight
Bowe

Summergold
GTwe Muir

Zeva
CSco GTwe Bowe

Redcurrant

Fay's New Prolific
Allg GTwe Bowe

Hollande Rose
GTwe

Jonkheer Van Tets
Early July. A heavy, cropping, large fruited, attractive redcurrant borne on long trusses. Very good flavour. Large, upright bushes. (Brog)
Allg Cast SDea SKee CSco GTwe Muir Bowe Edws

Junifer
Cast Muir

Laxton's No 1
Mid July. Medium sized, bright red berries borne on long trusses. A good cropper. Vigorous, upright to slightly spreading bushes. (Brog)
Allg Cast SDea WHig SKee Rog CSco GTwe Muir Bowe Edws

October Currant
GTwe

Portal Ruby
CSco

Raby Castle
GTwe

Red Dutch
Allg

Red Lake
Late July. Very large, bright red, juicy berries borne on very long trusses. A good cropper. Moderately vigorous, upright bushes. (Brog)
    SDea SKee Rog CSco GTwe LBuc Bowe Edws

** Redstart
August. Small to medium sized fruits produced on long strigs. Fruit has a well developed acid flavour. A heavy and consistent cropper. Makes a good quality jelly. A moderately vigorous, upright bush. (Brog)
    Cast SDea WHig SKee GTwe LBuc Bowe Edws

Rondom
SDea Bowe

Rovada
Cast Muir Bowe

Stanza
SDea GTwe Bowe

Wilson's Long Bunch
GTwe

Rhubarb

Cawood Delight
Mars

Champagne Early
see Early Red

Early Red
(Champagne Early.) Long, bright scarlet stalks of good flavour. Some of the plants will be exceptionally early. (Unwi)
    Mars Unwi

Glaskin's Perpetual
The one variety that can be cut in the first year of sowing. To do so, it is essential to get it off to an early start and keep it growing throughout the season. (OGC)
    Bloo Chil Dob EWK John JWB Mole OGC SbS SMM Suff

Holstein Blood Red
A vigorous grower, producing juicy dark blood-red stalks. (Dob)
    SbS

Large Victoria
A new variety strongly recommended. (JWB)
    JWB SbS

Prince Albert
SbS

Redstick
SbS

Strawberry
SbS

Timperley Early
Ideally plant February-March, but any time from October-January can succeed if soil conditions allow. This variety is suitable for forcing and produces thin, tasty stalks. (Tuck)
Brwn Mars Sore

Victoria
Much easier than you think to grow your own rhubarb from seed and so satisfying with this excellent variety. (Foth)
Brwn Foth John Milt Mole SbS Sutt Wall

Rock Samphire

Rock Samphire
A hardy perennial with glaucous, divided leaves and umbels of yellow flowers. A native of the sea cliffs of Britain, so it should do well planted in crevices in walls and in rock gardens. The salty leaves have an aromatic smell somewhat reminiscent of lemon curd, and can be used as a garnish, in salads, pickled, or steamed and eaten with butter.
Futu Poyn

Rocket

Rocket
The different varieties probably reflect different names for the same, essentially unselected, crop.
Biennial, 2 ft., full sun. Mustard flavoured leaves excellent in salads. (D&D)
Chil Futu Mars Poyn SbS Sutt Tuck VanH

Rucola
Can be sown in rows in April or May, keeping the rows at least 18 in. apart. The tender young leaves are used in salads asan addition to lettuce or endive. (OGC)
OGC

Salad Rocket
This is a superb salad vegetable with leaves of a delicious rich spicy flavour. Quite unlike anything else. Sow any time fromFebruary to September for an almost all year round supply. Very simple to grow and practically no pests or diseases. If you haven't a garden you can grow it in a pot on a window sill or include in a mustard and cress mix. An easy tasty crop that really ought to be better known. (Suff)
Suff

Rocket Turkish

Turkish Rocket
(Bunias orientalis) This is a hardy and vigorous perennial with pinnatifid, Dandelion-like leaves and heads full of bright yellow flowers in summer. Starting in growth very early in spring, when other fresh green vegetables are scarce in the garden, the young and tender leaves and shoots are highly recommended in salads or lightly boiled. 1-3ft. Perennial. (Chil)
Chil Futu

Rosette Pak Choi

Pueblo
Dob

Tatsoi
This is not a true variety name, but simply the Japanese for Rosette Pak Choi.
  EWK OGC SbS SMM Suff

Runner Bean

Achievement
Outstanding variety for table or exhibition. Top quality long pods. (Mars)
  Howe John Mars Mole RSlu S&G Sutt Toze Tuck Wall

Butler
This is a prolific cropper that is also completely stringless. Good sized tender pods on strong vigorous plants. Produces over a long period. (OGC)
  EWK OGC Sutt Wall

Crusader
Produces fine long exhibition pods of good cooking quality. (Brwn)
  EWK Foth John JWB Milt SMM Unwi VanH

Czar
A white seeded type with long rather rough pods. Good flavour cooked green, if left to dry it will give a crop of "butter" beans. (OGC)
  John OGC Suff Tuck

Desiree
A white seeded variety that produces long slender, fleshy pods, at least 10ins in length. Exceptional flavour and stringless, it crops very heavily. 40 pods per plant can be expected. Suitable for freezing. (OGC)
  Brwn EWK Foth John JWB Mars OGC SMM T&M VanH Wall

Enorma
An improved Prizewinner type with long pods of excellent quality. (Brwn)
  Brwn Dob EWK Foth Howe John Mars MAS Milt Mole

Fry Stringo
  S&G

Gulliver
High quality stringless runner bean on non-climbing plants approx. 12ins. No need for staking. Long straight smooth 9-10in. pods. Self-stopping, early, high yielding, difficult for exposed gardens needs cloches. (T&M)
  Cart Dob Toze

Hammonds Dwarf Scarlet
A bush runner bean for the smaller garden, tops may need to be pinched out to stop running. Easy to pick and and no poles needed. (OGC)
  EWK JWB OGC T&M Unwi VanH Wall

Ivanhoe
A quality early variety with long straight fleshy and thick up to 18in. pods which are stringless when young and reasonably so when mature. Scarlet flowers, unique lilac pink seeds. Recommended for exhibition. Early, high yielding. (T&M)
T&M

Kelvedon Marvel
Reading for picking ten days earlier than other varieties. A heavy cropper it is deservedly popular with both gardeners and growers. (OGC)
EWK Howe John JWB Mars Mole OGC RSlu S&G SbS Toze

Lady Di
Producing extra long and slender pods with a smooth skin and very slow to develop seed. Well worth a try. (OGC)
Brwn EWK Foth John Milt SMM T&M Tuck Unwi VanH

Liberty
Very smooth, thick flesh with a large number of beans per truss up to 35ins. in length. (JWB)
JWB Rob Wall

Mergoles
White-flowered and white-seeded, with long, fleshy pods in abundance right through the autumn. One of the best to grow for freezing. (Foth)
Bakk Brwn Dob Foth Sutt

Painted Lady
(1855) Add colour to the vegetable garden with the attractive red and white blossoms. Grow in the herbaceous border or against and unsightly fence. (OGC)
Dob EWK Foth John JWB Mars OGC SMM Suff Tuck Wall

Pickwick
(Unwi)
Brwn Foth John Mars Sutt Toze Tuck Unwi

Polestar
The scarlet flowers set easily and produce and abundant crop of 25cm long beans. Vigour is maintained throughout the season. In our opinion this one is simply the best stringless runner bean available. (Unwi)
Foth John Mars Mole Sutt Toze Unwi Wall

Prizetaker
Our own selected strain of outstanding quality. Good sized pods useful for freezing. (EWK)
EWK John SbS

Prizewinner
Large fleshy pods of fine quality and good flavour. (Unwi)
Cart Chil EWK John JWB MAS SbS Shar Sutt Tuck Unwi

Red Knight
Red flowered, this crops very heavily and the stringless beans are excellent for freezing. (OGC)
Brwn Cart EWK Foth JWB Mars OGC S&G SMM Suff VanH

Red Rum
Very early with a tremendous yield of 6-8in. fleshy, almost stringless, well flavoured pods. The first variety we know with some resistance to halo blight. Seed saved from the hybrid will not breed true. Very heavy yield, very early - can be used as a ground bean. Organic gardeners. (T&M)
T&M

Royal Standard
An impressive new variety. Smooth, bright green, fleshy, completely stringless, 20in. pods which are set well under adverse conditions. Early, heavy yielding. Exhibition. (T&M)
Dob T&M

Scarlet Emperor
(1906) A traditional variety that is as good today as when first introduced at the turn of the century. Preferred by many gardeners for its flavour. (OGC)
Brwn Cart Dob EWK Foth John OGC SbS Shar Suff Sutt

Streamline
A Chase speciality. Good pods of great length as well as excellent texture and flavour. The shape and uniformity of pods makes this useful for the exhibitor. (OGC)
Bakk Brwn Cart Chil Dob EWK Howe John JWB Mars

White Achievement
Sutt

White Emergo
White flowered and white seeded. Long slender pods of fine texture and fine flavour. Especially good for deep freezing. (Unwi)
Brwn EWK Foth Howe John Milt Mole RSlu SbS Shar

Salad Mallow

Salad Mallow
(Malva crispa) A vigorous annual that reaches m. or more and produces light green leaves with crinkled edges and pale pink flowers, making it an attractive plant. The leaves can be eaten in salads or stir-fried, and have excellent flavour and texture. Easily grown, with self-sown seedlings often surviving the winter.
Futu

Salsify

Giant
Called vegetable oyster because of its delicate, distinctive flavour. Long roots to be sliced and fried in butter, or boiled until tender. (Sutt)
Sutt

Mammoth
Long, tapering white roots which can be either boiled or fried. Of sweet, delicious flavour. (Mars)
Mars

Salsify
An interesting root vegetable that may be baked like parsnip, pureed for soup, or just grated raw into salads. (Poyn)
Futu Milt Poyn

Sandwich Island
Long, white tapering roots of smooth texture for Winter use. (EWK)
Chil Dob EWK John JWB OGC SbS SMM Suff T&M Tuck

Scorzonera

Duplex
Should not be sown too early, or it will form seed stalks. Harvest early Winter. Produces a good crop of long, unbranched roots. This variety is a real delicacy. Rich in vitamins. (Bakk)
Bakk

Giant Rooted
SbS

Habil
Long, straight, cylindrical roots with dark brown skin. Delicious sweet flavour somewhat similar to salsify. (Mars)
Mars

Lange Jan
Delicious when scraped and boiled in vinegar and salted water can be served like asparagus. Dark brown in colour, the roots are long and tapering. (Dob)
Dob SbS

Large Black
Another unusual and delicious vegetable looking not unlike salsify but with black-skinned roots. Easily raised, it can be grown and cooked like salsify. (Chil)
Chil

Long Black
The long roots should be scalded and cooked in salty water or sliced and fried in butter. Deliciously sweet flavour. (Foth)
EWK John JWB SbS

Long John
see Lange Jan

Maxima
Similar to salsify but with black roots. The small young leaves are eaten as salad. (OGC)
John OGC SbS SMM Tuck

Russian Giant
Black-skinned roots with unusual, delicate flavour. Scald and scrape before boiling in salted water; or slice, fry in butter, and serve garnished with parsley. (Sutt)
Sutt

Scorzonera
Cultural instructions as for salsify. Similar to salsify but with black skin. Reputed to deter carrot fly if sown with carrots. (Tuck)
Futu Milt Poyn Suff T&M Wall

Sea Kale

Lily White
A heavy cropper with well-flavoured shoots. (Futu)
Chil EWK Futu SbS SMM Suff T&M

Sea Kale
The long succulent blanched shoots are boiled and served like asparagus, with melted butter. Also can be eaten raw in salads. (Mars)
Mars Pask Poyn WKi

White
John

Shallot

Atlanta
EWK

Atlantic
Very firm crisp and crunchy golden brown skinned shallots with an excellent flavour. They are early, producing higher yields of better quality than standard types and have very long storing capabilities. Autumn harvested shallots can easily be kept until late spring in a cool dry room. (T&M)
Rog Sutt T&M Unwi

F1 Atlas
Bakk

F1 Creation
Cart Dob Sutt T&M Unwi

Delicato
Improved Red Shallot, with much better keeping qualities and less susceptible to virus. Strongly flavoured like the old Giant Red, the white flesh is attractively marked with pink rings. Large bulbs, with deep golden-brown skins. (Mars)
Mars

Dobies' Longkeeping Yellow
A reliable variety, crops well and keeps sound for months. Can be planted from February onwards. (Dob)
Dob

Dutch Yellow
High yielding and easy to grow. (Unwi)
OGC

Giant Yellow
Improved stock with better keeping quality. Each bulb planted will split to yield several shallots. Fine for salads or for pickling. (Mars)
Mars Sutt

Golden Gourmet
New much improved yellow variety. Firm even shallots, store well. (Tuck)
Bakk EWK John OGC Suff Tuck Unwi

Hative de Niort
Classic exhibition shallot. Bulbs of excellent form, deep flask-shaped and uniform, circular cross-section. Deep brown skins. (Mars)
Dob Mars Sutt

Pikant
Very well flavoured red shallots with very long keeping qualities. They are very early and high yielding too. Each bulb divided into many shallots at harvest time. (T&M)
EWK Mars Rog Sutt T&M Tuck

Red Sun
Red-fleshed shallot with a reddish skin. Strong, green plant which keeps well until late spring. Gives an extraordinarily high yield! (Bakk)
Bakk

Sante
Excellent for exhibition and kitchen use, producing large, round flavoursome bulbs well protected by reddish-brown skin. Yields up to 25% more than Longkeeping Yellow keeping in prime condition until March following. (Dob)
Brwn Dob EWK Foth Rog

Sante Red
A heavy yield of virus free bulbs of very high quality. Plant this non-hybrid type in mid-April, sowing before this may result in bolting in a difficult season, harvesting during August. (Tuck)
Tuck

Success
Mars

Topper
Big improvement on Giant Yellow. The plants are very vigorous, with stronger foliage and the crop is 30% bigger. Beautiful bright golden bulbs will store without rotting for an exceptionally long time, at least until May. Mild, refined onion flavour, excellent for cooking, salads or pickling. (Mars)
Mars

Yellow
Particularly fine, highly aromatic flavour. Many prefer these firm, small onions to the "ordinary" onions that have a somewhat sharper flavour. (Bakk)
EWK

Skirret

Skirret
Native of China and certainly an ancient vegetable. The plant produces a "bundle" of swollen edible roots which are tender and sweet and floury. Use in the same way as salsify. (Suff)
Chil Futu Poyn Suff

Solanum muricatum

Pepino
Futu

Solanum sisymbrifolium

Litchi Tomato
Futu

Spinach

America
Yate

Atlanta
Highly versatile variety. Sow March to May for May to June cropping and mid July to early October for use from early September to late November. High yielding, frost resistant strain with thick dark green leaves. (EWK)
EWK SbS

F1 Attica
S&G

F1 Bakan
Howe Milt

F1 Ballet
RSlu

Bazaroet
Ideal kitchen garden spinach, extremely prolific (exclusively female plants). Resistant to mildew. (Bakk)
Bakk

Bergola
An early maturing variety for use under glass. Sow at intervals from autumn to spring. Some resistance to Downy Mildew. (OGC)
OGC SbS

Bloomsdale
Deep green leaves with high vitamin C content. Slow running to seed. (Mars)
Chil Mars SbS

F1 Bolero
RSlu

Broad Leaved Prickly
Winter variety that stands well, and produces deep green fleshy leaves. Very hardy. (OGC)
Bakk Chil John JWB OGC SbS

Broad Leaved Prickly Standwell
SbS

F1 Chica
RSlu

F1 Correnta
RSlu

F1 Dash
SbS

Dominant
Thick, round, dark green leaves. Resistant to bolting. Heavycropper. Round seeded, for spring or autumn sowing. (Toze)
John JWB SbS Toze

Fabris
SbS

Giant Thick Leaved
see Broad Leaved Prickly

Giant Winter
Well-known, late autumn and winter spinach, very much in demand. Can withstand some frost. Strong variety, highly disease-resistant. (Bakk)
Bakk Toze

Grodane
Produces an abundance of fleshy leaves. Sow in spring, summer or autumn for an all year round supply. Good resistance to bolting. (Tuck)
EWK SbS Tuck

Hollandia
SbS

King of Denmark
SbS

Longstanding Round
Quick growing, with dark green leaves. (Sutt)
John T&M VanH

F1 Martine
RZ

F1 Mazurka
Foth RSlu SbS

Medania
This is a good variety for summer spinach which produces erect thick green smooth leaves. Vigorous, slow to bolt and resistant to mildew, it can be grown from spring through to late autumn. (OGC)
Brwn Howe John Milt OGC SbS Suff Toze Unwi Yate

F1 Melody
RSlu

Monarch Long Standing
A well-known and popular variety. (Unwi)
Unwi

Monnopa
Unique spinach, with low oxalic acid (an agent that causes loss of calcium from the blood). (T&M)
EWK OGC SbS T&M

New Zealand
Different to usual spinach. Low growing shoots can be picked during summer and autumn. Not frost hardy. Thrives in dry sunny places. Germination can be difficult: soak seed before sowing in pots or outside under cloches March to May. (D&D)
Chil Dob EWK Futu John JWB OGC SbS Suff Sutt Wall

Nobel
SbS

Nores
Late-bolting summer spinach; a strongly improved variety which is highly resistant to mildew. Produces extremely high yields. Flavour outstanding. (Bakk)
Bakk SbS

Norvak
Dob Mole SbS

F1 Novadane
Yate

F1 Oscar
SbS

F1 Pavana
RSlu

F1 Polka
John RSlu SbS

F1 Predane
Yate

Prickly New Giant
Mole SbS Wall

Prickly Winter
Sow in autumn for spring cutting. Strong growing, producing heavy crops of large, dark green leaves. (EWK)
EWK Tuck

F1 Rhythm
RSlu

Round Summer
Good cropping summer spinach. (D&D)
EWK

Sigmaleaf
Sutt

F1 Space
Foth Mole

F1 Spartacus
SbS

Spinoza
SbS

F1 Splendour
Brwn Mole Toze VanH

F1 Sprint
SbS

F1 Sputnik
SbS

F1 Symphony
Mars

F1 Teton
Toze

F1 Triade
Cart Foth

F1 Trias
S&G

F1 Triathlon
Mars

F1 Tribute
SbS

Trinidad
Mars

F1 Triton
Sutt Wall

F1 Valeta
RSlu

Viking
A first class variety rich in vitamins, minerals, protein and with a superb taste. One of the best. (Foth)
Foth SbS

Virkade
Round-seeded for autumn sowing. Resistant to cucumber mosaicand is therefore most useful wherever this disease causes yellowing and stunting in overwintered crops of susceptible varieties. (Toze)
SbS Toze

The Fruit and Veg Finder

Viroflay
For spring and autumn cultivation. Extremely suitable for wintering. Old, well-known variety which is still unbelievably popular. (Bakk)
SbS

Viroflex
RSlu

Wobli
Dark green, slow bolting variety for summer and autumn use. (Toze)
Mole SbS

F1 Wolter
Bakk

Spinach Beet

Erbette
Traditional cut and come again leaf beet from Italy. Grown for its fine tasting greens of good texture. (Suff)
SbS Suff

Fordhook Giant
Similar to Perpetual Spinach but has dark green leaves with a broad white rib. Provides greens throughout the summer and autumn. (OGC)
Dob Foth John JWB Milt Mole SbS Brwn Chil EWK Mars

Italian
White stemmed with dark green foliage. Sow March to August, and thin to eight inches. (Suff)
SbS Suff

Lucullus
A much more prolific form, with an abundance of large, tastyleaves and wide, white mid-ribs. Cook the succulent mid-rib like asparagus and serve with melted butter. (T&M)
Bakk Bloo SbS T&M

Lyon
Well-known variety. Excellent flavour. (Bakk)
Bakk

Perpetual Spinach
Should be cooked and eaten like spinach. Can be harvested several times. (Bakk)
Brwn Cart Chil Dob EWK Foth Howe John JWB Mars

Rhubarb Chard
Long stalks of bright crimson with dark green, deeply crumpled leaves. Highly decorative for floral arrangements as well as a valuable vegetable in the kitchen. Sow and grow as seakale. (Dob)
Bakk Bloo Chil Dob EWK John JWB Milt OGC SbS SMM

Rhubarb Chard Feurio
Mars

Ruby Chard
see Rhubarb Chard

Seakale Beet
Wall

Silver Chard
see Seakale Beet

Swiss Chard
see Fordhook Giant

Squash

F1 All Seasons
S&G

Chilacayote
A rampant, spreading vine that will trail for several yards or can be trained up fences and trellises. Produces enormous bright green and white mottled fruits, with white flesh containing black seeds. A native of South America, in Mexico it is used to make a dessert called Chilacayote. It is also eaten in France as a jam called Cheveux d'ange. Young fruits can be eaten like courgettes and when mature they can be stored for over a year. Tolerates cooler weather than other squashes, and is sometimes used as a disease-resistant rootstock for other Cucurbits. The seeds can be roasted and eaten, and are also grown for their high oil content. (Futu)
Futu

F1 Cream of the Crop
Bloo

F1 Delica
Mole SbS Toze

F1 Star Flower
S&G

F1 Summer Satellite
Bakk

F1 Sunburst
EWK OGC S&G SbS Suff Tuck

Squash Pumpkin

1826
SbS

Atlantic Giant
Holds the world record with a weight of 314 kg. Water and fertilize well. (Bakk)
Bakk Brwn Foth Mars Sutt T&M Unwi VanH

Autumn Gold
These interesting round, lemon yellow fruits, often reaching 7-10 lb. are produced on semi-trailing plants. (Sutt)
Sutt

Baby Bear
Toze

Big Max
Can grow very large under ideal conditions, large globe 17 in. X 17 in., orange pattern on pink background. Thick coarse skin, orange flesh. Long growing season. (Bree)
Rob

Big Moon
A novelty pumpkin with huge, late maturing fruit. The farm shop crowd puller. (Yate)
SbS Yate

F1 Buckskin
SbS

F1 Bushfire
SbS Yate

Cinderella
SbS Toze

Connecticut Field
Approx. 101 days to maturity. Weighs in at 15-25 lb. Large size and bright orange colour. (Suff)
SbS Suff

F1 Funny Face
SbS SbS Yate

Ghost Rider
Normally 12-20 lb. in weight. Deep orange colour. Fine quality with good strong handles. (Toze)
John SbS Toze

Golden Hubbard
John OGC SbS Sutt

Halloween
Normally 6-10lbs. in weight. High yielding variety maturingearly September. Fruit start life yellow in colour turning to
golden orange. (Brwn)
Brwn SbS Toze

Howden
Normally 15-25 lb. in weight. Deep orange, ribbed fruits. Good handles. (Toze)
SbS Toze

Hundredweight
A popular edible pumpkin. Will grow to a large size. (Tuck)
EWK Sutt Tuck Wall

Jack Be Little
The tiniest most decorative pumpkin. Bright orange and distinctly ribbed. They make charming table decorations. Eating quality is superb. Sweet and floury when baked. Perfect for stuffing. (Suff)
EWK OGC SbS Suff

Jack O' Lantern
Deep globe with flattened ends, medium orange colour. Size 8in., weight about 4-5 kg. Fine variety for Jack O' Lanterns. Medium maturity. (Bree)
EWK S&G SbS

Jackpot
Compact, bush-type plants produce a heavy crop of 25 cm. (10in.) diameter orange-yellow fruit which will store until Christmas. (Unwi)
Unwi

Jaune Gros de Paris
SbS

Large Yellow
SbS

F1 Little Lantern
SbS

Mammoth
A "biggy", producing yellow skinned and orange fleshed fruits. A favourite. (Foth)
Chil Dob Foth Howe John JWB Mars Milt Mole OGC SbS

Munchkin
Mole SbS Wall

F1 Pacifica
Yate

Peelless Pumpkin
Originally found in Styria, part of Austria, where it is still very popular, it has several culinary uses, the main one of which is the almost black seeds which can be eaten without peeling, hence peelless pumpkin, and which have a pleasant nut-like taste. A salad oil can be extracted from then and not least you can eat the pumpkin part as a pumpkin. The oil is said to be very effective for prostate problems and for strengthening the bladder. (Chil)
Chil

F1 Prince Regent
Yate

Pumpkin
SbS

Small Sugar
A trailing variety, not especially vigorous. Medium fruits with bright orange flesh which store well. (OGC)
EWK Howe John Milt OGC SbS Suff Toze Yate

Spellbound
Normally 8-12 lb. in weight. Semi-bush type, early maturing. High yields of bright orange, smooth, round fruits. (Toze)
SbS Toze

F1 Spirit
Bloo Mole SbS Yate

F1 Spooktacular
Yate

Sumo
Exhibition size pumpkin. Round in shape and bright orange in colour. (Toze)
SbS Toze

Sunny
see Halloween

Sweet Dumpling
Distinctive blocky fruits, creamy white with green stripes and mottling. (Brwn)
Brwn Chil EWK SbS Suff Toze Tuck

F1 Sweet Mama
EWK OGC SbS SMM

Triple Treat
Cucurbita moschata. Bright orange with delicate fine grain flesh and hull-less seeds (for sprouting, roasting or frying). Often grown for Halloween. Ideal for carving. (Suff)
EWK SbS Suff

Turk's Turban
EWK OGC SbS Suff Tuck

Uchiki Kuri
Japanese Pumpkin. Produces a heavy crop of bright orange, tear-drop shaped fruit with yellow flesh and a sweet and nutty flavour. (OGC)
EWK OGC SbS Suff Tuck

Squash Summer

Gold Nugget
A bush variety producing small orange fruits weighing up to 1kg, ideal for those with limited space. One of the earliest squashes to mature. (Futu)
EWK Futu OGC SbS Tuck

F1 Peter Pan
Sutt

F1 Tivoli
Dob Mars Milt Mole SbS SbS Sutt T&M Unwi Wall Yate

Yellow Crookneck
Suff

Squash Winter

Buttercup
Firm dense flesh with a superb sweet flavour. For soups, roasting round the joint and pumpkin pie and curd. Unusual shape and green/grey in colour. (Suff)
SbS Suff Toze

Butternut
The cylindrical fruits have only a small seed cavity and the bright orange flesh is sweet, fine-grained and of excellent quality. (Dob)
EWK Foth Mars Milt SbS Tuck Unwi

F1 Butternut Sprinter
Toze

Crown Prince
Steel blue in colour, bright orange flesh. Up to 10lb. in weight. Stores well. (Toze)
Mars SbS Sutt Toze Yate

F1 Early Butternut
Dob Mole Wall Yate

Gem
Cricket ball sized, black/green fruits maturing from mid August. Very high yielding. (Toze)
Mars Suff Toze

F1 Goldkeeper
SbS

Onion
Brilliant orange/red coloured fruits of onion shape. 1-3 lb.in weight. (Toze)
SbS Toze

Pompeon
Delicious Japanese winter squash; shiny almost black flat globe shape with golden flesh of superb eating quality as a sweet or savoury. (OGC)
OGC Suff

Ponca
Butternut type. Cylindrical buff coloured fruits with very dense flesh and small seed cavity. Weight from 2 lb. (Toze)
SbS Toze

Rolet
A well flavoured South African gem squash type. An improvement on Little Gem both in yield and fruit size. Better for the small garden. Compact, high yielding vines producing lotsof apple sized, black/green fruits which mature to bright orange.Excellent culinary qualities. (T&M)
SbS

F1 Table Ace
Brwn Foth Milt Mole SbS Toze Wall

Strawberry

** Aromel
August-October. Small to medium sized red, conical fruits with excellent flavour. Sometimes wedge-shaped. Produces a moderate crop. Susceptible to mildew. (Brog)
Allg WHig CSco GTwe Muir Bowe

** Bogota
Cast CSco GTwe Bowe

Bounty
GTwe Muir Bowe

Calypso
Cast WHig

Cambridge Favourite
Mid June-mid July. Medium sized, orange-red, round conical fruits with moderate flavour. Reliable cropper. Virus infection can be a problem. Once the most widely grown variety. (Brog)
Allg Cast SDea WHig Rog CSco GTwe Muir Bowe

Cambridge Late Pine
CSco Muir

Cambridge Rival
CSco

Cambridge Vigour
Early June-late June. Large, conical, bright red fruits withgood flavour. Firm, pale orange flesh. Moderate yields. Yield and
fruit size tend to decline after first year. (Brog)
Cast SDea Rog CSco GTwe Muir Bowe

Domanil
CSco Muir

** Elsanta
Mid June-mid July. Medium to large, round-concial, glossy orange-red fruits with a firm skin. Orange, firm flesh with a good flavour. A heavy cropper. A popular commercial variety. Susceptible to verticillium wilt and red core. (Brog)
Cast SDea WHig CSco GTwe Muir Bowe

** Elvira
Muir Bowe

Evita
Muir

Fern
Bowe

Gorella
Cast CSco Bowe

** Hapil
Mid June-mid July. Large, orange-red, firm fruits with a good flavour. Wedge shaped becoming conical. Crops well. Very susceptible to verticillium wilt. Runners freely. (Brog)
Cast Rog CSco GTwe Muir

Hedley
Bowe

Honeoye
Early June-late June. Medium to large, conical shaped fruits. Glossy red skin with firm red flesh. Acid flavour. Crops well. (Brog)
Cast SDea WHig CSco GTwe Muir Bowe

** Korona
Muir Bowe

** Kouril
Muir

Mara des Bois
Cast WHig GTwe Muir

Marastil
Muir

Maxim
Muir

Ostara
Bowe

** Pandora
Cast GTwe Bowe

Pantagruella
CSco GTwe

Pegasus
Late June-late July. Medium to large, round-concial, glossy orange-red fruits with good flavour. Heavy cropper. Resistant to verticillium wilt. Susceptible to red core. (Brog)
Cast WHig GTwe Muir Bowe

Providence
Bowe

Rabunda
Bowe

** Rapella
GTwe Bowe

Raritan
Bowe

Redgauntlet
Rog CSco Muir Bowe

** Rhapsody
Early July-late July. Medium to large, long conical, glossy red fruits with moderately firm orange-red flesh. Good flavour. Resistant to red core and moderately resistant to verticillium wilt. (Brog)
  Cast WHig GTwe Muir Bowe

Royal Sovereign
  CSco GTwe Muir Bowe

Saladin
  CSco Bowe

Selva
  Bowe

Shuksan
  Bowe

Silver Jubilee
  Bowe

F1 Sweet Sensation
  Dob Sutt

Talisman
  CSco GTwe

** Tamella
Mid June-mid July. Large, dark red berries with fair flavour. Very heavy cropper. (Brog)
  Allg Cast GTwe Muir Bowe

Tantallon
  Bowe

** Tenira
  GTwe Muir Bowe

Totem
  GTwe Bowe

Tribute
  Bowe

Tristar
  Bowe

Troubadour
  CSco Bowe

Strawberry Alpine

Alexandra
  Bowe

Baron Solemacher
  WHig CSco Bowe

Productive
  Bowe

Red Wonder
  Bowe

Rugen
  Bowe

Yellow Wonder
  Bowe

Swede

Acme
Popular fast growing variety with large fine textured roots. (D&D)
  Mole RSlu SbS Wall

Acme Garden Purple Top
Popular fast growing variety with large fine textured roots. (D&D)
Chil EWK John OGC SMM

Angela
Produces purple, globe shaped roots of uniform shape and size. Good resistance to powdery mildew. Suitable for early harvest. (Bree)
Howe John RSlu S&G

Best Of All
Yellow-fleshed globe with purple skin. Very hardy, will stand all winter. (Mars)
Brwn EWK Foth Mars MAS Mole SbS SMM T&M Unwi Wall

Blauwkop
Extremely heavy cropper with excellent keeping qualities. (VanH)
VanH

Champion Purple Top
SbS

Devon Champion
One of the most popular varieties outstanding for table use. (Tuck)
Toze Tuck

Doon Major
John

Joan
Yate

Laurentian
Dark purple, globe shaped roots, with very little neck and compact foliage. Ideal type for market swedes. (Bree)
John RSlu S&G SbS Yate

Lizzy
Bred specially for improved flavour, has a lovely sweet taste. Attractive internal and external coloration with excellenttolerance against root cracking and bolting. (Dob)
Brwn Cart Dob Foth John Milt SbS

Magnificent
Cart

Magres
A selection in Ruta Otofte with very high dry matter and very good resistance to powdery mildew. (Bree)
Howe John S&G SbS Toze Yate

Marian
A very high yielding variety of good flavour and texture, resistant to club root and mildew. (D&D)
Brwn Dob EWK Foth Howe John JWB Mars MAS Mole OGC

Peerless
SbS

Ruby
Mars Toze

Ruta Otofte
Purple skinned, round to slightly tankard shaped, with high dry matter and good winter hardiness. (Bree)
Howe John MAS S&G SbS

Western Perfection
Quick-growing, almost neckless, purple-topped roots with yellow flesh. Ready to lift as required from September. (Sutt)
Sutt

Sweetcorn

F1 Aztec
John

F1 Boston
S&G

F1 Butterscotch
T&M

F1 Candle
RSlu Sutt

F1 Challenger
SbS Toze

F1 Champ
Mars SbS T&M VanH

F1 Citation
SbS Toze

F1 Classic
SbS

F1 Cobham Sweet
SbS Toze

F1 Comanche
John

F1 Conquest
Brwn Dob Mole SbS T&M Toze Wall

F1 Crisp 'n' Sweet
Howe SbS

F1 Dawn
OGC SbS

F1 Dickson
S&G Sutt T&M VanH

F1 Dynasty
S&G Toze

F1 Earlibelle
SbS Sutt Toze Tuck

F1 Earliking
Chil Howe John JWB MAS Milt Mole OGC SbS Toze

F1 Earlivee
SbS Toze

F1 Early Cup
SbS

F1 Early Pac
EWK SbS Yate

F1 Early Pak
Suff

F1 Early Xtra Sweet
Howe SbS Unwi

F1 Festival
Brwn

F1 Fiesta
Foth Howe Milt Mole SbS Tuck

5th Edition

F1 First Of All
Sutt

F1 Florida Stay Sweet
Howe SbS

Golden Bantam
John Mole SbS

F1 Golden Sweet
EWK OGC SbS SMM

F1 Gourmet
Mars Toze

F1 Herald
Mole SbS Toze Wall

F1 Honey and Cream
Mars

F1 Honeycomb
SbS SMM Suff Tuck

F1 Honeydew
Foth JWB SbS

F1 Indian Dawn
SbS Toze

John Innes Hybrid
John

John Innes Hybrid Canada Cross
SbS

F1 Jubilee
Brwn EWK Howe John Milt Mole S&G SbS Suff Toze

Kelvedon Glory
Crops well, early and yields high quality, long, even cobs of exceptional flavour. (Foth)
Bloo Brwn EWK Foth John MAS Mole OGC SbS Unwi Wall

F1 Kelvedon Sweetheart
SbS

F1 Kodiak
SbS

F1 Lariat
SbS

F1 Lumidor
RSlu

F1 Mellogold
John

F1 Minisweet
Bloo OGC

F1 Minor
Foth John T&M

F1 Miracle
EWK SbS Wall

F1 Morning Sun
SbS Wall

F1 Northern Belle
EWK John Mole SbS Toze Tuck

F1 Northern Extra Sweet
SbS SbS Toze

F1 Northern Star
SbS

F1 October Gold
John SbS

F1 Ovation
SbS Toze

F1 Peppy
Bakk

F1 Pinnacle
SbS Toze

F1 RBS 9029
S&G

F1 Reliance
SbS

F1 Reward
Brwn John SbS

F1 Rosella 425
EWK SbS

F1 Royal Crest
SbS

F1 Seneca Horizon
SbS Toze

F1 Seneca Star
SbS

F1 Snogold
SbS

F1 Snosweet
Yate

F1 Spirit
S&G

F1 Starlite
Chil EWK OGC SbS

F1 Sugar Boy
EWK OGC SbS

F1 Sugar King
SbS

Summer Flavour
Very early maturing which makes it ideal for Northern districts, poor summers and late sowings. Plus gourmet sweet, very tender and tasty 6.5-7 in. cobs. (T&M)
T&M

F1 Summit
SbS

F1 Sun Up
SbS Toze

F1 Sundance
Brwn Dob SbS Sutt Toze Unwi

F1 Sunrise
Cart Dob Mars SbS Toze

F1 Sweet 77
John JWB Mole SbS Wall

F1 Sweet Bonus
EWK SbS

F1 Sweet Mexi
SbS

The Fruit and Veg Finder

F1 Sweet Nugget
EWK SbS

F1 Sweet Season
OGC SbS

F1 Sweet September
SbS Toze

F1 Sweet Treat
Tuck

F1 Tasty Gold
SbS

F1 Tasty Sweet
Bakk EWK SbS Suff

F1 Terrific
SbS

F1 Trophy
RSlu

F1 Two's Sweeter
T&M VanH

F1 Xtra Sweet Improved
Mars

F1 Yukon
SbS SMM

Texsel Greens

Ethiopian Rape
see Texsel Greens

Texsel Greens
(Brassica carinata) This leafy vegetable is milder in flavour than cabbage and much more tasty than spinach. Ideal to pick and eat fresh but will also keep in cold storage. Sow in the open and harvest when the plants reach 8-12inches. Sow: Mar-onwards. Harvest: after 50 days. (Brwn)
Brwn Futu OGC SbS Suff Yate

Tomatillo

Large Green
Large green fruits. (Futu)
Futu

Purple
Smaller fruit with a sharper flavour and purple colour, preferred by some Mexican cooks. (Futu)
Futu

Tomatillo
(Physalis ixiocarpa) Also known as Jamberry and Mexican Husk Tomato. This is an interesting plant that can be grown as an outdoor tomato with purple-blotched yellow flowers followed by golfball-sized, sticky, purplish fruits enclosed by a papery husk. Unripe, these are used in wide variety of Mexican dishes such as salsa verde, a mildly hot chili sauce. The ripe fruits are sweeter and can be eaten raw, out of hand or in salads, or used in pies and jams. 2-4ft. (Chil)
Chil

Tomato

F1 Abunda
John Mole RZ

Ailsa Craig
Greenhouse/outdoor, cordon. Medium size fruit, very regular and perfect in shape. For real flavour, this is still one of the very best and it's a heavy cropper. (Unwi)
Bloo Brwn Chil Dob EWK Foth Howe John JWB Mars

F1 Alfresco
John JWB SbS Toze

Alicante
Outdoor/greenhouse, cordon. An ideal variety for beginners, producing a heavy crop of high quality well flavoured fruit. (T&M)
Bloo Brwn Cart Dob EWK Foth Howe John JWB Mars

Amateur
Wall

F1 Andra
RZ

F1 Angela
John Mole SbS Wall

F1 Arasta
EWK John Mole SbS Wall

F1 Atlantic City
SbS

Aurega
Dwarf variety for outdoors, fruit medium to small. (CGar)
EWK SbS Suff

F1 Beefmaster
Bakk SbS SMM Wall

Beefsteak Improved
VanH

F1 Big Boy
Brwn Chil Dob EWK Foth John JWB Mars Milt Mole OGC

F1 Blizzard
EWK Foth Howe JWB Milt Mole SbS Toze Tuck Wall

Brasero
Small, succulent, sweet, early ripening fruits produced in abundance. Staking or pinching out of sideshoots is not required and with a spreading bushy habit, it is ideal for pots and containers or in grow bags or in borders. (Foth)
Foth

Britains Breakfast
Lemon shaped fruit, red and very sweet, standard habit, has a very large spreading truss with many having over 60 fruits. Fruit does not split when ripe. (Rob)
Rob Wall

F1 Buffalo
Bakk John

F1 Calypso
Mole SbS Toze

F1 Carmello
S&G

Carter's Fruit
Cart

F1 Chaser
S&G

F1 Cherry Belle
Cart Dob Sutt Yate

F1 Cherry Wonder
Foth Yate

F1 Choice
S&G

F1 Contessa
Bakk

F1 Cossack
SbS

F1 Counter
Toze Unwi

Craigella
Non greenback similar to Ailsa Craig. (CGar)
EWK

F1 Cumulus
Dob

F1 Cyclon
SbS Unwi

F1 Danny
John Mole

F1 Dario
Mars

F1 Dombello
Dob John Mole SbS Sutt Tuck Yate

F1 Dombito
Brwn JWB Mars SbS T&M Toze Yate

Earliana
SbS

F1 Estrella
Bakk Brwn Dob SbS Wall

F1 Eurocross BB
EWK John JWB Mole SbS Wall Yate

F1 Extase
EWK SbS

First In The Field
Very good for outdoor culture, vigorous growth. (CGar)
EWK John JWB Mole SbS Wall

F1 French Cross
Sutt

Freude
see Gardener's Delight

Gardener's Delight
Small cherry-type fruit of outstanding flavour, ideal for salads and sandwiches, which can also be frozen complete. An exceptional cropper both outdoors and under glass. (OGC)
Bloo Brwn Cart Chil Dob EWK Foth Howe John JWB

F1 Gemini
Dob

Golden Sunrise
For those who like a little variation in their tomatoes. As the name indicates this is golden yellow in colour, medium in size, round, thin skinned, excellent flavour and a heavy cropper. Early. (OGC)
Brwn Chil Dob EWK Foth John JWB Milt Mole OGC SbS

F1 Golden boy
Sutt

F1 Goldstar
Mole SbS

F1 Grenadier
S&G SbS Sutt

Harbinger
An old favourite from the beginning of the century when tomatoes had flavour! A good tall outdoor variety or for growing under plastic. Thin skinned medium size fruit which will ripen well off the plant. (Suff)
Dob EWK JWB OGC SbS Suff Sutt Toze

Heinz
SbS

F1 Herald
Mars

Histon Early
Outdoor, cordon. A heavy cropper with bright red fruit of good size and quality and fine flavour. (Unwi)
Unwi

F1 Isidro
RZ

F1 JR-6
SbS

Jubilee
Rob

F1 Libra
Brwn OGC

Maja
Bush type of compact growing habit with very good tolerance to cool conditions. Bright red fruits up to 35cms each plant with strong aromatic flavour. (EWK)
EWK SbS Suff

F1 Manhattan
S&G

Marglobe
Large red fruit, thick meaty flesh of excellent flavour can be grown to over 1 lb each tomato. (Rob)
Rob SbS

Marmande VR
Outdoor, cordon. Large, firm irregular fruits of the Continental type, with very few seeds. Ideal for slicing. A semi-determinate type producing terminal trusses. Early. (Unwi)
>Brwn Chil Unwi EWK

Marmande hative
see Marmande Super

Marmande super
A variety originating in Southern Europe, producing large, irregular shaped, fleshy tomatoes ideal for slicing and of a rich
flavour. Shows good natural resistance to disease, and best results are obtained when grown outdoors. Bushy habit. (OGC)
>Bakk Dob Foth John JWB Mars Mole OGC SbS Suff Sutt

F1 Master
>Bakk

F1 Matador
>SbS T&M

Minibel
Tasty bite-size tomatoes can be grown in pots on the patio, in window boxes or on your windowsill, novel, miniature bush variety. (Foth)
>Chil Foth

F1 Mirabell
>Foth Mars

Moneycross
Greenhouse, cordon. An improvement on the popular Moneymakervariety being a heavy cropper of non greenback fruit. (John)
>John JWB Mole SbS VanH

Moneymaker
Outdoor/greenhouse, cordon. Very reliable variety which has stood the test of time. (T&M)
>Bloo Brwn Cart Chil Dob EWK Foth Howe John Milt

Moneymaker Dutch Victory
>Toze

Moneymaker Stonor
A very heavy cropper, with fruits of medium size, bright scarlet in colour. (Barb)
>JWB

Montfavet 63-4
A so-called bush type tomato, early maturing and fleshy, with a beautiful round shape. Resistant to "bursting" and, therefore, a sure cropper. Very suitable for early cultivation under glass. Perfectly suited for making tomato juice and ketchup. (Bakk)
>Bakk

F1 Monza
>EWK

F1 Nimbus
>Sutt

F1 Ostona
>SbS

Outdoor Girl
This variety has been developed for outdoor cultivation, and its characteristics include extreme earliness, large trusses bearing many medium sized fruit, excellent flavour, a good red colour and sturdy plants. An ideal outdoor garden variety. (John)
Brwn EWK John JWB Mars Mole OGC SbS Wall

Oxheart
The traditional Italian garden tomato. Huge pink fruit shaped like a heart. Flesh is very meaty with not too much juice so ideal for slicing, sandwiches, &c. Produced an excellent crop under a polytunnel. (Suff)
SbS Suff

F1 Pannovy
S&G

F1 Patio
Bakk

F1 Phyra
Chil EWK Foth OGC SbS SMM Suff

F1 Piranto
Mars

F1 Pixie
Bloo EWK John JWB Mole OGC SbS Suff Wall

Plumito
Smooth straight sided red fruit, sweet and fleshy, ideal for freezer or bottling, standard habit. (Rob)
Rob

F1 Primato
Dob S&G Wall

F1 Prisca
Mars

Red Alert
Outdoor/greenhouse, bush. Small fruits roughly 1 oz each with a good flavour. Easy. No side shooting or training. (T&M)
Brwn Cart Dob EWK Foth John JWB Mars Mole OGC SbS

Red Cherry
Cherry sized fruit, good flavour, standard habit with long strings of fruit. (Rob)
Rob

Roma VF
Outdoor, bush. Continental type bearing brightly coloured long, fleshy fruits. Heavy cropping, and resistant to fusarium wilt. (Sutt)
Brwn Foth Mars SbS T&M VanH

Round Yellow Sunrise
Notably sweeter in flavour than most red tomatoes, standard habit. (Rob)
Rob

Rutgers
SbS

San Marzano 2
A typical "Italian" tomato, producing longish, firm fruit. Extremely suitable for making the sauce that goes with spaghetti Bolognese, for tomato soup or for garnishing your salads. It gives a high yield of egg-shaped, firm-fleshed fruit. (Bakk)
    Chil EWK JWB OGC SbS SMM Suff Wall

F1 Shirley
    Brwn Cart EWK Foth Howe John JWB Mars Milt Mole

F1 Sigmabush
    Sutt

F1 Sioux
    Unwi

F1 Sixtina
    Bakk

F1 Sleaford Abundance
    JWB Mars SbS

F1 Sonatine
    JWB Sutt

F1 Sonato
    Unwi

F1 Spartan
    Dob

F1 Spectra
    Mole SbS

St Pierre
A very tasty traditional French tomato. Produces a late crop of large tasty bright red fruit, superb sliced for salad and sprinkled with fresh basil. (Suff)
    Suff

Stonor Exhibition
Medium early, round red fruit excellent for the show bench, has the good old fashioned taste. (Rob)
    JWB Rob Wall

F1 Sungold
    Bloo T&M

F1 Super Cross
    SbS

F1 Supersteak
    T&M

F1 Supersweet 100
    S&G

F1 Sweet 100
    Bakk Bloo Brwn Chil EWK Foth John Mars Mole OGC

F1 Sweet Cherry
    Foth SbS SMM

F1 Sweet Million
    Unwi

The Amateur
Outdoor. A very popular bush tomato. Good yield and quality. (Unwi)
    Cart Chil EWK John JWB Mole SbS Sutt Unwi

Tigerella
Eye catching red fruit with pale stripes and a very good flavour. Produces high yileds opf early maturing fruits. (RHS AM) (Brwn)
>Brwn EWK Foth OGC SbS Suff Sutt T&M Wall

Tiny Tim
The ultimate in compact tomato plants. Perfect for pot or window box growing. Superb flavoured cherry sized fruit which arequite delicious whole in salads. (Suff)
>EWK SbS Suff Tuck Wall

F1 Tomboy
>EWK SbS Suff

F1 Tomboy Golden
>EWK OGC SbS

F1 Tornado
>Foth Mars Mole OGC SbS Sutt Wall

F1 Totem
>Bakk Dob John Mole SbS Tuck Unwi

F1 Trio
>SbS Yate

F1 Tumbler
>Brwn Cart Dob John Mars Mole SbS Sutt T&M VanH

F1 Turbo
>John Mole SbS Toze Wall

F1 Typhoon
>Brwn Dob Howe Milt Mole SbS Wall

F1 Vitador
>Yate

Yellow Canary
>Mole SbS Wall

Yellow Cocktail
Delightful miniature, pear-shaped, golden-yellow fruits. Best grown under glass, tall sturdy plants quick growing with large trusses. (EWK)
>Chil EWK SbS SMM

Yellow Currant
Small fruit, grape-like in appearance, long strings of tomatoes. Can be grown as a standard type in a pot or as a bush habit. (Rob)
>Rob Wall

F1 Yellow Debut
>S&G Toze

Yellow Pearshaped
Pear shape fruit, very sweet and solid with few seeds, standard habit. (Rob)
>Bakk Rob Suff Wall

Yellow Perfection
The earliest and most prolific tall yellow tomato in existence. Recommended for outdoors. Cordon. (Unwi)
>Mars Unwi

F1 Zorro
>EWK

Tree Tomato

Tree Tomato
A first-rate attraction for indoors. Sow early, prick seedlings out into pots and put in a frost-free place during the winter. This decorative tree will bear fruit from the second year onwards. A real treat, raw as well as cooked. (Bakk)
Bakk

Turnip

Aberdeen Green Top Yellow
SbS

Arcoat
SbS Yate

Audric
RZ

Champion Green Top Yellow
One of the most popular yellow fleshed turnips grown. Remains firm and palatable over a long period. (Tuck)
Tuck

De Norfolk a collet vert
see Imperial Green Globe

Early Snowball
Harvest when small, sweet and tender. Cook lightly and add a dab of butter. The variety grows quickly from a spring sowing.
(Suff)
Foth Suff

Early White
see Snowball

Early White Stone
John

Frisia
Sow late June and July for feeding July, August and early September. (MAS)
MAS

Golden Ball
Sow for succession from late spring onwards. Harvest when about tennis-ball size. Can be sown late August for winter storing in sand or peat. Good flavour. (D&D)
Brwn Cart Dob EWK John JWB Mars Mole OGC SbS Suff

Goudbal
see Golden Ball

Green Globe
see Imperial Green Globe

Green Top
SbS

Green Top Stone
see Manchester Market

John

Green Top Stone
see Manchester Market

F1 Hakutaka
Dob

Imperial Green Globe
Maincrop with round roots of pure white flesh. The best variety to grow for turnip top "greens". (Sutt)
Sutt

Manchester Market
Large white globe, green top. (Mars)
Brwn EWK Howe John JWB Mars Milt Mole RSlu S&G

F1 Market Express
Yate

Milan Early White Top
Very early, forces well under frame or cloche. (JWB)
JWB

Milan Purple Top Forcing
A very early garden turnip for sowing in the open, although it can also be sown in a frame. Sweet flavour, very rich in vitamins. (Bakk)
RSlu S&G SbS Toze Wall

Milan White
Flat shaped roots of pure white for early crops. (Dob)
EWK Howe John Milt SbS SbS Toze Wall

Milan White Top
see Milan White

Model White
see Stone

Norfolk Green Globe
see Imperial Green Globe

Orange Jelly
see Golden Ball

Presto
Aptly named, this is a very small, pure white turnip that can be picked in little more than a month after sowing when the roots will be about one inch in diameter. Sow in rows and thin out to three inches apart. The leaves can also be eaten, cooked as for greens. (Chil)
Chil

Purple Top Milan
Quick to mature and good for early sowings. It has distinctive white flat roots topped with purple which have an excellent flavour. (Foth)
Brwn Cart Dob EWK Foth John Mole SbS SMM Sutt Tuck

Purple Top White Globe
White globe shaped root with purple top. (Bree)
EWK John OGC S&G SbS

Red Milan
SbS

F1 Royal Crown
Suff Toze

Snowball
Very fast growing. Tender flesh suitable for salads if harvested when young. (D&D)
Brwn Cart Chil EWK John JWB Mars MAS Mole OGC SbS

Sprinter
see Milan Purple Top Forcing

Stanis
Round roots with deep pink shoulder. For late summer and autumn crops. (Toze)
SbS Toze

Stone
Dob Toze

Stubble Turnip
see Tyfon

F1 Tokyo Cross
Dob EWK Foth John OGC S&G SbS Suff Sutt T&M Tuck

Tokyo Market Sagami
see Presto

Tokyo Market Second Early
Maturing in 6 to 8 weeks from sowing is this tasty variety producing white-skinned roots, a couple of inches across, with crisp, solid, mild-flavoured, white flesh. (Chil)
Chil

F1 Tokyo Top
John SbS

Tyfon
Cook the tops like spinach, very nutritious for humans and goats. (JWB)
JWB MAS

Veitch's Red Globe
Smooth skinned roots with red top and pure white flesh. Fastmaturer. (OGC)
John Tuck

Unusual Fruits

American Elderberry (Sambucus canadensis 'Adams & York')
CSim

Arctic Raspberry (Rubus x stellarcticus)
CSim

Buartnut (Juglans x bixbyi)
CSim

Chilean Guava (Myrtus ugni)
CSim

Edible Honeysuckle (Lonicera caerulea edulis)
CSim

Edible Rowan (Sorbus aucuparia edulis)
CSim

Fruit Salad Plant (Feijoa sellowiana)
CSim

Juneberry (Amelanchier x lamarckii 'Ballerina')
CSim

Lingonberry (Vaccinium vitis-idaea)
CSim

Maypop/Apricot Vine (Passiflora incarnata)
CSim

Nanking Cherry (Prunus tomentosa)
CSim

Passiflora x exoniensis
CSim

Pepino (Solanum muricatum)
CSim

Rubus calycinoides 'Emerald Carpet'
CSim

Saskatoon (Amelanchier alnifolia)
CSim

Siberian Gooseberry (Actinidia arguta)
CSim

Water Chinquapin

Water Chinquapin
(Nelumbo lutea) A beautiful ornamental lotus from the USA, growing in shallow water. It produces round leaves that are held above the water and huge, pale-yellow, waterlily-like flowers. These are followed by unusual flat pepper-pot seedheads. The large seeds are delicious cooked like chestnuts. The young leaves were cooked like spinach by native tribes and the tubers were leached to remove bitterness and eaten, with a flavour likened to sweet potato.
Futu

Watercress

Imperial Large Leaved
SbS

Watercress
Will grow without running water, in constantly moist shady site, or in pots part sunk into gravel - (keep gravel wet). Very rich in vitamin C. Gives spice to salads and sandwiches. (Bloo)
Bloo Chil Dob EWK John JWB Mole OGC SbS Suff VanH

Watermelon

Charleston Gray
Fine eating variety with crisp red flesh and light greenish skin. Semi-long fruits which can grow to a large size. Needs a lot of watering. (EWK)
EWK John JWB Mole OGC SbS SMM Wall

Crimson Sweet
Produces large green-skinned fruit with a distinctive mouth watering aroma and very refreshing, juicy, scarlet flesh. (John)
John

F1 Dulzura
RZ

F1 Golden Crown
T&M

F1 King of Hearts
Bakk

Lucky Sweet
A hybrid which replaces the older type of water-melon because it has the merit of good fruit setting, even in low temperatures. (Bakk)
Bakk

Sugar Baby
Round fruits weighing up to 10 lbs. Sweet and juicy. Startseed early to get best results. 80 days. (Suff)
SbS Suff

Whitecurrant

White Dutch
CSco Bowe

White Grape
Rog GTwe Bowe

White Pearl
Bowe

White Transparent
GTwe

White Versailles
Early July. Large, pale yellow, sweet fruits produced on long trusses. A good reliable cropper. A vigorous, upright bush. (Brog)
Allg Cast SDea WHig SKee CSco GTwe Muir LBuc Bowe Edws

Yacon

Yacon
(Polymnia sochifolia) A frost-tender species from the Andes, which produces large storage tubers that look like dahlia roots, as well as vegetative tubers similar in appearance to Jerusalem artichokes. The plant is ornamental, producing large triangular leaves on thick stems, and reaches a height of 1.5 — m. under ideal conditions. It makes a good accent plant for edible landscapes. The storage tubers have no buds, so they do not sprout and can be stored for long periods in a frost-free place. Plants have produced storage tubers weighing 1 Kg. with a crunchy texture and sweet flavour. Traditionally they are left in the sun for a few days after harvesting before being eaten. They retain their crunchiness after cooking and are an ideal substitute for water chestnuts in Chinese cookery.
Futu

Allg   J.C. Allgrove Ltd

The Nursery, Middle Green
Langley
Bucks
Phone: 01753 520155
Fax:

Bakk   Bakker Holland

P.O. Box 111
Spalding
Lincs
PE12 6EL
Phone: 01775 711411
Fax: 01775 711381
An interesting selection of varieties, if you can work out how to use the catalogue.

Benn   Michael Bennett

Long Compton
Shipston on Stour
Warwickshire
CV36 5JN
Phone:
Fax:
A supplier of asparagus crowns and artichoke offsets, with good advice on growing.

Bir   Jennifer Birch

Garfield Villa
Belle Vue Road
Stroud, GLOS
Phone: 01453 750371
Fax:
A specialist supplier of garlic, who will also supply in bulk.

Bloo   Blooming Things

Y Bwthyn, Cymerau
Glandyfi
Machynlleth
Powys
SY20 8SS
Phone: 01654 781256
Fax:
New this year. An interesting departure, selling a range of organically grown flowers and vegetables as plugs and plants, ready for setting out in your garden.

Bowe   Chris Bowers & Sons

Whispering Trees Nursery
Wimbotsham
Norfolk
PE34 8QB
Phone: 01366 388752
Fax:

Brwn   D. T. Brown Ltd

Station Road
Poulton Le Fylde
Blackpool
Lancs
FY6 7HX
Phone: 01253 882371
Fax: 01253 890923
A good range of small packets, but also supplies in greater bulk. Flowers too.

The Fruit and Veg Finder

CGOG   Global Orange Groves UK

PO Box 644
Poole
Dorset
BH17 9YB
Phone: 01202 691699
Fax:

CSco   Scotts Nurseries (Merriott) Ltd

Merriott
Somerset
TA16 5PL
Phone: 01460 72306
Fax:

CTho   Thornhayes Nursery

St Andrews Wood
Dulford
Cullompton
Devon
EX15 2DF
Phone: 0188 246746
Fax: 01884 266739

Call   John Callum

Unit 51
Bandeath Ind. Estate
Throsk
Stirling
FK7 7NP
Phone: 01786 815357
Fax: 01786 814400
Potato specialist, who supplies large and small quantities.

Cart   Carters Tested Seeds Ltd

Hele Road
Torquay
Devon TQ2 7QJ
Phone: 01803 616156
Fax: 01803 615747

Cast   Castle Plant Company

38 Church Road
Wimsbotsham
King's Lynn
Norfolk
PE34 2QG
Phone: 01366 387237
Fax:

Chil   Chiltern Seeds

Bortree Stile
Ulverston
Cumbria
LA12 7PB
Phone: 01229 581137
Fax: 01229 584549
An astonishing range of seeds, apart from vegetables, and a wonderfully readable catalogue, if you like that sort of thing (which I do).

CSim   Clive Simms

Woodhurst
Essendine
Stamford
Lincolnshire
PE9 4LQ
Phone: 01780 55615
Fax:

Dob   Samuel Dobie & Son Ltd

Broomhill Way
Torquay
Devon
TQ2 7QW
Phone: 01803 616888
Fax: 01803 615150
A colourful catalogue with seeds, plants, and sundries.

EBal   Ballerina Trees Ltd.

Maris Lane
Trumpington
Cambridgeshire
CB2 2LQ
Phone: 01233 840411
Fax:

ERea   Reads Nursery

Hales Hall
Loddon
Norfolk
NR14 6QW
Phone: 01508 548395
Fax:

EWK   E.W.King & Co. Ltd

Monks Farm
Pantlings Lane
Coggeshall Road
Kelvedon
CO5 9PG
Phone: 01376 570000
Fax: 01376 571189
Bulk supplies and smaller packets. A major wholesaler for other seed suppliers.

Edws   Edwards Fruit Trees

Tryfan
24 Rodney Gardens
Pinner
Middlesex
HA5 2RR
Phone: 0181 8666434
Fax:

Foth   Mr Fothergill's Seeds Ltd

Gazeley Road
Kentford
Newmarket
Suffolk
CB8 7QB
Phone: 01638 751161
Fax: 01638 751624
A well-known supplier, with colourful catalogue and good range of flowers and vegetables.

Futu — Future Foods

20 Gastard Lane
Gastard
Corsham
Wiltshire
SN13 9QN
Phone: 01249 712749
Fax:
A truly wonderful catalogue, full of unusual edible plants. We have listed only the vegetables; Future Foods also supply trees and shrubs, unusual fruits, mushroom spawns, and starter cultures for fermented foods. Good selection of books, too. Although the business has changed hands — and will need to settle down — the range is still one of the most interesting available.

GTwe — J Tweedie Fruit Trees

Maryfield Road Nursery
Maryfield, Nr Terregles
Dumfries
Dumfriesshire
DG2 9TH
Phone: 01387 720880
Fax:

Hen — James Henderson & Sons

Kingholm Quay
Dumfries
DG1 4SU
Phone: 01387 52234
Fax: 01387 62302
A potato specialist.

Howe — Steve Howe Seeds Ltd

Fresh Fields
Long Hedges
Fishtoft
Boston, Lincs
PE22 0RH
Phone: 01205 360235
Fax: 01205 357794
Bulk seed supplier, exclusive agents for GZG Marne, Huizer Zaden and Van Der Have.

JWB — J.W. Boyce Seedsmen

Bush Pasture
Lower Carter Street
Fordham, Ely
Cambs
CB7 5JU
Phone: 01638 721158
Fax:
Good selection of varieties, with pansies and other flowers too.

John — W.W. Johnson and Son Ltd

London Road
Boston
Lincs
PE21 8AD
Phone: 01205 365051
Fax: 01205 310148
Supplies small packets and in bulk. Latest catalogue we have is from 1994.

LBuc   Buckingham Nurseries

14 Tingewick Road
Buckingham
Buckinghamshire
MK18 4AE
Phone: 01280 813556
Fax: 01280 815491

MAS   M.A.S.

9 Brevel Terrace
Charlton Kings
Cheltenham
GL53 8JZ
Phone: 01242 234355
Fax:
Bulk only. Specialist in grass mixtures for all purposes. Also wildflowers and conservation mixtures.

Mars   S.E. Marshall & Co Ltd

Wisbech
Cambs
PE13 2RF
Phone: 01945 583407
Fax: 01945 558235
A well-known supplier with a good range of potatoes as well as the more usual fruit, flowers and veg.

Mart   J.E. Martin

4 Church Street
Market Harborough
Leics
LE16 7AA
Phone: 01858 462751
Fax: 01858 434544
Potato specialist.

McL   Mrs M. MacLean

Dornock Farm
Crieff
Perthshire
PH7 3QN
Phone: 01764 652472
Fax:
Wonderful range of potatoes, but rather limited availability. Please send SAE when enquiring. Two information leaflets available: Fact Sheet on Special Properties of Potato Varieties (revised 1990, price 50p) and Growing Potatoes for Exhibition (1987, price 30p). The bad news is that Mrs McLean is retiring after the 1995 season; what will become of her unique collection?

Milt   Milton Seeds

3 Milton Avenue
Blackpool
Lancs
FY3 LY8
Phone: 01253 394377
Fax: 01253 305110
New this year. A fine range of flowers and veg in an informative catalogue.

Mole   J. W. Moles & Son

Turkey Cock Lane
Stanway
Colchester
Essex
CO3 5PD
Phone: 01206 213213
Fax: 01206 212876
Bulk only. Moles will not deal in small quantities, and agreed to be included in this year's edition only if we pointed out that they will not reply to enquiries from amateurs. Last catalogue we have is from 1994.

Muir   Ken Muir

Honeypot Farm
Weeley Heath
Clacton-on-Sea
Essex
CO16 9BJ
Phone: 01255 830181
Fax:
Soft fruit specialist.

OGC   Chase Organics (GB) Ltd

Coombelands House
Coombelands Lane
Addlestone
Weybridge
KT15 1HY
Phone: 01932 820958
Fax: 01932 821258
The HDRA's mail-order catalogue with many sundries for organic gardening in addition to seeds. Discount for HDRA members.

Pask   Michael Paske Farms Ltd

Estate Office
Honington
Grantham
Lincs
NG32 2PG
Phone: 01400 50449
Fax: 01400 50204
Specialist in thongs of sea kale, and also supplies asparagus plants, crowns and seeds, and artichoke plants. "We deal with every enquiry individually and try to supply our customers' requirements."

Poyn   Poyntzfield Herb Nursery

Black Isle
By Dingwall
Ross-shire
Scotland
IV7 8LX
Phone: 01381 610352
Fax: 01381 610352
Specialist herb nursery, with many unusual edible plants beyond those listed. Organically grown seeds and plants. Send 3 1st class stamps and SAE for catalogue.

RSlu — Royal Sluis Ltd

Unit 4, St Andrews Court
Rollesby Road
Hardwick Ind. Estate
King's Lynn
PE30 4LS
Phone: 01553 691133
Fax: 01553 691144
Bulk only supplies of seed, of varieties of interest mainly to commercial growers.

RZ — Rijk Zwaan UK Ltd

Pocklington Ind. Estate
Pocklington
York
YO4 2NR
Phone: 01759 305830
Fax: 01759 305848
The retail arm of the famous Dutch breeders. If you want to try the varieties the commercial growers use, this is the one.

Rob — W. Robinson & Sons Ltd

Sunny Bank
Forton
Nr Preston
Lancs
PR3 0BN
Phone: 01524 791210
Fax: 01524 791933
Specialist in giant and exhibition varieties.

Rog — R. V. Roger Ltd

The Nurseries
Pickering
North Yorkshire
YO18 7HG
Phone: 01751 472226
Fax: 01751 476749
A general supplier, with good list of fruits and also potatoes, onions, shallots &c. They do supply packet seeds, but they don't send out a list.

Roug — Rougham Hall Nurseries

Ipswich Road
Rougham
Bury St Edmunds
Suffolk
IP30 9LZ
Phone: 01359 270577
Fax:

S&G — S & G Seeds Ltd

17 Summerwood Lane
Halsall
Ormskirk
Lancs
L39 8RQ
Phone: 01704 840775
Fax: 01704 841099
S&G is an abbreviation for the Sluis & Groot brand name, part of the Sandoz company. This is the new incarnation of Breeders Seeds, and they supply commercial varieties in bulk, and in smaller quantities for trialling.

The Fruit and Veg Finder

SDea — Deacon's Nursery

Moor View
Godshill
Isle of Wigh
PO38 3HW
Phone: 01983 840750
Fax:

SFam — Family Trees

PO Box 3
Botley
Hampshire
SO3 2EA
Phone: 01329 834812
Fax:

SFru — The Fruit Garden

Mulberry Farm
Woodnesborough
Sandwich
Kent
CT13 0PT
Phone: 01304 813454
Fax: 01304 813454

SIgm — Tim Ingram

Copton Ash
105 Ashford Road
Faversham
Kent
ME13 8XW
Phone: 01795 535919
Fax:

SKee — Keepers Nursery

446 Wateringbury Road
East Malling
Kent
ME19 6JJ
Phone: 01622 813008
Fax:

SMM — S.M.McArd (Seeds)

39 West Road
Pointon
Sleaford
Lincs
NG34 0NA
Phone: 01529 240765
Fax: 01529 240765
Bulk & small supplies. Good range of no-nonsense packets at keen prices.

SbS — Seeds-By-Size

45 Crouchfield
Boxmoor
Hemel Hempstead
Herts
HP1 1PA
Phone: 01442 251458
Fax:
An outstanding range of vegetable varieties, available in any amount to suit every buyer.

Shar — Sharpes International Seeds Ltd

Sleaford
Lincs
NG34 7HA
Phone: 01529 304511
Fax: 01529 303908
Bulk only, mostly peas and beans. The company will accept orders for a minimum of 5 Kg, but all orders should be of multiples of 5 Kg.

Sore — T. and J.A. Sore

Marward House
Beck Row
Bury St Edmunds
Suffolk
Phone: 01638 712779
Fax:
New this year, a supplier of asparagus crowns and other vegetative material.

Suff — Suffolk Herbs Ltd

Monks Farm
Coggeshall Road
Kelvedon
Essex
CO5 9PG
Phone: 01376 572456
Fax: 01376 571189
Their extensive list features many old European varieties, and the catalogue is a delight to read with foods, recipes, sundries and much more.

Sutt — Suttons Seeds Ltd

Hele Road
Torquay
Devon
TQ2 7QJ
Phone: 01803 614455
Fax: 01803 615747
A colourful catalogue with a broad range of flowers, fruit and veg.

T&M — Thompson & Morgan (Ipswich) Ltd

Poplar Lane
Ipswich
Suffolk
IP8 3BU
Phone: 01473 688821
Fax: 01473 680199

Toze — A.L. Tozer Ltd

Pyports
Downside Bridge Road
Cobham
SURREY
KT11 3EH
Phone: 01932 862059
Fax: 01932 868973
Larger quantities only. Specialist in squashes.

Treh   J Trehane & Sons Ltd

Stapehill Road
Hampreston, Wimborne
Dorset
BH21 7NE
Phone: 01202 873490
Fax:

Tuck   Edwin Tucker and Sons Ltd

Brewery Meadow
Stonepark, Ashburton
Newton Abbot
Devon
TQ13 7DG
Phone: 01364 652403
Fax: 01364 654300
Good potato list among many general seeds.

Unwi   Unwins Seeds Ltd

Mail Order Department
Histon
Cambridge
CB4 4ZZ
Phone: 01945 588522
Fax:
Good selection of flower and veg seeds.

VanH   Van Hage Garden Company

Seed Department
Great Amwell
Ware
Herts
SG12 9RP
Phone: 01920 870811
Fax: 01920 871861
Specialises in Dutch varieties.

WHig   Highfield Plant & Garden Centre

Bristol Road
Whitminster
Gloucestersh
GL2 7PB
Phone: 01452 740266
Fax:

WJas   Paul Jasper (Trees & Roses)

The Lighthouse
Bridge Street
Leominster
Herefordshir
HR6 8DU
Phone: 01568 611540
Fax: 01568 616499

WKi	**West Kington Nurseries Ltd**	**Webs**	**Websters Seed Potatoes**

WKi — West Kington Nurseries Ltd

Pound Hill
West Kington
Near Chippenham
Wiltshire
SN14 7JG
Phone: 01249 782822
Fax: 01249 782953
Supplier of ornamentals, they also do thongs of true sea kale.

Wall — Wallis Seeds

Broads Green
Great Waltham
Chelmsford
Essex
CM3 1DS
Phone: 01245 360413
Fax:
General list.

Webs — Websters Seed Potatoes

Unit 16, Ogilvy Place
Arbroath
Tayside
DD11 4DE
Phone: 01241 871789
Fax:
Potato specialist. Some people have reported difficulties with supplies, so it may be worth checking first with Mr Webster.

Yate — Samuel Yates Ltd

Withyfold Drive
Macclesfield
Cheshire
SK10 2BE
Phone: 01625 427823
Fax: 01625 422843
Bulk only supplies of varieties of interest to the commercial grower.

The RHS Plant Finder
1995/96
Britain's No 1 gardening annual

This latest edition of *The RHS Plant Finder* lists 65,000 plants, including 4,000 new entries, and their stockists. From alpines to trees, tender perennials to fruits, roses to water plants - whether your interest is specific or wide-ranging - *The 1995/96 RHS Plant Finder* is essential for all serious gardeners. It can help you find the plant which has eluded you for years or discover new rarities, many never before available in Britain.

As the recognised authority on plant nomenclature, **The RHS Plant Finder** is updated annually. It regularly incorporates thousands of name changes and this year's edition has improved cross referencing to avoid any confusion in tracking down a familiar plant with an unfamiliar name.

Codes by each plant direct you to nurseries where it can be obtained. The address, telephone and fax number, opening times, mail order and export details are given for every nursery, and regional location maps pinpoint its exact position.

The 1995/96 edition is available now priced £12.99 from all good bookshops or from RHS Enterprises Ltd, RHS Garden, Wisley, Woking, Surrey GU23 6QB. For credit card orders telephone the RHS Mail Order department on 01483 211320 or write enclosing a sterling cheque made payable to RHS Enterprises Ltd at the above address. Price £12.99 plus postage and packing (£2.00 UK second class mail, £3.00 overseas surface mail).